Postemotional Society

Foreword by David Riesman

Stjepan G. Meštrović

D0002437

SAGE Publications
London • Thousand Oaks • New Delhi

© Stjepan G. Meštrović 1997

First published 1997

 SAGE Publications Ltd
6 Bonhill Street
London EC2A 4PU

SAGE Publications Inc
2455 Teller Road
Thousand Oaks, California 91320

SAGE Publications India Pvt Ltd
32, M-Block Market
Greater Kailash – I
New Delhi 110 048

British Library Cataloguing in Publication data
A catalogue record for this book is available
from the British Library

ISBN 0 7619 5128 8
ISBN 0 7619 5129 6 (pbk)

Library of Congress catalog card number   96–070410

Typeset by M Rules
Printed in Great Britain by Biddles Ltd, Guildford, Surrey

To my precious Victoria Noelle,
Daddy's little angel

'Passion individualizes, yet it also enslaves'

–Émile Durkheim

Contents

Foreword

It is from Stjepan Meštrović that I learned the meaning of the term 'postemotional society.' It is a society in which people do not react to what, in an earlier era, would have been stirring occurrences and crises. Rather, individuals have become blasé, allergic to involvement, yet intelligent enough to know that the events are significant, and perhaps even to know that in an earlier era individuals would have responded with deep emotional empathy, or equally deep emotional antipathy, to particular individuals, and to the events surrounding them.

At the time *Postemotional Society* was written, President Clinton had just injected the appearance of American power into the Balkan War, which Meštrović interprets, in my view quite appropriately, as the war of the Serbs against the Croats and the Muslims of the former Yugoslavia. The capture of cities, the killing of civilians, the apparently shameless braggadocio of the Serbian military–civilian leadership – all this reasonably educated people read in their newspapers and saw on their television screens, while erasing any sense of personal connection with events. Sympathy, perhaps Yes, but empathy, No.

The postemotional stance absolves those who hold it from any sense of obligation, or sense of responsibility for what occurs in that part of the planet, the more or less educated part, to which people have in the past felt some sense of engagement and responsibility.

Stjepan Meštrović has, so to speak, a family connection to the former Yugoslavia. He is a grandson of the great sculptor Ivan Meštrović, who left his native Croatia to become an American citizen, and to continue to contribute to the worlds of art. I have no such personal connection, and yet I have felt, since the Serbian aggressions began, that Western Europe and the United States ought to 'do something' to stop it and even to reverse it. (I do not feel comparable involvement in events world-wide, which would hardly leave me much peace of mind!) But, contrary to what is suggested in *Postemotional Society*, I feel at least as much involvement in what happens in the Balkans as I do in what happens in Italy – a country that makes an appearance, not always to its credit, in *Postemotional Society*.

Meštrović refers to the O.J. Simpson trial, in which Simpson was acquitted. He concludes that at least white Americans viewed the case with postemotional detachment, believing for the most part that O.J. Simpson was clearly guilty, but not concerned especially with whether the jury found him guilty or not, because of the detachment that 'postemotional' life makes possible.

At the age of 86, I am grateful that I was brought up in a world in which the disengagement implicit in the postemotional outlook did not yet have widespread currency. In my own life, not being postemotional has involved me in public affairs in contrast to my preference for privacy and noninvolvement. I had had no political concerns at all when I was a Harvard College undergraduate or Harvard Law student. With Pearl Harbor I became immediately involved in seeking to prevent the deportation of Japanese from the West Coast to the de facto concentration camps into which many were relocated, taking me to Washington, DC, to lobby with Attorney-General Biddle in the Justice Department, encouraged by the marginal connection my parents had with Biddle as fellow Philadelphians. From that time forward, I have been involved in intra-academic and also in national concerns, far more than is my personal preference. I believe I understand myself a little less badly because of the contrast with the postemotional outlook.

I believe that other readers of *Postemotional Society* may find themselves similarly enlightened about their own reactions as well as the reactions of those around them. Perhaps, but not inevitably, it is too much to hope for that *Postemotional Society* will help many literate individuals again to allow themselves to become engaged in the multiple worlds we inhabit.

David Riesman
Henry Ford II Professor of the Social Sciences Emeritus

Preface

In this book, I propose a new sociological concept, postemotionalism, as an alternative to both postmodernism and modernist theories such as Anthony Giddens's structuration theory which focus on the *knowledge* and skill of the human agent. The missing ingredient in most sociological theorizing is the role of the *emotions*. I argue that contemporary Western societies are entering a new phase of development in which synthetic, quasi-emotions become the basis for widespread manipulation by self, others, and the culture industry as a whole. I agree with the modernists that the contemporary individual knows more than our ancestors did, but argue against modernist theorists that knowledge is not enough to result in action. Action assumes a connection between the emotions and intellect, and that connection has been severed in postemotional societies. I agree with the postmodernists that the era in which we live is one of mass simulation and recycling the past, and that it is dominated by seemingly rootless circulating fictions. Some find this postmodern vision exhilarating while others regard it as nihilistic. But I argue that what seem to be postmodern circulating fictions are not really rootless or chaotic, and that postmodernism implies neither human freedom from traditional constraints nor nihilism. Rather, postemotional society introduces a new form of bondage, this time to carefully crafted emotions. The theorists and theories that I invoke in this discussion are wide in scope, from classical social theorists such as Freud and Durkheim to the critical theorists and Jean Baudrillard. Several sociological works and theories are particularly important, and are used as backdrop for developing the postemotionalism concept. I extend the insights of these theorists in novel ways that they may or may not agree with:

● George Ritzer's thesis in *The McDonaldization of Society* that McDonaldization represents modernity's push toward extreme efficiency and rationalization is extended to the McDonaldization of emotions. These are bite-size, pre-packaged, rationally manufactured emotions – a 'happy meal' of emotions – that are consumed by the masses.

● David Riesman's theory of other-directedness, found in *The Lonely Crowd*, is recontextualized and extended as follows: I agree with him that the other-directed type has become a powerless inside-dopester whose emotional life has been reduced mostly to curdled indignation and being 'nice.' But I disagree with him that the long-term trend for other-directedness is one of becoming unemotional. I argue instead that the post-other-directed or postemotional type takes cues from peers and the media as to when he or she should rationally choose to exhibit a vicarious indignation, niceness or other pre-packaged emotions.

• Émile Durkheim's sociological theory in *The Elementary Forms of the Religious Life* is re-analyzed and recontextualized in the following way: His category of the 'sacred' really pertains to the emotional side of humans, while the 'profane' is the languishing, dull, non-emotional side. But the sacred canopy has collapsed, 'nothing is sacred anymore,' and that which was formerly sacred and emotional has become public, pedestrian, accessible to all – in a word, it has been profaned. Thus, contemporary 'collective effervescence' is staged and rationally induced. The 'collective consciousness' no longer exists: It has succumbed to a process of fission, a Balkanization of social identity into fragmented group identities that are hostile to one another.

• Chris Rojek has shown himself to be a sophisticated theorist in addition to his expertise in leisure studies, especially in his *Ways of Escape* and *Decentring Leisure*. I agree with most of his arguments concerning the intellectualization and bureaucratization of leisure, which lend themselves easily to an extension of these processes to emotional life. I agree with him especially that both modernity and postmodernity have two faces, Modernity 1 and Modernity 2, diametrically opposed tendencies toward order *and* chaos. I extend his insights to argue that postemotionalism constitutes a new hybrid of emotions that stems from the fusion of Modernity 1 and Modernity 2, namely, rationally ordered emotions.

In addition to these and many other social theorists, such as Herbert Marcuse and his concept of the 'happy consciousness,' found in *One-Dimensional Man*, I invoke and extend literary and humanistic writings in a sociological vein. Thus, Henry Adams argued in his well-known essay 'The Dynamo and the Virgin' that the emotional 'power' of the Virgin was being replaced in modernity with the mechanized power of the dynamo. But I argue that emotion did not disappear in the age of the machine. Instead, emotion has been mechanized. Similarly, Fyodor Dostoevsky's character the underground man foreshadowed today's postemotional type whose connection between emotion and action has been severed. Postemotional types can 'feel' a vast range of quasi-emotions, from indignation to compassion, yet are unable to put these feelings into appropriate action. This characterization contradicts completely Anthony Giddens's claim that the human agent is skilled and knowledgeable in relation to social structure. I argue against Giddens's overly felicitous account of human agency that postemotional types are more clever and knowledgeable than our ancestors could have imagined, yet have been reduced to acting out the role of Riesman's impotent 'inside-dopesters': They want to know almost everything precisely because they have concluded, deep down, that they are really powerless to do anything significant to affect politics or change the course of world events.

George Orwell's writings constitute a particularly important backdrop for my development of the postemotionalism concept, especially his *Nineteen Eighty-Four* and *The Road to Wigan Pier*. I agree with his arguments overall concerning ideological manipulation in the West as well as a general trend toward mechanization. But again, curiously, it never seems to have occurred to Orwell that not only *cognitive* content was subject to manipulation. Emotions are also manipulated by the culture industry and thereby transformed into post-emotions. Orwell was too innocent to have conceived this truly frightening aspect of modernist, mechanized culture. His innocence is illustrated by the fact that he acted on his intellectual criticisms of fascism by fighting against the fascists in Spain. By contrast, how many intellectuals today have been willing to go to fight against new 'fascists' in Chechnya and Bosnia?

Without repeating the arguments made in this book, let me illustrate how postemotionalism draws on Orwell yet moves beyond him. I will draw on some of his best-known statements in *Nineteen Eighty-Four* and reformulate them in the context of postemotionalism:

• 'War is Peace.' Indeed. US Presidents in recent years routinely send American soldiers into combat without seeking approval of the Congress because – after all – the soldiers are sent to create peace, not to wage war. No need to invoke the Congressional War Powers Act! But there is something new. After the Vietnam War, the death of even one American soldier for the sake of peace is too much for the American public to accept. Soldiering no longer makes use of machismo emotions pertaining to war; rather, as a well-known slogan claims, the US Army is 'more than a job, it's an adventure.' Fascists and enemies of democracy are no longer demonized, as they were in World War II. Rather, 'dialogue' is used to bring indicted war criminals to the 'negotiating table.' The USA fights wars no longer in order to win, but to produce a 'balance of power.' US war planes still bomb 'enemy' targets, but Pentagon spokespersons insist that the USA is 'neutral.'

• 'Big Brother is watching you.' The peer group is watching you. If you don't seek the services of a competent public relations firm or if you disregard the advice of political 'pundits,' the opinion-makers will destroy you. There is no need for Big Brother to watch you when the power of the peer group is so much stronger than the power of government. And the peer group can be manipulated easily. Marcuse was right: Once a happy consciousness is established, people obey without thinking in a society without opposition.

• 'Newspeak.' Entertainmentspeak. For no one can tell the difference between news and entertainment any more. Newscasters depend on high ratings, and to achieve them they must not offend. They must bring in 'human interest' stories. They must be 'nice' no matter how heinous the news that they report. Conversely, the masses learn more about world events from psychodrama, *Entertainment Tonight*, Oliver Stone's films, and other forms of mass entertainment than they do from the 'news.'

• 'Doublethink.' Emotional cleansing. Contemporary politicians as well as media 'wizards' know that they have to 'hook' you emotionally to get your attention regarding an issue. Once you are 'hooked,' the rational arguments do not connect up with the emotional appeal. The original emotions disappear. Thus, opinion polls show that most Americans simply could not comprehend President Clinton's proposal to reform health care in the USA, although it seemed to be a compassionate alternative to the existing system. Newt Gingrich's Republican 'revolution' seemed to be a good idea at the time, as all revolutions do, but Americans did not realize that it would entail the loss of social services they deem essential.

● 'Freedom is Slavery.' Freedom is nice, and slavery is not. So long as consumers are free to choose from hundreds of different yet nice products, options, and opinions, why worry about slavery?

● 'Ignorance is Strength.' Ignorance is cool so long as it is nice. *Forrest Gump. Dumb and Dumber. Clueless. Ace Ventura, Pet Detective.* Peter Sellers's Inspector Clouseau movies. Being ignorant *but* nice ensures success. Strength just doesn't exist any more.

● 'Who controls the past controls the future: who controls the present controls the past.' History is no longer a matter concerning facts, but one concerning imagination. Who controls *emotional reactions* to the past controls the future. Who controls the *emotional reactions* to the present controls the past. Baudrillard is right: History does not exist.

● 'Power is in inflicting pain and humiliation. Power is in tearing human minds to pieces and putting them together again in new shapes of our own choosing.' Power is in being charming while inflicting pain and humiliation. Power is in tearing human *emotions* to pieces and putting them together again in new shapes without inducing the human agent to think about choosing.

In summary, Orwell's formulations served their purpose in the inner-directed era of yesteryear. They apply to Hitler, Stalin, Brezhnev, even Truman and Nixon. These were rough and obnoxious inner-directed types. They were not nice. Truman dropped the atomic bomb on Japan without much explanation before or after he did it, and few Americans doubted that this war crime had to be committed for the sake of peace. The inner-directed masses understood concepts such as power, strength, and slavery. Yet one could still oppose fascism, Communism, and Big Brother because they were repulsive. But things changed in the other-directed and postemotional eras. Nixon's Presidency was the watershed in the transition from inner- to other-directedness on a mass scale. Watergate might have been just another scandal in inner-directed times, but for other-directed types, Nixon just wasn't nice. Gorbachev was the transition figure from inner-directed to other-directed Communism. Gorbachev headed the 'Evil Empire,' as Reagan called the Soviet Union, but he was a nice Communist. Reagan got to like him, and Americans liked Gorbachev more than the Soviets did. Boris Yeltsin also represents the new, postemotional dictator: He bombs Muslims in Chechnya but is hailed as a champion of democracy. Isn't he better than the obnoxious Zhirinovsky? Slobodan Milošević played tenderly on the piano at the Dayton Peace Talks. The American delegation liked him. Jimmy Carter was the first nice President, but Bill Clinton is the nicest President ever. He has been carrying the Whitewater scandal with him for most of his Presidency, but it cannot bring him down like Watergate ruined Nixon. Americans cannot get indignant at Bill Clinton. He is too nice. And he is too much like them.

Clinton's 'I feel your pain' line is not something most people notice, or remember, for they tend to react as he does, with a false empathy where compassion would have been appropriate. In this book, I refer to Clinton as the postemotional President.

If there is any truth to Durkheim's dictum that political leaders are created by their constituencies as representatives of their social character, then Bill Clinton represents postemotional America. To be sure, some Americans complain that he is wishy-washy, but the truth is that most Americans are ambivalent about almost everything. Ambivalence and ambiguity are the hallmarks of the postemotional intellectual too: He or she must demonstrate the ability to see all points of view and take a stand against none (except for clearly obnoxious points of view, of course). Yet even representatives of racist, sexist, and other offensive points of view are learning how to package their views in increasingly charming ways. As of this writing, Slobodan Milošević of Serbia is the penultimate example of the charming racist. Even the policy of 'ethnic cleansing' has a nice, clean ring to it, far removed from old-fashioned genocide.

In this book, I argue that a neo-Orwellian process of emotional manipulation is dawning in the Western world. Its consequence is that any policy or event, no matter how repulsive it might be by old-fashioned inner-directed standards, will be acceptable as long as it is packaged properly. Proper packaging entails a nice exterior and the pre-planned channelling of indignation into pre-chosen channels. This constitutes a new form of totalitarianism that is distinct from inner-directed forms of totalitarianism. It bears some resemblance to the portrait of mass society found in Herbert Marcuse's *One-Dimensional Man* and other critical theorists. But it is significantly different. First, one cannot get really indignant at this new form because it has a nice face. Second, the mass society of yesteryear has given way to fractionalized group identities so that it will be less possible to form a unified front of resistance. Third, to the extent that one still gets indignant, the indignation will not lead to action because it will be cancelled out by competing, fractionalized indignation *vis-à-vis* splintered group identities: men against women, whites against other ethnic groups, gays against straights, and so on. Fourth, heightened rationality cannot save humanity from these trends, as the critical theorists, in their over-estimation of the Enlightenment, had hoped. This is because postemotional control is aimed at the emotions, not the mind. The power of rationality and of the mind enshrined by the Enlightenment has given way to an indolent mindlessness.

The scenario for the future that I sketch out in this book seems more horrifying than the one envisioned by Orwell or Marcuse. This is because both of them still had faith in what has come to be known as the Enlightenment project. They believed that heightened rationality could save humanity from totalitarian mind-control. But I argue that the Enlightenment project itself is a postemotional phenomenon, that it constitutes yet another instance of emotional clinging to a simulation of the Enlightenment. What serious observer of contemporary culture would *really* argue that the West values the 'mind' that was enshrined by the Enlightenment? Indolent mindlessness and kitsch emotional reactions to serious problems seem to better characterize the contemporary social landscape in the West. In addition, I draw on Rojek and Ritzer to suggest that the escape routes from postemotional society have been closed because the 'ways of escape' are also manipulated and controlled. Yet the reader would be wrong to conclude that I agree with them completely, or that my position is nihilistic. I drop plenty of hints throughout this discussion on how to find the real escape routes. But these hints remain undeveloped, given that the intent of this book is to sketch the parameters of postemotional society, not to find the escape routes.

Acknowledgements

I would like to thank colleagues who discussed with me various aspects of the argument put forth here: David Riesman, Keith Tester, Akbar Ahmed, Slaven Letica, Philip J. Cohen, C.G. Schoenfeld, and Thomas Cushman. I would also like to thank undergraduate as well as graduate students in my classes for their responses to the ideas that I later developed into this book. I could not have completed this book without the research and editorial assistance of Rebecca Wood. Finally, thanks to my wife, Amber, and my daughters, Ivy and Victoria, for generously letting me work on this book when I could have and probably should have been spending more time with them.

The author and publisher wish to thank the following for permission to use copyright material: The Free Press, a division of Simon and Schuster, from *The Elementary Forms of the Religious Life* by Émile Durkheim, translated by Joseph Ward Swain. Copyright © 1965 by The Free Press. Yale University Press, from *The Lonely Crowd* by David Riesman. Copyright © 1950 by Yale University Press.

1

Introduction

The following is a theoretical discussion that will attempt to introduce a new sociological concept, postemotionalism, to account for the lacunae and deficiencies of postmodernism as a theoretical construct, and to capture a distinct tendency in contemporary social life toward the mechanization of emotional life. Inspired by George Orwell's[1] and George Ritzer's[2] discussions of the mechanization of social life, I will extended their insights to include the mechanization of the emotions. I will also sociologize Orwell's insight by situating it within a larger social theoretical context. I will do this by recontextualizing the works of David Riesman and Émile Durkheim in addition to those of Herbert Marcuse, Georg Simmel, Henry Adams, Fyodor Dostoevsky, and other intellectuals who wrote on the happy consciousness of a society without opposition, the blasé attitude, the cultural power of the dynamo, and the modernist disjunction between thought and feeling.

Pauline Rosenau is undoubtedly right that postmodernism, despite being difficult to define, has two faces, which she calls affirmative and skeptical. The affirmative postmodernist rhetoric includes multiculturalism, tolerance, communitarianism, an ethics of openness and inclusion,[3] and the 'salad bowl' model of ethnic relations that is supposed to have replaced the old-fashioned 'melting pot' and assimilationist models. One should note immediately that these postmodern virtues have the ring of standardized formulas about them. Yet it is abundantly clear that something altogether different is occurring in the industrialized West in the 1990s. In fact, it is a great irony that President Clinton's Presidency will be remembered not for the communitarianism[4] and the overcoming of differences that he claimed he sought, but for the fission, divisiveness, and Balkanization – domestic and international – that has accompanied his Presidency.[5] The most salient feature of this new development is the tendency for *emotionally charged* collective representations to be abstracted from their cultural contexts and then manipulated artificially by self and others in new and artificially contrived contexts. The two most dominant quasi-emotions extant in the West today seem to be curdled indignation and a carefully managed 'niceness,' both prophesied by David Riesman in *The Lonely Crowd*.[6] So-called postmodern culture feeds parasitically on the dead emotions of other cultures and of the past in general. The result is that various groups become the reference point for synthetically created quasi-emotions and the notion of an all-encompassing cultural reference point such as Americanism has been replaced by Americanisms pertaining to women, Hispanics, African-Americans, other minorities, and various permutations of these and other groups.[7] Arthur Spiegelman writes of a 'catastrophic racial divide' in the USA and of a possible 'total racial meltdown' in the future.[8] A genuine Balkanization of the West[9] seems to be occurring in other industrial countries as well, despite the loud yet routinized, even forced rhetoric of unity. For example, Quebec almost seceded from Canada. The assassination of Israeli Prime Minister Yitzhak Rabin as well as Benjamin Netanyahu's very narrow election victory as his successor suggest that Israel has Balkanized over the issue of trading land for peace with the Palestinians. There are ominous signs that Scotland may wish to secede from the United Kingdom.

At first blush, this state of affairs seems to resemble the other, skeptical, even nihilistic version of the postmodern world conceived as a heap of contingent fictions, modelled after America as the dawning of the postmodern social universe.[10] This view has been promulgated especially by Jean Baudrillard.[11] It is true that the icons of American culture such as McDonald's and Coca-Cola are slowly but surely taking over the rest of the world, and that they carry with them a cultural mind-set that deliberately displaces indigent cultures. For example, Parisian cafés are on the decline largely because of the McDonaldization of Paris.[12] It is also true that a distinct neo-Orwellianism is emerging on the world scene, but: (1) in addition to Orwell's original depiction of the almost exclusive manipulation of *ideas*, rational content, and habits of the mind, *emotions* and habits of the heart are also manipulated; (2) what appears to be postmodern disorder or the circulation of random fictions, as depicted by Jean Baudrillard,[13] turns out to have a hidden order of its own, and to be highly automatized, rehearsed, and planned; (3) this internal and highly mechanized logic and order nevertheless lead to a larger pandemonium, as the title of one of Senator Daniel Patrick Moynihan's books suggests.[14]

An important aspect of postemotionalism is the recycling of dead emotions from the past. In this sense, postemotionalism seems to be a part of the generalized tendency toward widespread simulation and cultural recycling that is evident to most observers of the current *fin de siècle*:[15]

> Recycling is no longer confined to diet coke cans and evian water bottles. It's become one of the dominant impulses in American culture today. . . . Whether you call it nostalgia, postmodernism or a simple vandalizing of the past, all this recycling essentially amounts to the same thing; a self-conscious repudiation of originality.[16]

Chris Rojek offers a similar assessment of the times in which we live in his *Ways of Escape*:

> From a postmodernist standpoint the past bursts into the present through stage representations like Greenfield Village or the 'Way We Were' centre at Wigan Pier where actors wear the costume of turn-of-the-century schoolteachers and keep classes of day trippers in order. In addition, and more generally, branches of the mass media keep the past constantly 'alive' in the present. Nostalgia industries continuously recycle products which signify simultaneity between the past and the present. For example, hit television shows from the sixties are retransmitted in the

1980s and '90s and reproduce or beat their original success; top pop songs from the fifties, sixties and seventies are re-released and become number one hits all over again; and fashions that were discarded as infra dig in our twenties are triumphantly championed by our children thirty years later. Increasingly, popular culture is dominated by images of recurrence rather than originality.[17]

It is easy to extend Rojek's illustrations. Thus, a second Woodstock rock festival was held in 1994. Renaissance festivals are practically an institution in the United States with their re-engineering of the emotions that supposedly constituted the real Renaissance.[18] Celebrities repackage themselves as intellectuals, and vice versa, in the information media.[19] Journalists themselves have become celebrities.[20] The terrorist who killed people through the use of mail bombs – nicknamed the 'Unabomber' – tried to present himself as a scholar and insisted that the *New York Times* or *Washington Post* publish his manifesto. (If the paper refused, he threatened to kill more people and ask *Penthouse* magazine to publish it.[21] *Penthouse* was even willing to let him write a monthly column.)[22] The *Washington Post* did finally publish the manifesto written by this terrorist-as-sociologist on 19 September 1995. Similarly, the indicted international war criminal Ratko Mladić tried to pass himself off as a patriot and victim.[23] The United Nations continued to negotiate with other Serbian indicted war criminals, thereby putting them in the new and synthetic role of criminals-as-statesmen. Great Britain, which is losing its economic standing in the industrialized world, recently tried to repackage its image as a special nation by reminding the world that it is responsible for the Magna Carta, and is therefore still a great nation.[24] Along these lines, French President Jacques Chirac expressed the view that the French gave the world civilization even as he ordered his government to attack defenseless Greenpeace protesters in the South Pacific, and went ahead with nuclear testing that had been banned by the civilized world. One could expand greatly this list of illustrations.

Yet the easily accepted notions of repackaging, recycling, and simulating objects of *knowledge* as staples of a postmodern world – noted by Theodor Adorno[25] and other critical theorists long before the postmodernists arrived on the cultural stage – neglect the role of *emotions*, and beg important questions: (1) *What* is being recycled, intellectual content or emotion or both? The current literature in postmodernism seems to assume that cognitive *representations* are recycled, and that the world is basically a *mental* text. I am not satisfied with this assessment, and, through the use of the concept of postemotionalism, seek to incorporate the role of emotions in the postmodern discourse on the recycling of representations. It is more accurate to say that I seek to problematicize the age-old distinction between rationality and emotion, and to conceptualize a new hybrid of emotions-as-representations. (2) *How* is current cultural recycling different from authentic cultural experiences of emotion, and is this process of borrowing from the past different from rituals in traditional societies? Many participants in the postmodernist discourse assume that 'authenticity is no longer an issue under postmodernism,'[26] but I disagree. Our postmodern age is obsessed with the 'real thing' versus the phony in politics, leisure, advertisement, education, and other social arenas, even if most people cannot agree on how to make this distinction.[27] (3) *Who* is responsible for the recycling? In other words, is the recycling random or is it committed by the 'culture industry', as Theodor Adorno[28] argued? And if the culture industry is involved, the same question must be repeated: Is the process in the vast culture industry random and spontaneous, as argued by Baudrillard, or does it have a mechanized logic of its own? I question the now standard postmodernist claim that because of de-differentiation, former social, economic, and political distinctions are no longer valid.[29] I will argue that the old distinctions have been transformed, but are still important. It is worth pondering how former distinctions still operate in new, artificial forms despite the appearance of postmodern chaos and de-differentiation. (4) Finally, *why* is postemotionalism occurring at a time in Western history that most social forecasters thought would be characterized by the end of ideology, the end of history, the triumph of democratic ideals, post-industrialization, and the end of racism, sexism, and other forms of oppression? Relying on a recontextualized reading of David Riesman's *The Lonely Crowd*, I shall argue that the group-oriented social fission everyone is witnessing today is the logical next phase of what he called other-directedness. These are among the unresolved issues that I propose to problematicize and address in outlining the concept of postemotionalism.

Before turning to the theoretical scaffolding for apprehending this movement to postemotionalism, let us survey some more concrete examples with an eye on the issues discussed above. These are intended to serve as illustrations, not as proof of the existence of postemotionalism. While the illustrations I will use will eventually become dated, the underlying logic that I expose to describe them will probably remain relevant for many years to come. My intent in this section is to give the reader an intuitive, pre-theoretical feel for postemotionalism that will enable him or her to pick up a newspaper in the years to come and be able to discern postemotional logic in the description of events that will be 'current' in the future.

The Balkan War, for example, was depicted by the information media as well as diplomats and politicians as a war fought in the 1990s on the basis of Serb fears of Muslims that go back to 1389(!) and their fears of Croats based on Ustasha atrocities committed in World War II.[30] There are many curious aspects to this postemotional repackaging of reality. When the Croats and Bosnian Muslims won back territory that had been seized by the Serbs, the *New York Times* ran the headline, 'For Serbs, a Flashback to '43 Horror'. Nineteen-nineties' Serbs were quoted concerning their fears of non-existent 1990s' Ustashe:

> The chilling fears that have lived here for 52 years were confirmed. . . . [the Croatian campaign was] a continuation of the crusade to exterminate Serbs.[31]

How does a fear, or any other emotion, live for fifty-two years? Moreover, as this journalist noted in an aside, 'In explaining their fears today by what happened to them [Serbs] five decades ago, the people seemed to forget what happened to their neighbors [Croats and Muslims] only three years ago.'[32] What happened, of course, is that Serbs committed genocide against Croats and Muslims.[33] Indeed, if it were solely a matter of memory, it is curious that Serbs would remember a fear from fifty-two years ago and forget hatred from a few years ago.

Another interesting aspect of this postemotional repackaging of quasi-history is the assumption that Croats and Muslims have no flashbacks of horrors committed by Serbs in World War II. Serbian Chetniks, who were Nazi collaborators as well as Nazi resistors in World War II, are repackaged emotionally as freedom fighters and victims in the 1990s[34] while the Croats of the 1990s, who seceded from Yugoslavia, are repackaged as Nazis[35] fifty years after the fall of Nazism. And Bosnian Muslims are represented as 'the Turks' more than six hundred years after the Turks conquered Serbia. The French philosopher Alain Finkielkraut captures the gist of this seemingly confusing state of affairs with the pithy line: 'The Nazis [Serbs] of this story are trying to pass themselves off as the Jews.'[36] An editorial entitled 'If Bosnians Were Whales' argued that public indifference to the Bosnian victims of genocide contrasts sharply with widespread sympathy for whales.[37] If the emotions pertaining to whales could have been transferred postemotionally to Bosnian humans, would the indifference been overcome?

Similarly, the media coverage of the O.J. Simpson trial in the United States – dubbed the trial of the century, which is an interesting slight to both the Nuremberg war crimes trials and the Lindbergh kidnapping trial, which used to be thought of as the international and American trials of the century, respectively – was not just about O.J. Simpson's guilt or innocence:

> The OJ Simpson trial has become the OJ Simpson show. It is almost as if reality has become television. People talk about the trial with detachment. Few of those interviewed mentioned that two people had been killed or that two young children had lost their mother. . . . The case and the way people talk about it seem to reflect the country's cynical mood. There is suspense, but it is not about whether Mr. Simpson is guilty. It is about whether he will go free. . . . What a lot of people said is if they ever get into trouble they'd want Johnnie Cochran to defend them because he could get anybody off.[38]

Alongside Simpson, the Los Angeles Police Department was, in effect, put on trial for racism whose history was traced back to slavery – and the Simpson trial is one among many such postemotional trials involving race and memory.[39] Another interesting aspect of the media attention given to the Simpson trial is that it eclipsed completely the concurrent trial concerning one of the biggest terrorism-conspiracy cases in US history, the trial of Sheik Omar Abdel Rahman and his co-defendants.[40] The Sheik and others were charged with the February 1993 bombing of Manhattan's World Trade Center, but 'few people seem to care.'[41] (The news that they were convicted of conspiracy to commit terrorism seemed to come out of the blue.[42]) Similarly, the media tended to neglect corruption and brutality in police departments in cities other than Los Angeles, such as New Orleans, where 'four New Orleans police officers have been charged with murder' and Federal investigators estimated that '10 to 15 percent of the force . . . has engaged in criminal behavior,' primarily against Americans of Vietnamese descent.[43]

The closing arguments by the defense in the year-long Simpson trial were postemotional in the extreme. Commentators noted that the defense placed racism center stage over the issue of murder. The chief lawyer for Simpson's defense, Johnnie Cochran, accused Los Angeles police officer Mark Fuhrman of 'genocidal racism' and compared him with Adolf Hitler; asserted that O.J. Simpson was the real victim in the case; and asked the jury to acquit Simpson as a civil rights gesture.[44] Some Jewish groups and the victims' families expressed indignation at the comparison with Hitler, arguing that Hitler killed millions of people while Fuhrman uttered racist remarks.[45] Even Robert Shapiro, one of Simpson's lawyers, expressed indignation along these lines and stated that he would not work with Johnnie Cochran again: 'Mr. Shapiro also said he was "deeply offended" by Mr. Cochran's comparison of modern racist attitudes to the Nazis and the Holocaust.'[46] But Simpson's family was indignant at these expressions of indignation.[47] Women's groups expressed indignation at the fact that Simpson's brutality toward his ex-wife while they were married did not get the attention it deserved. The fact that this was a murder trial seemed to have become lost in the emotional outbursts, and the public's view of Simpson's guilt or innocence before, during, and after the trial was divided along mostly racial lines.[48] Simpson's acquittal on 3 October 1995 by a jury comprised mostly of African-Americans only exacerbated these ethnic cleavages in the USA.[49]

One could hardly avoid drawing the conclusion that the television media's presence in and outside the courtroom during the reading of the jury verdict contributed to staged emotions. Commentators spoke of the possibility of riots if the jury were to find Simpson guilty, with an anticipation that mirrored the crowd's apparent readiness to set off a 'spontaneous' disturbance:

> Lurking within the morning marathon was the threat of street commotion. The subject was treated gingerly: Peter Jennings spoke of a 'certain anticipation' that a verdict 'one way or the other' might lead to disturbances. . . . As it turned out, instead of burnings and beatings, there were cheers for the verdict. The pictures of the celebrants were not altogether clear, but it seemed like a mostly black party.[50]

It is important to note parallels between the Bosnia and Simpson cases. In Bosnia, Serb-sponsored genocide against Bosnian Muslims took second stage to Serb claims that they were the real victims on the basis of arguments harking back to World War II Ustashe. In the Simpson trial, murder took second stage to defense claims that the accused murderer was the real victim on the basis of arguments harking back to slavery. All too often, many other events in the 1990s were packaged and consumed as postemotional issues of racism and sexism rather than the more traditional issues of genocide, murder, rape, corruption, and so on. For example, US Congressman Mel Reynolds claimed that he was the victim of racism when he was sentenced to five years for sexual crimes and obstruction of justice.[51]

Let me tip my hand early in the discussion and suggest what is postemotional as opposed to emotional about the Bosnia and Simpson cases. A 'live' emotional response to genocide in Bosnia would have been outrage at the brutality as it was being reported. A 'live' emotional response in the Simpson case would have involved the desire to expiate the murders of Nicole Brown Simpson and Ron Goldman. Harking back to Durkheim's sociological theory of crime and punishment,[52] the desire to punish crime has been a traditionally emotional reaction, even if the earlier forms of revenge and expiation have been muted and softened *vis-à-vis* the contemporary criminal justice system, which results mainly in incarceration, not brutal physical injury to the criminal. But in both of the cases discussed above, the 'dead' emotions going back many and at times hundred of years became the central ones. Specifically, more indignation seems to have been expressed at historical Croatian Nazi collaboration than contemporary Serbian genocide. In the Simpson trial, more indignation was expressed at the racism in the USA going back to slavery than at the murder of the two victims. In subsequent chapters, I shall explore in more depth the difference between authentic versus dead emotions.

One more legal aspect in both cases needs to be mentioned with regard to postemotionalism. In the Simpson trial, Los Angeles police officer Mark Fuhrman invoked the Fifth Amendment to avoid possible self-recrimination. The Fifth Amendment originated when America was young as a reaction to the British forcing of confessions in the American colonies. Its continued use in the 1990s, under wholly different contexts, also constitutes postemotionalism. Similarly, the great care by the International War Crimes Tribunal in the 1990s that indicted war criminals suspected of perpetrating genocide receive a 'fair trial' draws postemotionally on historical times in which it was impossible to obtain a fair trial. But nowadays getting a 'fair trial' often means purchasing the services of extremely competent defense attorneys who are skilled at obtaining acquittals. The traditional emotional need for societies to punish criminals, with or without a fair trial, seems to have been lost. Consider, for example, the caption beneath a political cartoon that shows a Serbian messenger interrupting a card game in which Radovan Karadžić is present. The caption reads: 'The bad news is they wanna try us as war criminals . . . the good news is they're gonna try us in L.A.'[53]

The Oklahoma City bombing that occurred in the United States on 20 April 1995 immediately brought onto television screens images of present-day American militia leaders – always depicted with the American flag in the background – who invoked 20 April as a sacred date going back to the burning of Lexington in 1775 up to and including the burning of the Branch Davidians on 20 April 1993. Far from being a cut and dried case of American terrorism, this event was recast sentimentally in representations pertaining to American patriotism, the meaning of the American Republic, as well as racism and anti-Semitism. The emotional spillover became so vast that prominent US Republicans had to distance themselves from the emotional rhetoric used by the militias, because these Republicans had themselves used a similar rhetoric of challenging a big, bad US government that had to be tamed.

The deadly use of nerve gas against Tokyo subway riders in Japan in 1995 'evoked a thrill of horror and revived memories of the ghastly casualties inflicted by chemical warfare agents during World War I' – at least it evoked these memories for the Western media.[54] Affirmative Action in the USA – the subject of heated debate following the victory of Republicans in the US Congress in 1994[55] – is frequently depicted as involving collective guilt by the white majority for the enslavement of African-Americans, or, more euphemistically, as advocating group rights and quotas over individual rights.[56] It is also frequently depicted as involving collective guilt by all males for the enslavement of women dating back to pre-history.[57] Its psychological result is that the beneficiaries of Affirmative Action are haunted by the question 'Was I really qualified?' while some in the majority presume that this program's beneficiaries are inadequate,[58] and the hybrid phenomenon of reverse discrimination against the majority appears. Thus, Shannon Faulkner became a celebrity when she was admitted to the all-male military academy at the Citadel in South Carolina. One magazine featured her along postemotional lines as if she were fighting her own Civil War for women's rights.[59] But clearly, the contemporary culture industry would never entertain such a use of emotional imagery for an imaginary case of a male student trying to enter a famous women's college such as Wellesley in Massachusetts. Anita K. Blair notes that most people today believe that women's colleges 'are constitutionally valid because they serve as reparations for the past oppression of women by men.'[60] Only specific groups are allowed to wear the poignant mantle of victimhood. Paul Hollander expresses this point well:

> Clearly during the past quarter-century there has been a spectacular expansion in the numbers of people claiming victimhood. If we add them all up – women, blacks, Hispanics, Native Americans, the disabled, homosexuals, AIDS victims, the homeless, the children of abusive parents, the overweight etc. – it would emerge that not more than 15% of the population in the US is free of the injuries of victimhood. . . . White males say they believe they are being forced to pay for history they had no part in and that they feel weary, angry, and alienated.[61]

The climate of political correctness that has accompanied Affirmative Action has led to terror in the classroom: 'Teach but don't touch' is the new motto, or you may be charged with crimes as serious as molestation and harassment.[62] In the 1990s, more words carry emotional and political connotations than ever before in history:

> Shifts in terms have an unfortunate side effect. Many people who don't have a drop of malice or prejudice but happen to be older or distant from the university, media and government spheres find themselves tainted as bigots for innocently using passé terms like oriental or crippled.[63]

But political correctness has had its backlash. It has Balkanized most US university campuses.[64] The overuse of the word 'rape' to include even some instances of seduction and consensual sexual intercourse has deadened the emotional impact of this crime.[65] The very term 'date rape'[66] joins two constellations of emotions that are diametrically opposed to each other, the first as a leisure activity and the second as a crime. Closely related phenomena include sexual correctness,[67] in which men ask permission for every act of sexual intimacy with a female, and 'lookism,'[68] in which an admiring gaze can be construed as the crime of sexual harassment. Most of the time, these terms are used in relation to women as victims, such that men are assumed not to be potential victims of date rape, sexual harassment, lookism, or old-fashioned physical abuse. Thus, President Clinton asked every man to promise never to hit a woman.[69] The murder of women by men has been termed 'femicide,' but there is no special term for the murder of men by women or by other men.[70] Moreover, postemotionalism leads one to confront the question why *domestic* rape in the United States is the subject of intensely emotional reaction whereas the well-publicized rape of women and girls in Bosnia-Herzegovina was not stopped and went unpunished.[71] Again, the rape of Bosnian Muslim *men* by Serbian *men* was practically ignored.[72]

In general, the 1990s have witnessed a dramatic and highly visible increase in the rhetoric of victimhood:

> That rhetoric is everywhere. In the ultra-radical feminism that sees sexual intercourse as rape. In the campus speech codes that abridge free expression, to 'protect' minority students. In the daily diet of television shows where panelists claim – often to questionable motives – lifetimes of horrific abuse by their parents. Victimhood has become a celebrated state – and a license.[73]

But what is distinctive about this new cult of victimhood compared to previous eras is that it is no longer private but extremely public; that one qualifies as a victim only if one belongs to specific groups; that the postemotional victim is all too willing to re-enact or otherwise stage his or her emotions on camera; and that just about *any* phenomenon can be attached synthetically to the emotions that used to apply traditionally to very specific events. Thus, until recently, convicted criminals could not successfully use 'victimspeak' to gain sympathy, because such emotions were reserved for the 'legitimate' victims of crime. This is no longer the case, as the trial of Colin Ferguson demonstrated. Ferguson was convicted of a mass-murder on a New York subway, but

> Mr. Ferguson argued from the beginning that he was not the shooter and that he too was a victim. He said that he fell asleep on the train and that a white man stole his gun from a bag beneath his seat and did the shootings.[74]

Ferguson was found sane and defended himself. He rejected lawyers who sought to defend him on the grounds of insanity and

> a theory that his mental illness was aggravated by the cultural shock and bias he endured as a black man in the US. Mr. Ferguson emigrated 12 years ago from Kingston, Jamaica, where he was born 37 years ago and lived a privileged life as the member of a well-to-do family.[75]

Ferguson found sympathizers among radio talk-show listeners, one of whom called in to say:

> The mayhem on the 5:33 train was retribution for the whites' sins against blacks. . . . These [white] people who enslaved our fathers, enslaved our mothers – they earned it [death].[76]

The awesome emotions related to victims are now routinely attached to events that never would have qualified as victimhood until recently. As Charles J. Sykes demonstrates in *A Nation of Victims*, a politics of victimization has emerged such that, for example, obese people sue restaurants for not recognizing that large people cannot sit comfortably in their seats, and the National Association to Advance Fat Acceptance claims discrimination on television because 'You rarely see fat women as love interests.'[77]

The famous Jerry Lewis Labor Day telethon in the United States has come under criticism because Lewis called the objects of his charity 'cripples,' and allegedly because he invokes pity for them.[78] The postemotional aspect here is that the physically disabled in the 1990s are beginning to invoke the emotions pertaining to minority statuses. Another illustration of a dramatic shift in emotional attitudes concerns breast-feeding. Despite the rhetoric of tolerance regarding many feminist issues, mothers who breast-feed in the 1990s are faced with a public attitude that regards breast-feeding as disgusting. If it must be done at the workplace, it is confined to restrooms.[79] This is a sharp departure from tolerance and even encouragement of public breast-feeding found in most traditional societies and, until recently, in many European countries as well.[80] More importantly, it involves a displacement of feelings of disgust for bodily excretions such as excrement to breast milk.[81]

Another excellent illustration of postemotionalism is to be found in the activities of former US President Jimmy Carter, who made visible the concept of human rights in foreign affairs. In his many publicized efforts to prevent or ameliorate military action by the US military against Saddam Hussein, Kim Il Sung of North Korea, the Haitian dictator Raoul Cedras, and Bosnian Serb leader Radovan Karadžić (who was indicted as a war criminal by the International War Crimes Tribunal in the Hague), among other unsavory political types, Jimmy Carter has made these and other victimizers seem like victims. Roger Kagan asked the appropriate question, 'What accounts for the sympathy this supposed advocate of human rights displays toward brutal dictators?'[82] One reply is that Jimmy Carter is at home in a postemotional world which suddenly allows the transference of the traditional prestige associated with having been a US President as well as with being publicly religious to realms which previously would have been unthinkable,[83] such as the genocidal activities of Radovan Karadžić.[84] Jimmy Carter presented Karadžić with flowers when the two men met. And in general, Karadžić and his cause have their sympathizers in the media elite.[85]

Genghis Khan, who used to be regarded as a barbarian, was rediscovered as a hero in Mongolia following the collapse of Communism.[86] All postcommunist countries rediscovered and refurbished not just persons but names, dates, and images as well that the Communists had branded as fascist or barbarian but that were suddenly transformed into nationalist icons. On the other end of the spectrum, events that used to be regarded as sacred are routinely profaned. For example, the remembrance of events such as the Holocaust is being transformed recently into forms that some critics regard as borrowing from theme parks, thereby cheapening the meaning of the

Holocaust and making visitors into voyeurs.[87] The emotional power of *the* Holocaust as a sacred site of Jewish memory is frequently co-opted and transferred to other sites such as the African-American Holocaust, the Serbian Holocaust, the Atomic Holocaust[88] (Hiroshima), the Bosnian Holocaust,[89] and other borrowings that many Jews find offensive. Steven Spielberg, the director of the film about the Holocaust *Schindler's List*, was quoted as saying there are many holocausts, in response to a move by some Islamic nations to prevent his film from being shown.[90] Using modern conceptual distinctions, one can distinguish the Holocaust as a sacred site of Jewish memory from the Holocaust as an instance of genocide which can be compared and contrasted to other sites of genocide, but not as Holocausts.[91] But in the postmodern age of de-differentiation, this distinction is blurred, and has led to the misuse and overuse of both terms, holocaust and genocide, with results that do not promote tolerance. Both the Holocaust and genocide have been routinized.

Thus, at the commemoration of Auschwitz, Poles and Jews engaged in a visible dispute about which group was the real victim of the Holocaust/genocide. Elie Wiesel went to the Auschwitz commemoration 'to show the centrality of the Jewish experience.'[92] But the then President of Poland, Lech Wałesa, emphasized 'the suffering of the Polish people under the Nazis, did not mention the affliction of the Jews, and he did not send an emissary to Jewish prayers at Birkenau.'[93] British historian Norman Davies commented that Auschwitz

> is a huge source of resentment between Poles and Jews. Both sides lost colossal numbers during the war and feel that nobody understands them and that they don't want to share the victimization.[94]

For Jews, Auschwitz is one of the symbols of the Holocaust, but 'for non-Jewish Poles it became a symbol of their nation's martyrdom.'[95] And a third group-memory emerged, the memory of the Russian liberators of Auschwitz:

> It would seem fitting, at the very least, for leaders of these two groups [Jews and Poles] to stop, put aside their grief for just a moment to give thanks and pay some kind of tribute to the Russian people (whatever their faults, and their leaders), whose young men fought and died in enormous numbers in so many terrible battles.[96]

Postemotionally, the Holocaust is used increasingly as a badge of honor by competing groups. This was evident also from the closing arguments of the previously discussed Simpson trial:

> 'The fact that he had the nerve to compare Fuhrman to Hitler is the ultimate hypocrisy,' [Mr Joel Kotkin] said, referring to Mr. Cochran's closing arguments. But Danny Bakewell, chairman of the Brotherhood Crusade, a black community development organization, took strong issue with Jews who have criticized Mr. Cochran. 'I don't think it helps when anyone suggests that Cochran's use of the Holocaust doesn't compare in any way to the pain and suffering to those in the African-American community,' Mr. Bakewell said. 'Moreover, pain and suffering doesn't exclusively belong to anyone.'[97]

What might be called the genocide industry has emerged on the post-emotional scene, such that the emotional energy associated with the word 'genocide' is used for various purposes. Thus, 'Russia has accused NATO of genocide against the Serbs' in response to NATO's bombing of Bosnian Serb military targets in September of 1995.[98] When the Holocaust Museum exhibited photographs of Serbian-sponsored genocide in Bosnia and Croatia in the 1990s, Serbian-American groups protested loudly that Bosnian Muslims and Croats should not be portrayed as contemporary victims of genocide because they were perpetrators of genocide in World War II.[99] The man who is widely regarded as most responsible for the genocide against Bosnian Muslims, Slobodan Milošević, was transformed postemotionally by Western powers into a peacemaker. Thus, the key to the US-sponsored 'peace plan' in the war against Bosnia was 'the political reinvention of Mr. Milošević into a star statesman from potential war criminal.'[100]

Advertisements no longer even pretend to convince consumers of the superiority of their product on the modernist bases of ingredients, efficacy, or superiority in specific regards relative to competitors. Instead, advertisements these days sell *feelings* that often have no relationship to the product at all. Thus, Pepsi becomes the drink of a new generation. Nike tennis shoes are advertised with the strange phrase 'Just do it.' Benetton clothing is sold on the multicultural basis of 'the united colors of Benetton.' Calvin Klein has been accused of promoting child pornography in a recent advertising campaign. And not only the manufacturers of goods resort to such postemotionalism. Governments and institutions use a similar strategy. Consider, for example, an advertisement for the United Nations published in the *New York Times* on 20 September 1995:

> The people of New York City congratulate the people of the UN on their 50th anniversary. 'As the "capital of the world," New York City is particularly pleased to be hosting a series of cultural events and educational programs commemorating the United Nations 50th Anniversary. Here's to another 50 great years together!' – Mayor Rudolph W. Giuliani.

The photograph that accompanied this text shows two smiling gentlemen standing in front of a taxi cab with New York City skyscrapers in the background, with the captions: 'Jaswinder Singh, Cabdriver, Flushing, Queens. Richard Butler, Australian Ambassador to the United Nations.' One might well ask: What do any of these happy emotions have to do with commemorating the United Nations, which has been judged to have failed miserably in promoting peace and stopping genocide in the post-Cold War world? And of course, the UN avoids publicizing certain memories, such as the Nazi collaboration of its former Secretary-General, Kurt Waldheim.

Finally, consider the apparent paradox by which Speaker of the US House of Representatives Newt Gingrich, along with other Republicans, rode a wave of nostalgia for the 'good ol' days' of American Republicanism at the same time that they promoted a Toffleresque program of future shock, virtual reality, putting Thomas Jefferson 'on line,' and other aspects of centralized, classical, hierarchical bureaucracy.[101] It is the same old modernist bureaucracy and big government dressed up with a new emotional appeal.

Skepticism

For some readers, the immediate tendency will be to dismiss these and other examples as just old-fashioned instances of scapegoating, demagoguery, and propaganda. But I would suggest that even if the phenomena used for illustration above are somewhat similar to traditional phenomena, several things are new: (1) The camera is now ubiquitous and therefore makes all these emotional phenomena potentially staged, artificial, and second-hand.[102] (2) What David Riesman called other-directed 'inside-dopesterism' is also a ubiquitous mode of consuming information nowadays, thereby transforming most persons into voyeuristic consumers of these second-hand emotions. (3) Even twenty years ago, there were no full-time, professional 'opinion-makers' or 'newsmakers.' People were not sure what opinions they held or ought to hold, and newsmakers were recognized much after the fact. By contrast, the 1990s is the age of live newsmaking created by persons designed as *newsmakers* whose opinions are immediately refracted by designated *opinion-makers* and whose impact is gauged almost as quickly by opinion polls, which are broadcast back to the inside-dopesters. It is difficult to conceive of the possibility of feeling a genuine, spontaneous emotion in such a social structure. (4) Finally, in all of the illustrations that have been examined, and others that the reader can supply, one cannot help suspecting a climate of affected, feigned emotion, as if it were rehearsed and planned ahead of time.

Thus, the genocide committed by Hitler during World War II was a state secret for the most part, and it is *still* being analyzed, more than fifty years after the fact. By contrast, Serb leaders in the 1990s openly proclaim their genocidal aims in the cloak of victimhood on CNN and other prominent media sites. The point is that Hitler *was not able to* boast about the genocide he was committing on prime time television. Whereas the brutality at Auschwitz might be characterized as a high-tech but extremely low-visibility phenomenon, due to the elementary state of the information media at the time, the genocide in Bosnia is low-tech (the use of knives and bare hands) but extremely high-visibility:[103] Media coverage of Bosnia is second only to the coverage of the O.J. Simpson trial, which was the most covered news event in US history. The refrain that comes to us from World War II as rationalization for not stopping Hitler is 'We didn't know.' In the 1990s, nearly everyone on the planet knew about genocide in Bosnia, and the contemporary refrain might be summarized as 'We're confused (because we can't make out the victim) and we have compassion fatigue (because all sides seem worthy of our sympathy).' All this is definitely new.

Moreover, a new and distinctive aspect of contemporary news coverage is that journalists take pictures of each other taking pictures of staged assaults by US Marines on the beaches of Somalia, for example, or, to take another example, they hover on street corners notorious for producing victims of Serbian snipers in Sarajevo. The intent is to capture, on film, the live death and the immediate reaction by others in the vicinity to the suffering, and then supply the emotional packaging to the television audience for apprehending the event as they view it. Similarly, the Tiananmen Square massacre became a graphic media sensation of the sort of government repression that people formerly only read about, much after the fact, and had to imagine privately.[104] This vulture-like feature of the media feeding on sensationalism is a definite departure from norms that governed the presentation of phenomena related to death until recently. And far from being an illustration of postmodern de-differentiation, these and other examples of filming death so that it appeals to voyeurs are clearly motivated by the monetary rewards that such 'staged live' sensationalism brings to the journalists and the corporations they serve.[105] One headline captures an important truth about the contemporary media: 'As TV Sows Outrage, Guess What It Reaps?'[106]

Russia's counter-charge that NATO was committing genocide against Serbs in response to Western findings that Serbia was committing genocide against Croats and Bosnian Muslims constitutes more than postmodern de-differentiation. Taken in context of other actions by post-Cold War Russia – the massacre of the Chechens, the killing of American balloonists over Belarus, the anti-Western rhetoric emanating from Moscow, the open declaration of support for Serbs, the belligerent rhetoric toward the newly independent Baltic Republics – this act and others like it point to an organized logic behind the charge of genocide levelled at NATO.[107] Post-Cold War Russia is moving in the direction of reviving the Cold War: 'The truth is that Moscow has never accepted the breakup of the Soviet Union and . . . [engaged in] efforts to restore the Russian empire.'[108] I predicted something of this sort in my *The Balkanization of the West*: 'Western diplomats and intellectuals failed to see that the Yugoslav and Soviet communist systems were also internal Serbian and Russian Empires. . . . I predict that . . . Russia will take on the role of Serbia relative to the other, formerly Soviet republics.'[109]

The doctrine of collective guilt that was used by Hitler against Jews, though widely promulgated, was perceived to be anti-Semitic even at the time, and as contrary to ideals derived from the Enlightenment that focus on individual not collective responsibility. Although appeasement and cowardice enabled Hitler to make use of this anti-Enlightenment doctrine, people at the time knew that it was a morally dubious if not reprehensible doctrine. Ironically, the doctrine of collective guilt in the 1990s in which Croats and Muslims as whole peoples were stained with the guilt of Nazi collaboration during World War II was perceived as a banal truth, not worthy of indignation or protest. The implied doctrine of collective guilt in Affirmative Action is also not challenged even by those who express indignation at its other aspects.

As stated previously, the O.J. Simpson trial has been hailed as the trial of the century. Prior to Simpson's trial, the US trial of the century was the Lindburgh kidnapping case. But the Lindburgh case really focused on the guilt or innocence of the accused, not the question of whether he would 'get off' even if guilty. Moreover, at the time of the Lindburgh kidnapping trial, no one would have entertained the idea of putting the government on trial alongside the accused. But in the USA, this formerly anarchical idea is now the staple of analyzing many government actions, from Ruby Ridge (where US government agents killed a tax protestor's wife while attempting to arrest him) to Waco to the Internal Revenue Service. One should not underestimate the depth of anti-government sentiment in the USA.

Regarding the Oklahoma City bombing (along with the related sites of the Branch Davidian compound in Waco, Texas, and the incident at Ruby Ridge), the widespread hatred of the US government now broadcast throughout America is again different from old-fashioned anarchy because these new anarchists are treated as celebrity 'guests' on television programs who have a point of view that needs to be heard. Curiously, many of these anarchists are filmed with the US flag deliberately and carefully draped in the background, much as one is used to seeing the President of the United States portrayed. The postemotional blurring of emotions ascribed to anarchists, patriots, and television celebrities would have been unthinkable in historical instances of anarchy.

As for the Affirmative Action debate, this, too, is different from Napoleon granting Jews their rights as French citizens in the nineteenth century, for example. Jews, as a group, were not granted special rights, only rights given to other French citizens. By contrast, Affirmative Action today grants exclusive group rights to minorities based on *historical* grievances. Thus, minority members in the United States have special rights that citizens in the majority do not enjoy, and this state of affairs is rationalized on the basis of arguments that rely on *collective* guilt. Previous historical instances of emancipation in the West, by contrast, granted oppressed peoples some of the *individual* rights enjoyed by the majority, and even then, not all of the rights of the majority. Thus, women had to wait a long time in democratic nations to obtain the right to vote. So-called minority issues nowadays are not really minority issues because they are used as a steamroller by various groups for very specific ends.

In the past, victims mostly suffered in silence. This was especially true of children, who, if unfortunate enough to suffer parental abuse or disease or hazing from peers, took their calamity as if it were the order of nature. Historically, people did not get as indignant over as many things as so many contemporaries do. To be sure, there were insults, but they were of a traditional sort (insulting someone's mother or wife, for example, or desecrating the flag), and the response was a traditionally sanctioned one for justifiable anger. It is quite another matter when people today feel victimized by a look, word, phrase, or touch based on the subjective interpretation of the alleged victimizer's motive and on the synthetic construction of their victimhood status as based on membership in a specific group deemed to be a victim. The resulting indignation by victims is often manipulative, resulting in a new form of ressentiment. Saul Bellow expresses this insight eloquently:

> Rage is now brilliantly prestigious. Rage, the reverse of bourgeois prudence, is a luxury. Rage is distinguished; it is a patrician passion. The rage of rappers and rioters takes as its premise the majority's admission of guilt for past and present injustices, and counts on the admiration of the repressed for the emotional

power of the uninhibited and 'justly' angry. Rage can also be manipulative; it can be an instrument of censorship and despotism. . . . We can't open our mouths without being denounced as racists, misogynists, supremacists, imperialists, and fascists.[110]

And note that whereas traditional societies devised ways of deflecting the male gaze through methods such as the veil used in Islamic societies or the non-revealing clothing of the Victorian era, contemporary societies have established a new, double-bind puritanism in which the body is systematically displayed as an integral aspect of contemporary fashion at the same time that the gaze is just as systematically prohibited and often punished. Akbar Ahmed argues convincingly that, dating back to the Greeks, Western cultures have sought to display the naked or nearly naked body, in sharp contrast to the norm of modesty in Islamic societies.[111] It really is quite new that modesty in Western culture is decreasing while the policing of desire and thought is increasing.

The phenomenon of televising trials and other cultural events is also quite recent and new. Harking back to Walter Benjamin's celebrated essay 'The Work of Art in the Age of Mechanical Reproduction,'[112] one wonders how the aura of the trial or any other event can be preserved *vis-à-vis* the television medium. I will discuss this problem later, but for now wish to note that television, which surfaced as a powerful social force in the USA in the 1960s following the Nixon–Kennedy debates, is devouring an increasingly large chunk of social life. After forcing itself on the American judicial system and thereby transforming the trial into a soap opera, television is now moving into the arena of international war crimes trials. As such, it cannot avoid postemotional borrowing from the Nuremberg trials.[113] Consider the rhetoric in the following full-page advertisement in the *New York Times*:

> Sometimes it takes the whole world to bring one man to trial. Duško Tadić. A Serbian café owner who reportedly got along well with his Muslim customers. But when *civil war* broke out in the former Yugoslavia, Tadić – according to a United Nations' team of prosecutors – turned on his neighbors with a vengeance. This fall Tadić will face a special United Nations Tribunal. He's accused of torturing, mutilating and murdering men and raping a woman held in a Serbian prison camp in 1993. Tadić denies all charges. He says he wasn't there. The U.N. prosecutors claim he's a sadistic war criminal; and they say his trial could begin to redeem the rule of law around the world. Court TV will bring you LIVE coverage from the Hague, Netherlands of this first multinational war crimes tribunal convened since Nuremberg. *It's a real trial of the century. A trial the whole world should watch. A trial you can watch only on Court TV.*[114] (emphasis added)

Note that the upcoming trial is already framed for the viewer as a 'trial of the century,' and the war is staged in terms of a 'civil war,' not a Belgrade-sponsored war of genocide against the sovereign nation of Bosnia-Herzegovina. After the spectacle of the other trial of the century, the O.J. Simpson trial, the culture industry is deliberately gearing up for another, 'real,' trial of the century. Nor should one overlook the bottom line for Court TV, the income to be generated from this spectacle. No doubt Tadić's defense will follow the formula already uncovered in the Simpson trial: Tadić will be made out to be a victim of Croatian and Bosnian Muslim alleged racists.

There are many other contemporary illustrations of how postemotionalism differs from previous uses and misuses of emotion, but these will have to suffice for now. Facts do not speak for themselves, and require theory to illuminate them. In the remainder of this book, I will put forth the theoretical scaffolding for postemotionalism and then refer back to some of the examples found in this chapter for further explication.

Notes

1. George Orwell, *The Road to Wigan Pier* (New York: Harcourt Brace, [1937] 1958).
2. George Ritzer, *The McDonaldization of Society* (London: Sage, 1992).
3. See, for example, Zygmunt Bauman, *Postmodern Ethics* (Oxford: Basil Blackwell, 1993).
4. William A. Galston, 'Clinton and the Promise of Communitarianism,' *Chronicle of Higher Education*, 2 December 1992, p. A52.
5. Stjepan G. Meštrović, *The Balkanization of the West* (London: Routledge, 1994).
6. David Riesman, *The Lonely Crowd* (New Haven, CT: Yale University Press, [1950] 1969).
7. For an excellent discussion, see Georgie Anne Geyer, 'Foreign-Born Americans Should Receive Civic Education,' United Press International, 1 September 1995.
8. Arthur Spiegelman, 'Catastrophic Racial Divide in America Predicted by Some Observers,' *Houston Chronicle*, 20 October 1995, p. A12.
9. A separate theme that I pursue at length in *The Balkanization of the West*.
10. Jean Baudrillard, *America* (London: Verso, 1986).
11. Jean Baudrillard, *The Mirror of Production* (New York: Telos Press, 1975).
12. For an excellent discussion of McDonald's *vis-à-vis* culture, see Ritzer, *The McDonaldization of Society*.
13. Jean Baudrillard, *The Ecstasy of Communication* (New York: Semiotext(e), 1987).
14. Daniel Patrick Moynihan, *Pandaemonium* (New York: Oxford University Press, 1993).
15. Jean Baudrillard, *Simulations* (New York: Semiotext(e), 1983). For an excellent recent discussion of the role of simulation in contemporary life, see Chris Rojek, *Decentring Leisure* (London: Sage, 1995).
16. Michiko Kakutani, 'Art is Easier the Second Time Around,' *New York Times*, 30 October 1994, p. E4.
17. Chris Rojek, *Ways of Escape: Modern Transformations in Leisure and Travel* (Lanham, MD: Rowman and Littlefield, 1994), p. 4.
18. Quentin Hardy, 'Ye Olde Bottom Line is a New Attraction at Renaissance Faires,' *Wall Street Journal*, 28 September 1995, p. A1.
19. Holman Jenkins, 'Madonna, Cindy and George,' *Wall Street Journal*, 14 September 1995, p. A18.
20. Stephen Kinzer, 'Where There's War There's Amanpour,' *New York Times Magazine*, 9 October 1994, pp. 57–63.
21. Robert D. McFadden, 'Mail Bomber Links an End to Killings to His Manifesto,' *New York Times* 30 June 1995, p. A1.
22. Ibid.
23. David Binder, 'Ratko Mladić: Pariah as Patriot,' *New York Times Magazine*, 4 September 1994, pp. 26–42.
24. Robert Zoellick, 'Mother Country No More, Britain is Still Special,' *Wall Street Journal*, 3 April 1995, p. A18.
25. Theodor W. Adorno, *The Culture Industry* (London: Routledge, 1991).
26. Rojek, *Ways of Escape*, p. 134.
27. Thus, the *New York Times*, for example, carried two editorials on 18 September 1995, p. A11, that focused on authenticity: 'The Authentic Quality' by Anthony Lewis and 'The Phony Air War' by William Safire. Lewis argues that undeclared Presidential candidate Colin Powell appeals to many Americans because he seems genuine, while Safire argues that the 'massive air strikes'

against the Serbs, carried out in September 1995, were phony, that 'NATO does not have the will to kill killers.'

28. Adorno, *The Culture Industry*.

29. Rojek, *Ways of Escape*, p. 5.

30. Roger Thurow and Tony Horowitz, 'Paranoid and Vengeful, Serbs Claim Their War is to Right Old Wrongs,' *Wall Street Journal*, 18 September 1992, p. A1; Dan Morgan, 'Haunted Serbia: My Journey Back in Time to a Self-Defeated Nation,' *Washington Post*, 19 June 1994, p. A12.

31. Mike O'Connor, 'For Serbs, a Flashback to '43 Horror,' *New York Times*, 21 September 1995, p. A6.

32. Ibid.

33. Norman Cigar, *Genocide in Bosnia-Herzegovina* (College Station, TX: Texas A&M University Press, 1995).

34. For detailed documentation of this assertion, see Philip J. Cohen, *Serbia at War With History*, (College Station, TX: Texas A&M University Press, 1996).

35. Stephen Kinzer, 'Pro-Nazi Legacy Lingers for Croatia,' *New York Times*, 31 October 1993, p. A6.

36. Alain Finkielkraut, *Comment peut-on être Croate?* (Paris: Gallimard, 1992), p. 42.

37. Meir Shalev, 'If Bosnians Were Whales,' *New York Times*, 29 August 1992, p. A15.

38. Sara Rimer, 'A Bit Reluctantly, a Nation Succumbs to a Trial's Spell,' *New York Times*, 7 February 1995, p. A1.

39. Benjamin A. Holden, Laurie P. Cohen, and Eleena de Lisser, 'Race Seems to Play an Increasing Role in Many Jury Verdicts,' *Wall Street Journal*, 4 October 1995, p. A1:

> Increasingly, jury watchers are concluding that . . . race plays a far more significant role in jury verdicts than many people involved in the justice system prefer to acknowledge. . . . [black jurors] are choosing to disregard the evidence, however powerful, because they seek to protest racial injustice and to refrain from adding to the already large number of blacks behind bars. . . . The race factor seems particularly evident in such urban environments as the New York City borough of the Bronx, where juries are more than 80% black and Hispanic. There, black defendants are acquitted in felony cases 47.6% of the time – nearly three times the national acquittal rate of 17% for all races. . . . Washington Mayor Marion Barry, who was acquitted on all but one of 14 counts against him smoking crack cocaine; the string of acquittals of defendants charged with beating Reginald Denny during the Los Angeles riots in 1992. . . . Representing himself in an Atlanta trial last summer, Erick Bozeman openly pleaded with a jury to acquit him of serious federal drug charges because he is [*sic*] black. In his opening statement, he told jurors that the US war on drugs was part of the same war on black people that 'has existed in one way or another since African prisoners arrived in 1619 as slaves'. . . . The case ended in a hung jury on the central charge.

40. Peter Waldman and Frances A. McMorris, 'As Sheik Omar Case Nears End, Neither Side Looks a Winner,' *Wall Street Journal*, 22 September 1995, p. A1.

41. Ibid.

42. Joseph P. Fried, 'Sheik and 9 Followers Guilty of a Conspiracy of Terrorism,' *New York Times*, 2 October 1995, p. A1.

43. Bob Herbert, 'Killer Cops,' *New York Times*, 15 September 1995, p. A15.

44. David Margolick, 'With Tales of Racism and Error, Simpson Lawyers Seek Acquittal,' *New York Times*, 29 September 1995, p. A1:

> Mr. Cochran's orations today were thick with evangelical imagery and emotional appeals tailored to the largely minority jury . . . [he] focused most of his fire on Mr. Fuhrman, whom he called a 'genocidal racist,' likened to Adolf Hitler. . . . After many of his remarks, one half-expected to hear an 'Amen.' . . . Mr. Scheck [another defense attorney] recited far more facts. But in his own way he was every bit as emotional. That was far heavier on frowns and scowls, as if a whole school of dead fish had been placed under his nose.

45. Ibid.

46. Seth Mydans, 'In the Joy of Victory, Defense Team Is in Discord,' *New York Times*, 4 October 1995, p. A11.

47. Ibid.

48. Don Terry, 'Distrust Fuels Racial Divide on Just Verdict for Simpson,' *New York Times*, 2 October 1995, p. A9.

49. A sampling of excerpts and headlines from the *New York Times* on 4 October 1995, the day after the verdict was handed down, illustrates this well: David Margolick, 'Jury Clears Simpson in Double Murder; Spellbound Nation Divides on Verdict,' p. A1: 'The case turned when the black jurors pivoted from looking at the murder to looking at the police. . . . In a sentiment expressed by numerous people around the country, Daid Epps, 26, who is white and was also at the restaurant, said: "If you've got enough money to hire Johnnie Cochran and Robert Shapiro, you get off. If it was you or me, we'd go to jail." Around the country, too, many women also said they were hit hard by the verdict because of an empathy for Simpson's former wife, Nicole, who, according to testimony, endured years of abuse'; N.R. Kleinfeld, 'A Day (10 Minutes of It) the Country Stood Still,' p. A1; James Sterngold, 'Simpson Walks Out of the Courtroom a Free Man and into the Lucrative Free Market,' p. A10: 'It was also clear that the past that has dogged him [Mr Simpson] so mercilessly could also prove a financial bonanza, potentially making Mr. Simpson far wealthier than he was before his former wife and a friend were slain on June 12, 1994'; Deirdre Carmody, 'In the World of Books, a Rush to Publish,' p. A10; Charisse Jones, 'In the Seats Reserved for Relatives, Joy and Pain, Relief and Disbelief,' p. A11; Timothy Egan, 'One Juror Smiled; Then They Knew,' p. A11; 'Cacophony of Reaction: From One Woman's Cries to a College's Shouts of Joy,' p. A13: 'This is a statement from black America,' yelled a cheering Myron Burney, a 19-year-old sophomore from Chadbourn, N.C.'; Kenneth B. Noble, 'In the City of the Beautiful People, Trial Hinged on Uglier Issues,' p. A13:

> Many conflicting forces are likely to have combined in the acquittal of O.J. Simpson, but perhaps none has loomed larger than the role of the Los Angeles Police Department, as personified by Mark Fuhrman, the detective whose racist views caused him to be vilified by both defense and prosecution. In effect. . . . Nearly four years after the convulsions, turmoil and fear that followed the beating of the black motorist Rodney King, the police are still considered an occupying force in large segments of the community. And the not-guilty verdict in the Simpson trial, many fear, is likely to fortify that view. Indeed, while in a narrow sense, the Simpson case was simply about whether the wealthy and charming athlete killed his former wife and her friend, many Angelenos suggested that the jurors ultimately cast their vote on the very fate of this sprawling city's social fabric. . . . Suspicion and fear have infected the political climate here like a deadly virus. . . . When the defense lawyer Johnnie L. Cochran Jr. showed up at the courthouse last week surrounded by bodyguards from the Nation of Islam, many Jews, including Ronald Goldman's father, took deep offense, recalling the group's reputation for anti-white and anti-Semitic invective.

See also George F. Will, 'Simpson Jury Yielded to Politics of Race,' *Houston Chronicle*, 4 October 1995, p. 24A. I agree with Mr Will that

> For more than a generation now, public policies such as affirmative action, the racial spoils system and the cult of 'diversity' have been teaching the nation that groupthink is virtuous. Such policies have taught this by encouraging identity politics – the politics of thinking that you are but a fragment of the racial or ethnic group to which you belong and you have few if any obligations beyond it. Such policies have taught this by making it admirable – and lucrative – to identify with grievance groups defined by their resentments of the larger society. . . . Given all this, it is not surprising that the jurors had no pangs of conscience about regarding Simpson merely as a member of a group – and not seeing his victims at all.

50. Walter Goodman, 'Vivid Images Dispel Abundance of Hot Air,' *New York Times*, 4 October 1995, p. A12.

51. 'Congressman is Sentenced,' *New York Times*, 29 September 1995, p. A8.

52. Émile Durkheim, *The Division of Labor in Society* (New York: Free Press, [1893] 1933).

53. Political cartoon by Bill Schorr, *New York Times*, 17 December 1995, p. E4.

54. Malcolm W. Browne, 'Sarin is Just One of Many Gases Terrorists Could Use,' *New York Times*, 22 March 1995, p. A7.

55. See, for example, 'Affirmative Action: But Some Are More Equal Than Others,' *The Economist*, 15 April 1995, pp. 21–3; Stephen Labaton, 'Affirmative Action Case Embroils Clinton,' *New York Times*, 25 April 1995, p. A15; Farrell Bloch, 'Affirmative Action Hasn't Helped Blacks,' *Wall Street Journal*, 1 March 1995, p. A14; Shelby Steele, 'Affirmative Action Must Go,' *New York Times*, 1 March 1995, p. A19; Joe Klein, 'Affirmative Inaction?' *Newsweek*, 26 June 1995, p. 23; Geoffrey C. Clayton, 'Astronomy in the '90s: Angry, White, and Male?' *Mercury*, May/June 1995, pp. 33–4; Steven A. Holmes, 'Backlash Against Affirmative Action Troubles Advocates,' *New York Times*, 7 February 1995, p. B9; 'California Governor Moves Quickly Against Affirmative Action,' *New York Times*, 2 June 1995, p. A15; Paul Roberts and Lawrence Stratton, 'Color Code,' *National Review*, 20 March 1995, p. 36; Edmund L. Andrews, 'F.C.C. is Said to Seek an End to Preferences on Sex and Race,' *New York Times*, 22 June 1995, p. D1; Linda Greenhouse, 'Justices, 5 to 4, Cast Doubts on U.S. Programs That Give Preferences Based on Race,' *New York Times*, 13 June 1995, p. A1.

56. John Edwards, 'Group Rights Versus Individual Rights,' *Journal of Social Policy*, January 1994, pp. 55–70; Thomas Sowell, 'Quota Enforcers,' *Forbes*, 10 October 1994, p. 64; Damon Darlin, 'Quota Queen,' *Forbes*, 20 June 1994, p. 42.

57. Thus, some have charged that when male professors mention anything of a sexual nature in the classroom, they may be engaging in sexual harassment, but female professors who do the same thing are engaging in academic freedom. See, for example, Asra Q. Nomani, 'Was Professor's Lecture Academic Freedom or Sex Harassment?' *Wall Street Journal*, 7 March 1995, p. A1.

58. Brent Staples, 'The Presumption of Stupidity,' *New York Times*, 5 March 1995, p. 14; Howard Fineman, 'Race and Rage,' *Newsweek*, 3 April 1995, pp. 22–5; Roger W. Wilkins, 'Racism Has Its Privileges,' *The Nation*, 27 March 1995, p. 409; Mortimer Zuckerman, 'Remember the Real Victims,' *U.S. News & World Report*, 26 June 1995, p. 68; Michael Kinsley, 'The Spoils of Victimhood,' *New Yorker*, 27 March 1995, pp. 62–9; Ellis Cose, 'Affirmative Action and the Dilemma of the Qualified,' *Black Enterprise*, October 1994, pp. 158–62.

59. However, she entered Citadel without meeting the physical requirements set for other cadets because of a court order, and quit after a few days. See the story by Associated Press, 'First Day for Female Cadet Ends in Citadel Infirmary,' *New York Times*, 15 August 1995, p. A1; 'Faulkner Spends First Days as Cadet in Bed,' *Houston Chronicle*, 16 August 1995, p. A1; Catherine S. Manegold, 'Female Cadet Quits the Citadel, Citing Stress of Her Legal Battle,' *New York Times*, 19 August 1995, p. A3.

60. Anita K. Blair, 'Separate and Equal,' *New York Times*, 20 November 1995, p. A11.

61. Paul Hollander, 'We are all (sniffle, sniffle) Victims Now,' *Wall Street Journal*, 18 January 1995, p. A16.

62. Carole Feldman, 'Teachers Grapple With Harassment,' *Bryan-College Station Eagle*, 5 July 1994, p. A1.

63. Steven Pinker, 'The Name of the Game,' *New York Times*, 5 April 1994, p. A15.

64. See, for example, Wes Swift, 'College Republicans Brought Up on Charges,' *The Battalion*, 20 September 1995, p. 1. The story refers to a letter written by College Republicans at Texas A&M University in which they charge that multicultural courses are a form of brainwashing, and that charges against them for expressing this view violate free speech.

65. For a sampling of the vast literature on this subject as it might pertain to postemotionalism, see Christiane Brems and Patricia Wagner, 'Blame of Victim and Perpetrator in Rape Versus Theft,' *The Journal of Social Psychology*, 134 (1994), pp. 363–74; 'Can a Woman Who Drinks be Raped?' *Glamour*, July 1991, p. 59; 'Cowboys' Williams and Friend are Accused of Raping 17-year-old Dallas Dancer,' *Jet*, 8 May 1995, p. 52; Robert T. Sigler and Donna Haygood, 'The Criminalization of Forced Marital Intercourse,' *Marriage and Family Review*, 12 (1987), pp. 71–85; Margaret D. Bonilla, 'Cultural Assault: What Feminists Are Doing to Rape Ought to be a Crime,' *Policy Review*, 66 (1993), pp. 22–9; Henry McNulty, 'Did the Tyson Trial Belong in the Sports Section?' *The Fourth Estate*, 29 February 1992, p. 5; Eugene J. Kanin, 'False Rape Allegations,' *Archives of Sexual Behavior*, 23 (1994), pp. 81–92; Patricia L. Donat and John D'Emilio, 'A Feminist Redefinition of Rape and Sexual Assault,' *Journal of Social Issues*, 48

(1992), pp. 9–22; Norman Podhoretz, 'Rape in Feminist Eyes,' *Commentary*, October 1991, pp. 29–35; Lisa Jackson, 'Society Loves a Good Victim,' *Newsweek*, 24 July 1989, p. 8; Sheila Weller, 'Why is Date Rape so Hard to Prove?' *Health*, July/August 1992, p. 62; 'Wrong on Rape: Neither Naming Rape Victims Against Their Will, Nor Broadening the Definition of Rape to Include Seduction, Helps the Cause of Feminism,' *The Economist*, 18 May 1991, pp. 14–15.

66. Kathy Dobie, 'Between Seduction and Rape,' *Vogue*, December 1991, p. 154; Calvin Fussman, 'Consent of a Woman,' *Lear's*, October 1993, pp. 32–3; 'Dangerous Dates,' *Glamour*, June 1992, p. 102; Renee D. Turner, 'Date Rape,' *Ebony*, December 1990, p. 104; David R. Carlin, 'Date Rape Fallacies,' *Commonweal*, 25 February 1994, pp. 11–12; Carl Mollins, 'His Word or Hers?' *Maclean's*, 17 February 1992, p. 2; 'Inflated Definition of Rape,' *Society* September/October 1991, p. 2; Norman Podhoretz, 'Rape and the Feminists,' *Commentary*, March 1992, pp. 2–8; 'Seduction or Date Rape?' *The Wilson Quarterly*, Winter 1992, pp. 138–9.

67. 'Sexual Correctness: Has it Gone Too Far?' *Newsweek*, 25 October 1993, pp. 52–8; Alan W. McEvoy, 'Talking About Date Rape to Male Students,' *Education Digest*, March 1992, pp. 42–3.

68. Elizabeth Kuster, '"Lookism": The Work-place's Dirty Little Secret,' *Glamour*, September 1993, p. 133.

69. *New York Times*, 14 October 1995, p. A4.

70. *Houston Chronicle*, 1 October 1995, p. 4C.

71. See Jeri Laber, 'Bosnia: Questions About Rape,' *New York Review of Books*, 25 March 1993, p. 3; Marlise Simons, 'Bosnian Rapes Go Untried by the UN,' *New York Times*, 7 December 1994, p. A12; Laura Eggertson, 'Children of Rape,' *Maclean's*, 24 May 1993, p. 22; Nina Kadić, 'Dispatches From Bosnia and Herzegovina: Young Survivors Testify to Systematic Rape,' *Ms.*, January/February 1993, pp. 12–13; 'Make Mass Rape a War Crime, UN Urged,' *Christian Century*, 28 April 1993, p. 448; Tony Scherman, 'Our Times,' *Life*, May 1993, p. 20; Tom Post, 'A Pattern of Rape,' *Newsweek* 4 January 1993, pp. 32–6; 'Rape is a Crime, Not an Act of War,' *Glamour*, April 1993, p. 96; Paul Lewis, 'Rape Was Weapon of Serbs, UN Says,' *New York Times*, 20 October 1993, p. A1; Catharine A. MacKinnon, 'Turning Rape Into Pornography: Postmodern Genocide,' *Ms.*, July/August 1993, pp. 24–30; Lance Morrow, 'Unspeakable,' *Time*, 22 February 1993, pp. 48–50; Ann Leslie, 'A Weapon Called Rape,' *Ladies' Home Journal*, August 1993, p. 120; Slavenka Drakulić, 'Women Hide Behind a Wall of Silence,' *The Nation*, 1 March 1993, p. 253; Aryeh Neier, 'Watching Rights,' *The Nation*, 1 March 1993, p. 259.

72. Male rape of men is barely mentioned in Alexandra Stiglmayer, *Mass Rape: The War Against Women in Bosnia-Herzegovina* (Lincoln, NE: University of Nebraska Press, 1994).

73. Brent Staples, 'The Rhetoric of Victimhood,' *New York Times*, 13 February 1994, p. E15.

74. John T. McQuiston, 'Colin Ferguson Convicted of L.I.R.R. Train Massacre,' *New York Times*, 18 February 1995, p. A1.

75. John T. McQuiston, 'Long Island Killer's Appeal Plan is to Question His Sanity,' *New York Times*, 19 February 1995, p. A18.

76. Quoted in Minoo Southgate, 'Balkanization in the Air,' *National Review*, 21 February 1994, p. 28.

77. Charles J. Sykes, *A Nation of Victims: The Decay of the American Character*. (New York: St Martin's Press, 1992).

78. CNN broadcast, 5 September 1992.

79. Karen Koman, 'Wrong Way to a Mother-Friendly Workplace,' *Wall Street Journal*, 24 November 1993, p. A14: 'To pump milk in a restroom is "like telling someone to go eat your lunch in the bathroom"'.

80. A. Bamisaiye and M.A. Oyediran, 'Breast-feeding Among Female Employees at a Major Health Institution in Lagos, Nigeria,' *Social Science and Medicine*, 17 (1983), pp. 1867–71; Cui Lili, 'China Encourages Breast Feeding,' *Beijing Review*, 21 September 1992, pp. 40–1; Anne L. Wright, Mark Bauer, and Clarina Clark, 'Cultural Interpretations and Intracultural Variability in Navajo Beliefs About Breastfeeding,' *American Ethnologist*, 20 (1993), pp. 781–96; Marylyn Salmon, 'The Cultural Significance of Breastfeeding and Infant Care in Early Modern England and America,' *Journal of Social History*, 28 (1994), pp. 247–69.

81. For a sampling of the vast literature on this topic, see Robert Boostrom, 'Baring the

Breast: Love, Defilement, and Breast-Feeding,' *Perspectives in Biology and Medicine*, 38 (1995), pp. 406–21; Esther Davidowitz, 'The Breast-Feeding Taboo,' *Redbook*, July 1992, pp. 92–5; Liza Habiby, 'Decent Exposure,' *Health*, November/December 1994, pp. 52–3; Natalie Kurinij, 'Does Maternal Employment Affect Breast-Feeding?' *American Journal of Public Health*, 79 (1989), pp. 1247–50; Jared Diamond, 'Father's Milk,' *Discover*, 16 (1994), pp. 82–7.

82. Roger Kagan, 'Hero of Haiti Finds Dictators to His Liking,' *Wall Street Journal*, 22 September 1994, p. A14.

83. Rick Bragg, 'Varying View on Role of Haiti General's Wife,' *New York Times*, 26 September 1994, p. A7. Bragg noted that Jimmy Carter said that Mrs Cedras 'was slim and very attractive.' See also Stephen Schwartz, 'Jimmy Carter Bobbles Nicaragua's Property Issues,' *Wall Street Journal*, 8 July 1994, p. A11; James M. Wall, 'Passion in Public,' *Christian Century*, 2 November 1994, p. 10003; David Skidmore, 'Foreign Policy Interest Groups and Presidential Power: Jimmy Carter and the Battle Over Ratification of the Panama Canal Treaties,' *Presidential Studies Quarterly*, 23 (1993), pp. 477–97; P.J. O'Rourke, '100 Reasons Why Jimmy Carter Was a Better President than Bill Clinton,' *American Spectator* 26 (1993), pp. 18–21; Joe Klein, 'Russia's Jimmy Carter,' *New York*, 18 February 1991, p. 14; Vicki Quade, 'Jimmy Carter Works the World,' *Human Rights*, 17 (1990), pp. 22–5; David Riesman, 'Prospects for Human Rights,' *Society*, 15 (1977), pp. 28–33.

84. Kevin Fedarko, 'Bad Blood and Broken Promises: As Bosnian Serbs Continue Harassing UN Peacekeepers, Jimmy Carter Jumps Into the Fray,' *Time*, 26 December 1995, pp. 121–2; 'A Little Help From Jimmy Carter,' *New York Times*, 21 December 1994, p. A26; Elaine Sciolino, 'Carter's Bosnia Effort Provokes Skepticism,' *New York Times*, 16 December 1994, p. A3; Roger Cohen, 'Serbs, Meeting With Carter, Agree to Bosnian Cease-fire,' *New York Times*, 20 December 1994, p. A1.

85. Perhaps the most visible sympathizer for the Bosnian Serb cause is A.M. Rosenthal, 'For American Worth,' *New York Times*, 12 September 1995, p. A13.

86. Tim Severin, *In Search of Genghis Khan* (New York: Atheneum, 1992).

87. Jane Perlez, 'Decay of a 20th Century Relic: What is the Future of Auschwitz?' *New York Times*, 5 January 1994, p. A4.

88. Richard H. Minear, 'Atomic Holocaust, Nazi Holocaust: Some Reflections,' *Diplomatic History*, Spring 1995, pp. 347–65.

89. A.M. Rosenthal, 'Bosnia and the Holocaust,' *New York Times*, 26 April 1994, p. A23.

90. Bernard Weinraub, 'Islamic Nations Move to Keep Out "Schindler's List",' *New York Times*, 7 April 1994, p. C15.

91. See Irving Louis Horowitz, *The Decomposition of Sociology* (New York: Oxford University Press, 1994).

92. Jane Perlez, 'Elie Wiesel Now Agrees to Go to Auschwitz Rites,' *New York Times*, 20 January 1995, p. A4.

93. Jane Perlez, 'Poles and Jews Honor Dead of Auschwitz,' *New York Times*, 27 January 1995, p. A1.

94. Quoted in Barbara Demick, 'Remembrance of Auschwitz Liberation Reopens Old Wounds,' *Bryan-College Station Eagle*, 26 January 1995, p. A3.

95. Frank Bajak, 'Fifty Years Later, Much Remains Unresolved at Nazi Death Camp,' *Bryan-College Station Eagle*, 28 January 1995, p. A4.

96. Letter to the Editor, 'Remember Liberators,' *New York Times*, 31 January 1995, p. A10.

97. Noble, 'In the City of the Beautiful People,' p. A13.

98. *New York Times*, 18 September 1995, p. A4.

99. Steven A. Holmes, 'Photographs of Balkans Draw Fire,' *New York Times*, 24 September 1994, p. A6.

100. Elaine Sciolino, 'Sarajevo Pact: Diplomacy on a Roll,' *New York Times*, 15 September 1995, p. A6.

101. Maureen Dowd, 'King Newt and His Court Explore Virtual America,' *New York Times*, 11 January 1995, p. A1.

102. See Arnold Gehlen, *Man in the Age of Technology* (New York: Columbia University Press, 1980).

103. I owe this insight to Daniel Kofman.

104. 'The Death of Democracy,' *Newsweek*, 4 June 1990, pp. 28–9.

105. See, for example, Joe Mandese, 'Seeking Killer Ratings, NBC Plans Snuff TV,' *Advertising Age*, 13 December 1993, p. 1.

106. Walter Goodman, 'As TV Sows Outrage, Guess What it Reaps?' *New York Times*, 28 March 1995, p. C26.

107. See William Safire, 'Tale of Two Treaties,' *New York Times*, 2 October 1995, p. A15: 'As Russia recovers and rearms, as history suggests it will, Moscow's imperialist urge might well rise again – and then it would be too late and "provocative" to redraw the defense line.'

108. George Melloan, 'If Russia Wants Another Cold War, Fine,' *Wall Street Journal* 18 September 1995, p. A19.

109. Meštrović, *The Balkanization of the West*, pp. 55 and 176.

110. Saul Bellow, 'Papuans and Zulus,' *New York Times*, 10 March 1994, p. A25.

111. Akbar Ahmed, *Postmodernism and Islam* (London: Routledge, 1992).

112. Walter Benjamin, 'The Work of Art in the Age of Mechanical Reproduction,' in *Illuminations*, ed. Hannah Arendt (New York: Harcourt, Brace and World, 1968), pp. 219–66.

113. Alex Ross, 'Watching for a Judgment of Real Evil,' *New York Times* 12 November 1995, p. H37. 'As Court TV prepares for its next "trial of the century," Nuremberg is the point of reference.'

114. 27 September 1995, p. A9.

2

The End of Passion?

In this chapter, my aim is to show how postemotionalism as a concept is able to transcend some of the limitations of postmodernism and the conceptual dilemmas it has caused. Many contemporary authors have taken their lead from Friedrich Nietzsche's claim in *The Will to Power* that rationalism will eventually destroy unreflective spontaneity.[1] In *The Birth of Tragedy* as well, Nietzsche singles out Socrates as the villain in Western history because of his high esteem for logic and rationality. Nietzsche argued that natural, healthy creativity can be achieved only by a return to primordial myth or what he calls the forces of Dionysus. Many intellectuals today accept Nietzsche's thumbnail sketch of modernity as the triumph of Apollo.

Some well-known literature from the previous *fin de siècle*, such as Dostoevsky's *Notes From the Underground*,[2] also portrays heightened consciousness as the hallmark of the modern person who is unable to feel spontaneously. Dostoevsky's lead character, the underground man, is simply unable to cross a modern barrier between desire and action. Stupid people, Dostoevsky's character writes, are able to act immediately on their feelings, but the modern person with sensitive consciousness is distracted by his or her own brain and its endless rationalizations. The underground man is born from ideas, not nature, very much like the city in which he lives, St Petersburg, which is built on a swamp and has not evolved organically. In this novel, as well as many others, Dostoevsky clearly intended to indict modernity as an unnatural sickness in which human reason overrides natural feelings.

Émile Durkheim lamented about a century ago that 'We have reasoned so much!' If his sociological treatises are read as humanistic manifestos – as I argued they can be read in my *The Barbarian Temperament* – one can discern easily the *fin de siècle* lines of argumentation found in Nietzsche, Dostoevsky, and other literary authors. For example, Durkheim depicts the overly sensitive and highly intelligent neurasthenic as the prime candidate for suicide. His misunderstood concept of anomie is actually an indictment of modernity as the over-stimulation of the mind because the widening of one's scope of consciousness is the root cause of the 'infinity of desires' that constitutes anomie. Durkheim's anomie concept, in a nutshell, holds that: The more we know, the more we want, and our desires can never be satiated. Traditional people – whom Dostoevsky's character would have called stupid – desire pretty much along the lines of what their societies allow them to desire. But modern and, by extension, postmodern societies offer so many choices and such an infinite number of objects of desire that in the end Durkheim's anomic type succumbs to the infinity of wanting, and, consequently, to an exasperated state of weariness.[3] Did Durkheim foreshadow the idea of desire fatigue?

Daniel Bell follows Nietzsche's lead to argue in *The End of Ideology*[4] that the twentieth century has witnessed the end of passionate ideological movements. David Riesman concludes his *The Lonely Crowd* with a discussion of other-directed 'loss of emotion.'[5] Francis Fukuyama[6] revitalized Hegel's concept of the 'end of history,'[7] which might be subtitled as the 'end of emotion' due to the triumph of rationality. Even Marxism, that extremely popular sociological doctrine that influenced non-sociologists more than any other, expresses a rhetoric of cognition much more than emotion. For example, in *The German Ideology*,[8] one finds Marx and Engels using terms such as 'phantoms of the brain,' 'conceiving,' 'thinking,' 'chimeras,' 'ideas,' 'dogmas,' and 'forms of consciousness.' They sought to rebel against a 'rule of thought'[9] they found abhorrent only to replace it with a different rule of thought. One of their central claims is that 'men are the producers of their conceptions,'[10] which may be true to some extent, yet omits both the role of emotions and the role of the collective consciousness, which individuals cannot control. When Marxists do touch on emotions, it is usually in the context of the 'fetishism of commodities,' alienation, or the irrationality of religion. But their attitude is that these emotional aspects of human nature can and must be overcome through heightened consciousness. In general, the widespread progress of science, positivism, and rationalism in the West in the twentieth century seem to signal the victory of the 'mind' over the 'heart' in Pascal's famous dualism.

If one were to accept this position, one might interpret the 'post' in my use of 'postemotionalism' as 'after-emotion.' In this reading, I would be seen as agreeing that spontaneous emotion is dead, and postemotionalism is a concept that falls into a well-recognized Western tradition emanating from Nietzsche and culminating in Marx. While this might make matters simpler, it is not an accurate assessment of my use of postemotionalism. In chapter 3, I show that Riesman's concept of the 'loss of emotion' is much more complicated than first meets the eye, and throughout this book I explore the nuances of postemotionalism. But at this juncture in the discussion, let me tip my hand and outline how my position differs from the Nietzschean and Marxist trajectories, and what I intend by postemotionalism.

I do not think that Nietzsche's dualism between heart and mind, emotions and the intellect, and, in general, Apollonian and Dionysian forces is any longer relevant to understanding contemporary societies. In chapter 23 of *The Birth of Tragedy*, Nietzsche argued that in modernity, myth (as fiction or invention) is approached via intellectual constructs. He argued for the return to myth as a liberating force for the human spirit, but from Nazism to the postmodernist embrace of circulating fiction, one can no longer believe that myth will save humanity. Against Nietzsche, I argue that in the twentieth century *emotion* is approached via intellectual constructs. It is worth noting that postmodernism has uncovered and revels in simulations, which are the rough equivalent of Nietzsche's myths. But this vast postmodern mythology has not resulted in the liberation of the human spirit that Nietzsche as well as some postmodernists envisioned. Against Nietzsche, I would point out that abstract mores, laws, and government are not the problem – for what else could they be but abstract? – but that *abstract emotions* are. The notion of an abstract emotion seems to be an oxymoron, yet it is exactly what I intend in the theory of postemotionalism. It is not cultural sterility but *emotional sterility* that plagues our present *fin de siècle*. With the postemotional concept, I am proposing something new, not a struggle or balance between will and idea, but the will *as* representation or idea.

Thus, postemotionalism refers to the use of *dead*, abstracted emotions by the culture industry in a neo-Orwellian, mechanical, and petrified manner. The use of 'post' in the concept of postemotionalism is deliberately ambiguous: It refers to the many endgames that postmodernists discuss, including post- or after-emotion. But the distinctive aspect of the theoretical construct I am trying to develop is that emotions did not really disappear, so that the 'emotional' in postemotional is still relevant. A new hybrid of intellectualized, mechanical, mass-produced emotions has appeared on the world scene. Thus, Baudrillard is wrong to claim that – following the Nietzschean and Marxist trajectories – there is no pity or compassion in the postmodern world. On the contrary, there is so much compassion that people complain of 'compassion fatigue.' Yet this distracted compassion is not the *caritas* of traditional times, but a displaced, viscerated compassion churned out by the culture industry that is really more like pity. *Caritas* binds humanity together whereas pity isolates and divides people into those who have the luxury to look down on others versus those who are desperate.

Moreover, the theoretical scaffolding of most of the intellectuals cited above carries with it the expectation that the alleged triumph of rationality will – or can – lead to tolerance. Nietzsche would not have approved of tolerance, had such a word been popular in his time, but I think he would have agreed that post-Socratic Apollonianism leads to tolerance as yet another manifestation of what he called 'sickliness.' The Marxists were too cocky about having found the right path to the end of history to even bother with tolerance. The Communist version of this myth was the utopia of brotherhood and unity. But against this premature conclusion, I agree with Akbar Ahmed that, world-wide, intolerance and ethnic strife, not tolerance, seem to be the rule, not the exception, in the years that have accompanied the postmodernist discourse: Ethnic cleansing has become a metaphor for our times.[11] And against Bell, in some senses, it seems that much of this intolerance is fuelled by passions of sorts.

Life for Life's Sake

Another entry point among many into the vast literature on modernity, modernism, and postmodernism lies in the distinction many authors wish to make between two forms of modernity. Thus, Matei Calinescu distinguishes between *modernity* as a stage in history and *modernism* as an aesthetic, avant-garde attitude in the arts.[12] Hence, with the advent of modernity, modernism opposes modern bourgeois society. Art is freed from traditional constraints of religion and custom. Modernist art, almost by definition, has to constantly change, move, defy, and stick out its tongue at the bourgeoisie. Modernist art has no duty. It does not have to serve social aims. It revels in 'uselessness,' in being art for art's sake.

Postemotionalism denies this neat and tidy division between modernity and modernism. Harking back to Thorstein Veblen's notion of the useless and wasteful as prestigious, set forth in 1899 in the classic but misunderstood *The Theory of the Leisure Class*,[13] postemotionalism assumes that almost all aspects of contemporary social life revel in the useless, in luxury. The habits of the leisure class in Veblen's time have permeated to the middle and lower classes, indeed all social classes, in contemporary times. Another way of phrasing this is that nearly everything in society becomes an aesthetic, and that the aesthetic is not confined to the fields of culture and art. Modernism escapes the boundaries of art and permeates other modern societal institutions such as politics, the law, and education (among others) such that a great deal of social life operates on the modernist model of art for art's sake. While many credit Daniel Bell with first making this claim, it can be found much earlier, in the writings of Thorstein Veblen as well as those of his colleagues who wrote in the spirit of the previous *fin de siècle*, among them Émile Durkheim, Georg Simmel, and Henry Adams, to name a few.[14] Modern, rational, capitalist institutions and their products themselves become aesthetic and useless. For example, the United Nations is increasingly perceived as a useless, wasteful, and highly expensive luxury organization whose many conferences, peacekeeping operations, and other activities are usually judged to be failures, but whose prestige seems to be unaffected by this judgement. One might paraphrase this with the motto 'UN for UN's sake.' (Or, as a Dutch UN Peacekeeper referred to the UN, during a flight we shared from Amsterdam to Zagreb, 'United Nothing.') Another telling sign is that in order to promote its high image for the fiftieth anniversary of the establishment of the United Nations, celebrated in 1995, the UN printed full-page advertisements in prestigious newspapers. Yet these advertisements featured photographs of the faces of celebrities who endorsed the UN with emotional truisms about peace, not any factual information about the UN's actual productivity. For example, one such advertisement featured a photograph of Norman Mailer and his claim that:

> The UN has endured through the massive maneuvers of the Cold War and all the chaos that has followed. If our hope of peace is to be achieved, it can probably not be realized without the presence of the UN as mediator.[15]

The best that Mailer can say for the UN is that it has endured. Clearly, the important point is that this UN strategy reflects the fact that advertisements for phenomena ranging from consumer products to presidential campaigns sell synthetic, rehearsed *feelings*, not information about usefulness.

Other illustrations abound: The Los Angeles Police Department tried to salvage its reputation following charges of racism made against it in the O.J. Simpson trial in 1995 not by releasing facts and figures to counter these charges, but by promoting a new television series, *L.A.P.D.* This television program would show real police personnel engaged in 'real' police work while cameras rolled, in order to reassure the public emotionally that its main task is to apprehend criminals, not to engage in racism. But the obvious rebuttal is that one cannot imagine members of the LAPD engaging in racist brutality for the cameras knowing that the cameras are rolling.

Similarly, consider NATO's decision to 'get tough' with Serbs in September 1995 after years of being humiliated by them. The television media showed images of bombs exploding on selected targets to demonstrate this allegedly new get-tough policy. One was supposed to believe that NATO realized that its credibility was at stake, that it had to prove it was more than an expensive luxury item for Western governments and the taxpayers who support it. William Safire and Anthony Lewis pointed out the *facts* that, contrary to this fiction of NATO as effective, NATO jets bombed the same thirty-five targets over and over again for many days, and deliberately avoided destroying 300 targets (tanks and heavy artillery) that would have made a difference in lifting the siege of Sarajevo.[16] But Safire and Lewis were drowned out in the emotional impact of the television images, which amounted to nothing less than a staged exhibit of NATO for NATO's sake.

Daniel Bell claims in *The Cultural Contradictions of Capitalism* that there exist three societal realms and that each follows its own rhythm (in contradistinction to the social system theorists who posit an integrated society); that these three realms are the techno-economic, political, and cultural; that the cultural realm is one of expressive meanings necessary for human existence; and that, for centuries, 'culture has been fused with religion.'[17] Bell's criticisms of the counter-culture of the 1960s and of modernist self-expression for its own sake have – in sharp departure from Bell's vision of the socially constrained uses of culture in history – led Marshall Berman to label Bell as a conservative who is implying that culture must be yoked again to religion:

> 'Modernism has [thus] been the seducer,' Daniel Bell wrote. . . . If only the modernist snake could be expelled from the modern garden, space, time and the cosmos would straighten themselves out. Then, presumably, a techno-pastoral golden age would return, and men and machines could lie down together happily forevermore.[18]

For Berman, Bell's three social realms *are* connected, and culture – in the form of modernist art for art's sake – is a response to the present. For Berman, modernism should be expressive, and not be constrained by religion[19] or any other societal institution, as a way of coping with modernity. Contrary to Berman's assertions, Bell clearly feels that modernism produces anomic contradictions:

> Modernism has thus been the seducer. Its power derived from the idolatry of the self. Its appeal stemmed from the idea that life itself should be a work of art, and that art could only express itself against the conventions of society, particularly bourgeois society. When tied to politics, as it has sometimes been, modernism

became subversive of contemporary society. . . . Today modernism is exhausted. There is no tension. The creative impulses have gone slack. It has become an empty vessel. The impulse to rebellion has been institutionalized.[20]

Conservatives are supposed to be those who uphold social integration, unity, and homogeneity while bemoaning the anomie, disintegration, cultural fraying, decay, barbarism, pornography, and general breakdown of societal institutions.[21] Conservatives typically aim their negative rhetoric at the artists and cultural expressors who are depicted as poisoning, polluting, and politicizing young minds. On the other extreme, the liberal self-expressors call conservatives Yahoos, Philistines, fascists, Nazis, and homophobes who want to stifle freedom, anti-conformity, self-expression, thought, authenticity, and individualism.[22] The conservatives complain that today's multiculturalists are separatist and divisive (although one could accuse conservatives of promoting their own brand of separatism and divisiveness) while the liberal multiculturalists complain of living in a near-fascist state, even those in so-called liberal democratic states. Of course, the situation becomes even more complex when liberals are accused of promoting 'left-wing fascism'[23] by insisting on politically correct speech and thought; when liberals adopt some of the conservative rhetoric of the need for society to unify and overcome divisiveness; and when conservatives claim that their right to self-expression has been curtailed by liberals!

I intend to avoid the liberal–conservative polemic in my discussion of the conceptual problems that emerge in Berman's critique of Bell. This is because, first, too many contemporary discussions in sociology are reduced to ideology, and, second, it is self-evident that both liberals and conservatives can be and have been accused of taking both moral and immoral stands, of being pro- and anti-fascist, and, in general, of mirroring each other's charges. Third, anti-Semitism emerges as yet another covert dimension to such ideological battles. In *The Decomposition of Society*, Irving Louis Horowitz claims that:

> Increasingly an attack upon the Jew can be registered as part of that overall critical anti-American thrust with which sociology has become increasingly identified. . . . Because of identifying with the field so closely, the Jewish scholar has come to be seen not only as an architect of 'mainstream sociology,' whatever that hydra-headed beast turned out to be, but also as the apotheosis of the swashbuckling capitalist.[24]

What is a 'critical anti-American thrust?' Its reality probably lies in the eyes of the beholder, and it is not clear that Jews fall more on one side or the other of Americanism or American mainstream sociology. But it is clear that the liberal attack on allegedly conservative sociologists for their support of social integration has been recast by some as a form of anti-Semitism. Horowitz is explicit in claiming that following World War II and the Cold War, America's ascendancy as a haven of liberalism drew Jewish scholars from abroad, such as the Frankfurt School, but also drew American Jews into sociology:

> Daniel Bell came from journalism, Nathan Glazer from editing, and David Riesman from law; they were perhaps the most noticeable. The field soon became populated by Jews to such a degree that jokes abounded: one did not need the synagogue, the *minyan* was to be found in sociology departments; or, one did not need a sociology of

Jewish life, since the two had become synonymous. This brilliant roster of postwar sociologists went on to populate departments in the great American diaspora.[25]

For Horowitz, the success of Jews in American sociology gradually led to a new form of 'acerbic left-oriented anti-Semitism'[26] in which criticisms of mainstream sociology are actually attacks on Jews. Thus, Daniel Bell is a successful sociologist whose writings have been interpreted as being conservative because he links religion to culture. To take up the significance of Bell's thesis for the postmodernist debate is to necessarily take up the corollary that criticisms of mainstream sociology can be perceived as a covert form of anti-Semitism. It should go without saying that I regard as postemotional even this aspect of contemporary intellectual debate. Furthermore, I reject the claim that criticizing American or Western society, as well as criticizing Jewish authors such as Daniel Bell or David Riesman, implies anti-Semitism.

Bell's claim is an echo of Durkheim's famous linkage between religion and culture made in *The Elementary Forms of the Religious Life*.[27] Durkheim observed in his classic work *Suicide* that Jews are able, in what seems to be a paradox, to combine a spirit of modernism with traditionalism:

> The Jew, therefore, seeks to learn, not in order to replace his collective prejudices by reflective thought, but merely to be better armed for the struggle. For him it is a means of offsetting the unfavorable position on him by opinion and sometimes by law. And since knowledge by itself has no influence upon a tradition in full vigor, he superimposes this intellectual life upon his habitual routine with no effect of the former upon the latter. This is the reason for the complexity he presents. Primitive in certain respects, in others he is an intellectual and man of culture. He thus combines the advantages of the severe discipline characteristic of small and ancient groups with the benefits of the intense culture enjoyed by our great societies. He has all the intelligence of modern man without sharing his despair.[28]

To make Durkheim seem politically correct, one needs to substitute the word 'traditional' for his use of the word 'primitive' above. In any event, Durkheim's assessment is a vitally important departure from the almost standard contemporary assessments of modernity, exemplified by Berman and many other theorists, that modernity is a stage in history that necessarily overcomes traditionalism. Durkheim, who was Jewish, alerts one to the tension-filled unity between universalism and particularism, collectivism and individualism, cosmopolitanism versus provincialism, and other seeming opposites as the hallmarks of Jewish cultural identity (hence, Durkheim's enigmatic pronouncement that modern individualism is itself a collective phenomenon guaranteed by one's society!).[29] I believe that these complex Durkheimian observations are still applicable to today's postmodernist discourse concerned with marginal versus mainstream theorizing, criticizing the Enlightenment project versus embracing it, and other related debates, including the liberal–conservative diatribes.

Postemotionalism assumes that modernity as well as modernism must borrow emotional content from other contexts in the present in addition to emotional content taken from traditions and history. This occurs even as modernity and modernism both seem to be concerned with the new, with the avant-garde, and with overcoming the inertia of tradition. The state of affairs envisioned by modernists and postmodernists of constant rebellion against the past is impossible to imagine. The 'new' must always involve some aspect of the 'old.' Despite the liberal rhetoric of self-expression and emancipation from the past, one cannot find or imagine a single instance of such expression or freedom that does not derive some of its emotional power from a previous 'sacred' site, person, image, or other phenomenon that is synthetically charged with an aura.

It is not true that, as Berman put the matter, echoing Marx, 'all that is solid melts into air.' It is more accurate to say that this appears to be the case, but that in reality the ghosts of the past emerge immediately in a different form. Similarly, it is not true, as Anthony Giddens claims, that modernity is a juggernaut that demolishes everything in its path toward the new.[30] Rather, modernity absorbs, refracts, and recasts bits and pieces of the past as it seems to create the new.

Baudrillard's Notes From the Underground

Jean Baudrillard's writings constitute another interesting point of departure for postemotional theory. Baudrillard is fascinating because he denies that he is a postmodernist even though he is frequently hailed as the spokesperson for postmodernism.[31] Baudrillard's style as well as the content of his writing are irritating, provocative, but above all difficult to pin down, prompting many in the academy to 'forget Baudrillard'[32] at the same time that others continue to be inspired by him. But in line with postemotional theory, even Baudrillard's message, style, and reception are easily comparable to Dostoevsky's *Notes From the Underground*, first published in 1864. Both Baudrillard and the underground man erase their assertions as they make them; stick out their tongues at those who take comfort in bourgeois modernity; and provoke the reader at the same time that they make it impossible for the reader to ascertain whether they mean what they say. Is Baudrillard serious when he claims that one can learn more from travelling on America's highways than from all the social science institutes put together?[33] Nobody knows. Is *Notes From the Underground* a real novel or an in-your-face critique of the novel? Literature professors still debate this question. Sociologists cannot make up their minds if Baudrillard's *America* is a travelog or a serious work of social theory.[34] But Baudrillard does not help resolve these 'serious' questions, and instead seems to revel in the ambiguity he has created. Both Baudrillard and the underground man – who may or may not represent Dostoevsky's feelings – engage in diatribes, are venomous in their criticisms, and seem capricious in their assertions even as they appeal immensely to students and other readers because their portraits of their respective social worlds seem to resonate with personal experience. After my students read Dostoevsky and Baudrillard, they are able to come up with numerous illustrations of what these authors allegedly intended.

It is certain that part of the provocative attitude found in Baudrillard as well as Dostoevsky's central character in *Notes From the Underground* stems from a desire to remain free, to not be pinned down, with regard to each as an author, and also as part of a general philosophy of life. Dostoevsky has his character dismiss socialized modernists as people who have allowed themselves to become 'piano keys' and 'doorstops' – the equivalent of the better-known phrase 'cogs in the machine.' Baudrillard and Dostoevsky want to annoy us, confuse us, to deny that the unpredictable can be predicted. The appeal to freedom is powerful, and one finds traces of it even in the manifesto of the underground man of the 1990s, the 'Unabomber,' who accuses technology and modernity in general of dehumanizing the masses. The Unabomber's manifesto comes across as cut from the same cloth of societal criticism that one finds in graduate student papers written by sociologists as well as some of the writings of the Frankfurt School. But it is another matter when Baudrillard wants to make the assertion that the social universe *really is* as chaotic, random, and disorderly as he perhaps wishes (and ambivalently does not wish) it were.

And that is precisely Baudrillard's message, and also the precise point where I challenge him with the new theory of postemotionalism. Baudrillard claims that the postmodern social world is nothing but a heap of simulations and contingent, rootless, circulating fictions – and at times, he seems to revel in this newfound freedom. *But I claim that what appear to be rootless, circulating fictions can be broken down into rooted and emotionally laden fictions with definite trajectories.* Moreover, Baudrillard's many writings can be read as exercises in helpless indignation, along the lines of David Riesman's other-directed type. The grounds for his indignation are convincing enough, but there is something unsatisfying about his conclusions that, for example, the Vietnam War was just a television war,[35] the Gulf War did not really happen,[36] everything is an illusion, and the have-nots must exit. Baudrillard never offers solutions, alternatives, or constructive criticisms.

Nevertheless, there exists considerable overlap between Baudrillard's version of postmodernism and what I am calling postemotionalism. We both agree that America is the 'dawning of the universe';[37] that a rupture has occurred with a previous era of modernity; and that the main characteristic of the contemporary era is simulation. But the more profound difference between us is that he focuses almost exclusively on the simulation of cognitive categories whereas I focus on the simulation of emotions. In fact, emotions are noticeably absent in most of his provocative claims. Consider, for example, Baudrillard's rhetoric in *America*, wherein he claims that America is cold and dead, like the desert;[38] that America has achieved the extermination of meaning;[39] that the spectacle of the brain *vis-à-vis* the computer and information technologies has become central;[40] that the 'orgy is over';[41] that America as the desert 'banishes all sentimentality';[42] that America as the desert represents 'no desire';[43] that there is no charm and no seduction left, and 'what is arresting is the absence of all these things.'[44] In contradistinction to Baudrillard, I see America not as the desert, but as an artificially contrived hothouse of luxurious and exotic emotions that do not necessarily translate into actions. Americans today feel things their ancestors did not feel: They feel the pain of whales, baby seals, and Bosnian refugees; they feel the joy of victory in the Gulf War, technological superiority and a leisure class life-style that used to be reserved for the real leisure class; they experience fear of each other, of saying something politically incorrect, of getting sued for actions that used to be passed off as mistakes; and so on. But all this luxuri-ous emotion leads to compassion fatigue, anomie as the malady of infinite desires that can never be satisfied, and a diffuse anxiety that colors almost every waking hour, among other pathologies.

Or consider Baudrillard's rhetoric in *The Transparency of Evil*.[45] He claims that the West is dead and can only 'simulate liberation,'[46] produce 'total con-fusion,'[47] and whitewash violence through cultural surgery.[48] 'All we do is psychodrama' such that we simulate the differences of others, simulate the Rights of Man, and simulate other core Western values.[49] There is consider-able truth in these bold generalizations, yet Baudrillard overlooks the authentic, tortured feelings of doubt, disgust, and helplessness that this state of affairs produces. He never ventures into the realm of manufactured emo-tional attachments to these core values by a populace who clings to them even if they realize that they are part of a process of self-manipulation and manip-ulation by others. Finally, he does not explain how postmodern simulation is different from traditional simulations of totemism, historical rites, and the past in general.

However, and because Baudrillard's writings have been analyzed by so many authors, I have decided to focus on his relatively lesser known writings concerning the Balkan War. Baudrillard published three such essays in *La Libération* on 7 January 1993, 3 July 1995, and 17 July 1995.[50] To my mind, though the subject matter of the Balkans is new for him, the style, tone, and message are vintage Baudrillard, and therefore constitute a suitable aspect of his work for analysis. I shall analyze the three essays in the order in which they were published, starting with 'No Pity for Sarajevo.'

Baudrillard begins by justifying the anger expressed at the West by a citizen of Sarajevo, who said, 'I spit on Europe.' Next, Baudrillard expresses his own indignation at 'Susan Sontag who came to Sarajevo to stage *Waiting for Godot*. Why not bring *Bouvard & Pecuchet* to Somalia or Afghanistan?' Whereas I would interpret Sontag's action (and the actions of many other Westerners who staged concerts in Sarajevo) as postemotional displacement of compassion, Baudrillard is put off by

> the condescension and the inability to distinguish positions of strength from positions of weakness. They [the people of Sarajevo] are strong, and we, who look to them for something, anything, to revive our strength and our lost sense of reality, are weak.

'Our sole reality is indeed at stake,' according to Baudrillard, but we delude ourselves with false pity while the suffering of the victims in Sarajevo is a real-ity. 'This explains why they are alive, and why we are dead.' Baudrillard seems to contradict himself a bit when he claims later that their life is hell, 'but a somewhat hyper-real hell' and that they live 'amid a type of spectral war.' But in general, I agree with him that the West behaves almost parasitically toward the real suffering of the people in Sarajevo.

I agree with him also that 'ours is a victim-society,' and that 'in the guise of ecumenical pathos, our society as a whole is literally on a path of "commiseration".' In my *The Barbarian Temperament*[51] I noted that, true to Schopenhauer's predictions that the expansion of consciousness leads to suffering, our *fin de siècle* is obsessed with suffering, albeit not the sort of obsession that leads to *caritas* but one that leads to pity and narcissism (which are compatible) instead. Baudrillard claims that the West feeds vicariously on the suffering of others in order to find the reality of its values. And this reality is far from comforting. According to Baudrillard:

> The fine point of the story is the following: in carrying out ethnic cleansing, the Serbs are Europe's cutting edge. . . . It is as if all European nationalities and policies had acted in concert to take out a contract for murder with the Serbs, who have become the agents of the West's dirty jobs.

As usual with his writings, it is difficult to distinguish Baudrillard the *provocateur* from Baudrillard the accurate social critic. It certainly seems to be the case that Europe (and the USA) is guilty of appeasement in the face of Serbian aggression. However, even if one were to argue that Europe is actively collaborating with the Serbs, there are several loose ends left out by Baudrillard, among them: (1) Europe and the West in general have passed resolutions condemning Serbian aggression at the same time that they have not stopped it. The self-torture for the West in advocating this discrepancy is not noted by Baudrillard, but is food for thought in postemotional discourse. (2) Europe's racism is not confined to non-whites, but includes the attitude that all Balkan peoples are sub-civilized, at Europe's 'backdoor.' Why, then, would Europe overcome its racism toward the Balkan people as a whole to collaborate with the Balkan Serbs in racism against 'Muslims and Arabs'? Even if true, this would require a truly complicated feat in postemotional management. But lest I be misunderstood, let me state that there is an important grain of truth in Baudrillard's assertions about the West's collaboration with Serbia.

In the second essay, 'The West's Serbianization,' Baudrillard notes astutely that the West has finally concluded that 'the Serbs are the aggressors,' but that this fact will not move the West to stop the Serbs. 'This rather platonic recognition of the executioners as executioners does not imply that the victims will be recognized as victims.' I tend to agree with Baudrillard that, at least as of this writing, 'there is no reason that the criminal will not maintain his monopoly over arrogance and crime.' Repeating part of his claim in an earlier essay, Baudrillard claims that the West will not act to stop the Serbs because they

> *are our objective allies in this cleansing operation for a future Europe.* (emphasis added)

Perhaps it is also true that, as Baudrillard claims, 'We suggest our job is done once we have declared the Serbs the "bad guys", but not the enemy.' As in the previous essay, he claims that Europeans 'are fighting exactly the same enemies as the Serbs: Islam, the Muslims,' from Chechnya to Algeria. The West's collaboration with Serbia is the real reason for not ending the war in the Balkans, according to Baudrillard. He makes an interesting allusion to the Gulf War in this regard:

> The scenario is the same as with Saddam Hussein: in our battle against him, we deployed a great deal of media and technology. In the final analysis, however, he was, and is, our objective ally. Reviled, denounced, and discredited in the name of human rights, he remains our objective ally against Iran, against the Kurds, and against the Shiites. *This is also why the Gulf War never really took place: Saddam was never our true enemy. This is also the case with the Serbs. By banishing them from the human community, we are actually protecting them, and continuing to let them carry out their work.* (emphasis added)

Clearly, Baudrillard is treating the current Balkan War with the same formula he has used to assess other postmodern wars. They are all 'unreal.' But the context of his remarks on the current Balkan War clarify what he meant with regard to the Gulf War and other wars. Apparently, he did not mean only that they were unreal because they were televised, as so many analysts concluded.[52] Apparently he also meant that Saddam Hussein and Slobodan Milošević were Western collaborationists despite the fact that the West seemed to vilify them. I do not deny that Baudrillard's provocative assessment contains an important kernel of truth. Albert Wohlstetter has published essays in which he concludes that the USA perceived Saddam Hussein as preferable to the Islamic fundamentalists who might have replaced him had he been vanquished.[53] Similarly, the USA, which is the real motor behind Western alliances, seeks a balance of power in the Balkans, not the defeat of Serbia.[54] Nevertheless, I have not changed my position, expressed elsewhere,[55] that there is something cruel in Baudrillard's dismissal of these and other wars as unreal exercises in hyperreality. Real people died in them, and they left real scars in national psyches. The Vietnam War, in particular, regardless of America's real motives in it, wounded America's collective belief that it was invincible, and no doubt contributed to limited warfare in both Iraq and the Balkans that would keep American casualties near zero. This emotional reality, which became the basis for postemotional maneuvering in the Gulf War as well as the Balkans, is nonetheless a reality, not a hyperreality or a non-reality.

My criticism of Baudrillard on this point should not obscure my admiration for his courage to state the almost unthinkable, that the West is collaborating with Serbian genocidal aggression against the Bosnian Muslims. This point is worth dissecting and analyzing in some detail. Empirical support for Baudrillard's charge is to be found in the meticulously documented book by Norman Cigar, *Genocide in Bosnia-Herzegovina*.[56] If this is true, then the Western powers (especially Great Britain and France) who have covertly favored the Serbs and have done their secret best to manipulate the United Nations so as to prevent effective action being taken against the Serbs are not simply guilty of failing to meet their legal obligations to prevent genocide (under the UN Charter), but are also guilty of complicity in it. The West, in short, is an *accomplice* to Serbian genocide. This seems to be Baudrillard's point.

Western leaders, UN officials and 'mediators' have given three basic reasons for what they have done or not done in this regard, by stating publicly that they: (1) tried to bring an end to the slaughter; (2) tried to relieve suffering with humanitarian aid; (3) tried to prevent the fighting from spreading to other areas. Yet closer scrutiny reveals that the first goal has been largely sacrificed, and that the second and third goals have been used as the postemotional reasons for this sacrifice. In other words, the seemingly emotional goals of humanitarianism and concern that the fighting does not spread have actually been used to disguise collaboration. It is a pity that Baudrillard does not delve into this use of postemotionalism, but then it could well be the case that postmodernism is not up to the task of analyzing such intricate motives. In any event, it is clear that the public juggling of these goals has been used by Western leaders, UN officials, and mediators to justify whatever they have wanted to do; what they wanted to do most of the time favored or at least allowed the Serbs to fulfill their goal; and it has made it difficult indeed to try to break down their rationalizations and to try to reveal their true motives. Thus, Baudrillard's charge of Western collaboration is next to impossible to prove rationally or empirically. It is convincing intuitively, and in the context of postemotionalism, which highlights the manipulation of emotions for achieving hidden goals.

Another important drawback to Baudrillard's excellent essay is that neither the West nor Islam is as monolithic as Baudrillard suggests. As I have argued elsewhere, and will only summarize here, Western nations are 'Balkanized' in their apparent unity, and so is Islam. France and Britain make strange bedfellows in Western policy toward the Balkan War, for their relations have been anything but amicable in the past; Russia is ambivalent about wanting to join the Western orbit of values at the same time that it claims to uphold its 'little Slavic brothers,' the Serbs; Germany has decided to play it neutral; Italy is the silent player for the most part but it did recently refuse to allow US F-117 bombers to use Aviano Air Base in Italy to bomb the Serbs; Greece, a NATO member, is openly pro-Serbian. The Islamic world, too, is far from unified in its support for the Bosnian Muslims. For many Islamic countries, the Bosnian Muslims are not sufficiently Muslim in practices to warrant support. While Turkey, Iran, Pakistan, and Malaysia have been active in supporting the Bosnian Muslims, Egypt has tended to remain neutral, while Libya, Iraq, and the United Arab Emirates have actually supported the Serbs. It is *not* quite the West versus Islam as Baudrillard suggests.

A serious deficiency in Baudrillard's explanations, here as in his other writings, is that he constantly focuses on reality versus hyperreality, but does not explain how people in various Western or other countries maintain those realities. My point is that cognitive realities are embedded in emotional and, more precisely, postemotional narratives. The one emotion that Baudrillard uses for explanation in this case is the crudest, racism. While racism in Europe toward Muslims (and, I repeat, toward others as well) is undeniable, it seems simplistic to argue that this racism alone is fuelling European collaboration with Serbia. But to his credit, Baudrillard's focus on crude Western racism is a refreshing alternative to the unrealistic claims put forth by Leah Greenfeld[57] and others that Western nationalism is not based on ethnicity and is based instead on civic individualism, while non-Western nations engage in ethnic nationalism. In the first place, many non-Western nations have their own forms of civic individualism: The West does not hold a patent on individualism. Second, Western nations do engage in crude racism. Witness the harsh French crackdown on Muslims in 1995 or the immediate mistreatment of Muslims in the USA following the Oklahoma City bombing, among many other examples.

In his concluding paragraph, Baudrillard asserts that imperialism has changed faces:

> What the West wants to impose on the world, from here on out and in the guise of universals, are not completely disjointed values, but its lack of values.

Again, this is a typical conclusion for Baudrillard, who writes elsewhere about the chaos, fragmented meanings, and circulation of fictions in the West. Yet it makes no sense to me that the West is suffering from a lack of values. It holds values galore, derived mainly from its Enlightenment traditions, but is apparently unable to act on many of them. This is more the result of a postemotional barrier between genuine emotion and action than of not having the values in the first place.

In the final essay, 'When the West Stands in for the Dead,' Baudrillard begins with the line, 'The West's military inability to react to Serb aggression is equalled by its inability to put the life of a single soldier at risk.' The USA seems to suffer from this neurosis the most, but, clearly, the French and the British have put many soldiers at risk in Bosnia, and have suffered many casualties there. For the USA, it might be true that, as Baudrillard claims, 'the body-count must be zero: this is the leitmotif of a clean war, and the decisive factor of a perfect war: a flawless athletic performance.' Unlike Baudrillard, I attribute the technological perfection in the Gulf War to the postemotional scars left on the USA by the Vietnam War, not technology for technology's sake. The Serbs have convinced the USA that Bosnia would be another Vietnam quagmire, and this is one reason among many that the USA has not led the West in seeking a military victory over the Serbs. As in his previous essays, Baudrillard adds that, regarding the slaughter of the Bosnian Muslims, the West watched helplessly as 'this dirty little job (with international status) [was] carried out by intermediary mercenaries,' the Serbs.

Baudrillard goes on to claim that the soldier of old has become the 'virtual soldier' whose life 'can be sacrificed to nothing – something we do not value cannot really be put at risk.' According to Baudrillard, we have reached the stage of 'the last man mentioned by Nietzsche,' the terminal individual. 'Thus, this last man cannot be sacrificed, since he is the last.' For Baudrillard, the West seeks to encapsulate itself from death, to opt for survival as the only value that is left in the ruins of Western culture: 'In Bosnia we are witnessing this infinite reproduction, this macabre parody, and this sinister confusion of history unraveling. We are witness to the face of history where the military and the humanitarian converge.'

Again, I agree with Baudrillard regarding the centrality of the issue that he uncovers, but not with his explanation. My explanation relies on David Riesman's concept of other-directedness, in which contemporary individuals are unable to commit themselves to any one value such as freedom, stopping aggression, or the rule of law because (1) each of these values can be deconstructed cynically into its apparent opposite and (2) there are too many competing values to engage the individual's commitment. In short, tradition-directed and inner-directed soldiers held some firm values for which they were willing to make sacrifices, including the ultimate sacrifice. But other-directed individuals – the soldiers who are directly involved as well as the population at home who participate vicariously – find no transcendent value worthy of sacrifice. In the end, the only value left is survival of the self.

Summary and Conclusions

In this chapter, I have examined three broad and major differences between the assumptions of postemotional theory and the assumptions in other theories. First, and against the many theories that take their inspiration from Nietzsche's claims that modernity has witnessed the triumph of rationality over emotion, enshrined in 'the last man,' postemotionalism suggests that emotion has not disappeared. Emotion has now been transformed into a quasi-intellectual phenomenon that makes it suitable for manipulation by self and others. Thus, I disagree with Daniel Bell that humanity has reached the end of ideology. Second, while I agree with Daniel Bell and others that the philosophy of 'art for art's sake' has left the studio and gallery to become 'life for life's sake,' I disagree that the old ideological distinction between liberal and conservative applies any longer to this new philosophy. Both extremes of the ideological spectrum, and all positions that lie between them, make use of postemotional arguments. The idealized nostalgia for the 'good ol' days' by the conservatives (for they were not really good days when one considers the documented racism, sexism, and other forms of oppression) manipulates emotional reality every bit as much as the idealized liberal utopia of a 'politically correct' multiethnic society, which is correctly considered to be oppressive by many persons. Third, postemotionalism and postmodernism share a concern with debunking, demystifying, decentering, deconstructing and otherwise not being taken in by presentations of reality. My admiration for Baudrillard in these regards is self-evident. But I criticize Baudrillard and the other postmodernists for reducing the world to a cognitive text and for being insensitive to the ambiguous and ambivalent *emotional realities* operative in the social reality. It is not true that reality has been replaced by simulations of cognitive reality or by what they call hyperreality. Beneath the surface of apparent hyperreality, a structured, mechanical postemotional reality is still at work.

In these broad ways, it seems that postemotionalism holds more explanatory power than the now fashionable concept of postmodernism. Postmodernism refers to that broad intellectual movement that centers on nostalgia, the blurring of the distinction between fiction and reality, and other anti-modern tendencies. But the phenomena described in this book are more than nostalgia; rather, they involve the transference of 'dead emotions' from the past into the living present. Instead of the circulation of fictions described by Baudrillard, it is more accurate to point to the co-existence of reality with emotionally charged 'fictions,' or what might be termed circulating emotions: for example, carefully documented Helsinki Watch reports condemning Serbian aggression alongside sympathy for Serb fears of the Muslims and Croats; a carefully documented prosecution case against O.J. Simpson alongside emotional anger at the history of racism in the USA. Thus, there appears to be a need to move beyond the parameters of postmodernism in cultural studies.

Let me return one more time to Baudrillard's frequently cited observations that the Gulf, Vietnam, and Balkan Wars did not happen (one awaits his next essay on the non-reality of the O.J. Simpson trial). It is not enough to dismiss cruel genocidal wars as fictions. The more interesting question becomes: Why is it that the world's postmodern culture industry as well as audience treat wars – current as well as past – *as if* they were fictions, but fictions charged with emotionalism borrowed from the past?

Another interesting question posed by postemotional theory is: How has 'reality' – out of reach for the West from the days of Kant to Baudrillard – been transformed into various metaphors, euphemisms, and other emotionally laden phenomena? These examples analyzed in this book seem to point to a new and distinctive Orwellian 'Newspeak' that has been perfected by the culture industry according to the rules of Marketing 101 with the aim of postemotional displacement. Examples include 'friendly fire,' 'ethnic cleansing,' 'safe areas,' 'peace is our profession' (the motto of the Strategic Air Command during the Vietnam War), and so on.

The modernists have depicted a reified, bounded, and fixed world of bloodless categories; the postmodernists seem to imply an abstract world of rootless fictions devoid of emotions; while I am implying a concrete world of rooted fictions saturated with emotions that are *displaced*, misplaced, and manipulated by the culture industry.

Bill Clinton might be termed the postemotional President. He 'fits' the postemotional times in which he lives (in a Durkheimian sense) in that he 'plays' on the old emotional images of the 1960s, of John F. Kennedy (with whom he has been compared frequently), and, in general, on the emotional needs of aging Baby Boomers who are looking back at their collective youth in the 1960s with considerable nostalgia, and transferring some of that emotional energy onto the present.

In general, the concept of postemotionalism captures with more elegance than is currently the case the confusion, hypocrisies, hysteria, nostalgia, ironies, paradoxes, and other emotional excesses that seem to color most events in contemporary Western social life. Postemotionalism holds greater explanatory power than postmodernism, because postmodernism holds that one should revel or feel comfortable in the face of ironies, inconsistencies, and contradictions. But in contradistinction to the many postmodernists who hope for a world of tolerance to emerge from all this de-differentation, openness, and deconstruction,[58] I have noted that the postmodern goal of tolerance is not being achieved: Extreme intolerance seems to be the rule, not the exception, in the postcommunist world as we head for the end of the century.

Nietzsche's philosophy may be read as a reaction to German Romanticism and as rebellion against his teacher, Arthur Schopenhauer, who held that passions were stronger than the intellect. Critical theory was largely a response to the horrors of modernism exemplified by Stalin and Hitler. Modernists such as Daniel Bell concluded too early that the postindustrial society would make the critical theorists seem irrelevant. Postmodernism was largely a foreshadowing of the collapse of the modernist system in Communism and a reaction to the last stages of modernist capitalism. I propose that postemotionalism ought to be regarded as a new theoretical construct to capture the fission, Balkanization, ethnic violence, and other highly *emotional* phenomena of the late 1990s that are being treated mechanically – and not just in the Balkans, but throughout the industrialized West.

Notes

1. Friedrich Nietzsche, *The Will to Power* (New York: Random House [1888] 1967).

2. Fyodor Dostoevsky, *Notes From the Underground* (Lanham, MD: University Press of America, [1864] 1982).

3. As I demonstrate in detail in *Émile Durkheim and the Reformation of Sociology* (Totowa, NJ: Rowman and Littlefield, 1988).

4. Daniel Bell, *The End of Ideology* (Cambridge, MA: Harvard University Press, 1988).

5. David Riesman, *The Lonely Crowd* (New Haven, CT: Yale University Press, 1950), p. 180.

6. Francis Fukuyama, *The End of History and the Last Man* (New York: Free Press, 1992).

7. G.F.W. Hegel, *The Philosophy of History* (New York: Dover Press, [1899] 1967).

8. Karl Marx and Friedrich Engels, *The German Ideology* (New York: International Publishers, [1846] 1960).

9. Ibid., p. 39.

10. Ibid., p. 47.

11. Akbar Ahmed, 'Ethnic Cleansing: A Metaphor for Our Time?' *Ethnic and Racial Studies*, 18, 1 (1995), pp. 1–25.

12. Matei Calinescu, *Five Faces of Modernity* (Durham, NC: Duke University Press, 1987), p. 41.

13. Thorstein Veblen, *The Theory of the Leisure Class* (New York: Penguin Books, [1899] 1967).

14. As I argue in *The Coming Fin de Siècle* (London: Routledge, 1991).

15. *Wall Street Journal*, 25 July 1995, p. A11.

16. William Safire, 'The Phony Air War,' *New York Times*, 18 September 1995, p. A11; Anthony Lewis, 'Weakness as Policy,' *New York Times*, 14 July 1995, p. A25.

17. Daniel Bell, *The Cultural Contradictions of Capitalism* (New York: Basic Books, 1976), p. 12.

18. Marshall Berman, *All That Is Solid Melts Into Air: The Experience of Modernity* (New York: Simon and Schuster, 1982), p. 31.

19. Perhaps Bell can be interpreted as a conservative. See Daniel Bell, *The Cultural Contradictions of Capitalism* (New York: Basic Books, 1976), p. 30: 'What religion can restore is the continuity of generations, returning us to the existential predicaments which are the ground of humility and care for others.'

20. Ibid., pp. 19–20.

21. See, for example, Robert Hughes, 'Pulling the Fuse on Culture,' *Time*, 7 August 1995, pp. 61–71.

22. For a sampling of the extremist rhetoric on both sides of the political spectrum, see Richard Bolton (ed.), *Culture Wars: Documents From Recent Controversies in the Arts* (New York: New Press, 1992).

23. See Irving Louis Horowitz, *The Decomposition of Society* (New York: Oxford University Press, 1994).

24. Ibid., p. 90.

25. Ibid., p. 77.

26. Ibid., p. 92.

27. Émile Durkheim, *The Elementary Forms of the Religious Life* (New York: Free Press, [1912] 1965).

28. Émile Durkheim, *Suicide* (New York: Free Press, [1897] 1951), p. 168.

29. Ibid., p. 334.

30. Anthony Giddens, *The Consequences of Modernity* (Stanford, CA: Stanford University Press, 1990).

31. As observed by Mike Gane, *Baudrillard: Critical and Fatal Theory* (London: Routledge, 1991).

32. This is aptly captured in the title of the collection edited by Chris Rojek and Bryan S. Turner, *Forget Baudrillard?* (London: Routledge, 1993).

33. Jean Baudrillard, *America* (London: Verso, 1986), p. 55: 'Drive ten thousand miles across America and you will know more about the country than all the institutes of sociology and political science put together.'

34. Rojek and Turner (eds), *Forget Baudrillard?*

35. Baudrillard, *America*.

36. Jean Baudrillard, 'The Reality Gulf,' *Guardian*, 11 January 1991, p. 25.

37. Baudrillard, *America*, p. 23.

38. Ibid., p. 5.

39. Ibid., p. 10.

40. Ibid., p. 36.

41. Ibid., p. 46.

42. Ibid., p. 71.

43. Ibid., p. 123.

44. Ibid.

45. Jean Baudrillard, *The Transparency of Evil* (London: Verso, 1993).

46. Ibid., p. 3.

47. Ibid., p. 10.

48. Ibid., p. 45.

49. Ibid., p. 125.

50. All three essays were translated into English by James Petterson of Wellesley College and are reprinted in Thomas Cushman and Stjepan G. Meštrović (eds), *This Time We Knew* (New York: New York University Press, 1996). The essays are entitled 'No Pity for Sarajevo,' 'The West's Serbianization,' and 'When the West Stands in for the Dead,' pp. 79–89.

51. Stjepan G. Meštrović, *The Barbarian Temperament* (London: Routledge, 1993).

52. Rojek and Turner (eds), *Forget Baudrillard?*.

53. Albert Wohlstetter, 'Wide Open Secret Coup,' *National Review*, 44 (1992) pp. 34–6; 'High

Time,' *National Review*, 45 (1993), pp. 45:30–3; 'The Bitter End,' *New Republic*, 29 April 1991, pp. 20–4.

54. Albert Wohlstetter, 'Creating a Greater Serbia,' *The New Republic*, 1 August 1994, pp. 22–7.

55. Stjepan G. Meštrović, 'Postemotional Politics in the Balkans,' *Society*, 32 (1995), pp. 69–77.

56. Norman Cigar, *Genocide in Bosnia-Herzegovina* (College Station, TX: Texas A&M University Press, 1995).

57. Leah Greenfeld, *Nationalism: Five Roads to Modernity* (Cambridge, MA: Harvard University Press, 1992).

58. See, for example, Zygmunt Bauman, *Postmodern Ethics* (Oxford: Basil Blackwell, 1993).

3

Recontextualizing David Riesman's
The Lonely Crowd

In this chapter I will reread David Riesman's much celebrated *The Lonely Crowd*, as I have many times privately as well as with my students, with an eye toward showing its continued relevance to the 1990s and, more importantly, suggesting that what I am calling the postemotional type can be read as an extension of Riesman's other-directed type. To put the matter differently: the other-directed type of the 1950s has become the postemotional type of the 1990s. I admit that I offer less an exegesis of Riesman's classic than I seem to read along with him, and, in the process, offer a new interpretation. It is a reading that he and others might not agree with in many respects, but it is one that takes him seriously, and does not treat him or his book as museum pieces. It is striking that Riesman's emphases in *The Lonely Crowd* on the media, culture, tolerance, the cults of fun and being nice, consumerism in politics, and eventual dissolution of authentic passion into a shallow manipulation of instantaneous feelings all seem remarkably fresh. In many ways, he was engaging in what has come to be known as the postmodernist discourse before the term came into vogue (and before many postmodernists were even born). Yet despite the remarkable success of and high esteem for Riesman's *The Lonely Crowd* – a book that has sold over one million copies world-wide – intellectuals engaged in the postmodernist discourse have not invoked him. Despite the fact that Erich Fromm, a critical theorist, was Riesman's most important mentor, Riesman is not typically read as a critical theorist. These are curious oversights. Those who have read both Riesman's *The Lonely Crowd* and Baudrillard's *America* will be struck by the remarkable similarities between the two visions of contemporary societies, as will readers of Marcuse's *One-Dimensional Man*. The similarities have to do primarily with the 'happy consciousness' (Marcuse), 'happy face' (Baudrillard), and 'nice' (Riesman) veneer that is placed on mass conformity. Yet there are significant differences between their portraits, and they are worth discussing.

Quite apart from social theory, Riesman's depiction of modernity prophetically foretold and still captures the most visible icons, landmarks, and markers of the 1990s: The other-directed focus on tolerance blossomed into the full-blown and highly organized cults of multiculturalism and political correctness. Fun is now so institutionalized that the children's television program *Sesame Street* has transformed the act of learning for children – which used to be painful until the 1950s – into the remarkably new notion that all education must be deliberately painless. The times of food scarcity gave way to the quest for nutrition and finally became the 'happy meal' of the 1990s, in which the family does not necessarily eat together or nutritiously, but is 'happy.' Nowadays, almost everyone who interacts with the public is 'nice,' or they might lose business, or even get sued. (This is remarkably similar to Marcuse's notion of the 'happy consciousness.') The electronic media have become so omnipresent, and omnivorous, that there is serious talk of cyber-societies based entirely on so-called virtual reality. When Riesman wrote about other-directed types subjecting themselves to the jury of their peers, could he have dreamed of the talk shows on today's television as well as radio in which ordinary people as well as celebrities literally bare all, disclose details of their lives that are so intimate that previous generations could not have imagined such confessions?[1] The focus in children's stories has moved away from the inner-directed hero as someone who struggled against heavy odds to an always winning other-directed hero sensitive to group needs. But the post-other-directed hero now follows the standardized formula in which the most popular children's programs feature groups of tolerant individuals, such as Barney and Friends, the Teenage Ninja Mutant Turtles, and the Power Rangers. When he wrote about language as a consumer good, could Riesman have imagined today's climate of political correctness? But above all, I will suggest, Riesman's book contains the germs for what I call postemotionalism, the manipulation of emotions by self and others into a bland, mechanical, mass-produced yet oppressive ethic of niceness. In Riesman's words:

> It has now become difficult for thoughtful Western men, not encapsulated by prejudice and ignorance, to take their own cultures and practices as absolutes. . . . The most important passion left in the world is not for distinctive practices, cultures, and beliefs, but for certain achievements – the technology and organization of the West – whose immediate consequence is the dissolution of all distinctive practices, cultures, and beliefs.[2]

The sentiment expressed by Riesman, above, resonates with the social landscape painted by George Orwell. David Riesman's theory in *The Lonely Crowd* is based in part on an eclectic and distilled blend of insights by Thorstein Veblen, Sigmund Freud, Georg Simmel, Erich Fromm, Émile Durkheim, and Alexis de Tocqueville (among others).[3] Interestingly, I rely on the same eclectic blend in the present discussion as well as other works. One should note that Karl Marx, whose intellectual legacy is important to many postmodernists as well as critical theorists, does not inspire Riesman's or my works. Thus, Riesman's multifaceted notion of the public consumption of fun, politics, news, and of the media in general is a creative extension of Veblen's concept of conspicuous consumption. Riesman's analysis of the inner-directed child's and adult's psychic battles with passions, authority, and conscience is a refraction of Freud's theory of the personality. The theory of social character is self-consciously taken from the works of Erich Fromm, including the seemingly paradoxical notion that the other-directed type is a conformist in his or her seeming non-conformity. (The notion of social character is also a distant refraction of *Völkerpsychologie*, and resonates with Durkheim's notion of the collective consciousness.) Riesman's portrait of the other-directed type's 'objectless craving'[4] and of feeling confused by the 'Milky Way'[5] of goals and objects of desire (in contrast to the inner-directed type's wishing upon a single star) is a fascinating extension of Durkheim's concept of anomie as the modernist infinity of desires. From Tocqueville, Riesman takes the cultural notion of 'habits of the heart' as a precursor to 'social character,' as well as a captivation with American culture. It is worth repeating that I share this attitude toward America as a cultural center with both Riesman and Baudrillard.

I do not point out these obvious ingredients in Riesman's work in order to reduce it to its elements nor to dissect it. On the contrary, and like all other literary works that have stood the test of time, *The Lonely Crowd* is a creative product that captures the times in which Riesman wrote it, as well as the time in which we live. (And although his book is empirically driven and is a work in social science, its literary qualities cannot be ignored, and do not detract from its science. Moreover, many literary works are frankly sociological.) As such, it defies easy categorization or analysis. My purpose in pointing out Riesman's eclectic assumptions is to suggest that we're not yet done with Riesman's work. It still contains rich kernels of thought that in some ways capture the 1990s much better than they do the 1950s. In any event, I believe that it contains the theoretical framework for the new concept of postemotionalism that I am proposing.

Borrowing an analogy from music, one could argue that in contrast to the many notes that Riesman can reach, Baudrillard's work, as well as the work of many other postmodernists, seems limited to a monotone. The works of the critical theorists, also, start to sound like a broken record, with their overworked allusions to the Enlightenment. Put another way, Riesman refracts ideas while Baudrillard beams one steady idea concerning simulation and the critical theorists beam one steady idea concerning authentic rationality. I do not disagree with Douglas Kellner[6] that Baudrillard's most important theoretical framework is Marxism, despite Baudrillard's repudiation of Marx. The image of Marx as the rationalist liberator from the slavery of self-imposed ignorance also animates all of the works of the critical theorists. And I do not mean this as a reproach on ideological grounds nor on the basis of any antipathy to Marx's thought. It is rather the case, already noted, that Marx limited himself almost exclusively to discussions of conceptions, representations, consciousness, and other rational derivatives of the mind at the expense of feelings and passions. Riesman's *The Lonely Crowd* is constantly mindful of the importance of feelings, whereas Baudrillard seems to reduce the entire social universe to a cognitive text, or, better yet, TV screen: simulations, fictions, hyperrealities, and other phenomena I regard as postemotional. The critical theorists also always return to rationality, despite their penetrating insights into the irrationalities of modern life. To be sure, Mike Gane[7] has found other influences on Baudrillard, such as Nietzsche's, but this discordant note only serves to account for Baudrillard's nihilism. Many astute commentators, such as the ones in Rojek and Turner's fascinating collection of essays entitled *Forget Baudrillard?*,[8] clearly find Baudrillard provocative

yet are disturbed by his conclusions, such as the one that in a world dominated by simulations, the have-nots must simply exit. One cannot simply
exit. I have addressed Baudrillard's works at length in my other books,[9] and
address him further throughout the present work, so I will not dwell on him
in this chapter. The reader would be wrong to conclude that I am dissmissive
of Baudrillard, because, as I have stated above, I believe that his social portrait of our times resonates closely with social reality in significant ways.
Similarly, my respect for critical theory is self-evident, but I ask: How much
more rationality must we adopt before humanity is saved from irrationality?
We have reasoned *so much*! Is it not high time to look for an alternative to
more rationality to cure the excesses of rationality?

Riesman's Basic Framework

I will not comment on those aspects of Riesman's argument in *The Lonely
Crowd* that have already been analyzed by scores of others, especially the
impact of population growth on social character. Instead, let me begin with
a basic summary of Riesman's argument: The tradition-directed types are
conformists who basically reproduce the societies of their ancestors. The
inner-directed type emerged with the Renaissance and Reformation and is the
one suited to individualism, constant expansion in exploration, colonization,
and imperialism.[10] (Let us recall that Durkheim was contemptuous of the
Renaissance and Reformation, periods that he deemed anomic.)[11] Riesman
remarks that his analysis of the other-directed character is 'at once an analysis of the American and of contemporary man'[12] – we must keep in mind that
this statement was first published in 1950. Yet Riesman's Americanization
and internationalization of the other-directed type is in keeping with
Baudrillard's claim that America has become the center of the inauthentic
universe. Baudrillard would also probably agree with Riesman that 'the
American is said to be shallower, freer with his money, friendlier, more uncer-
tain of himself and his values, more demanding of approval than the
European.'[13] Much like Baudrillard describes the importance of mass communication and language for producing a hyperreality, Riesman places great
importance on language and the information media for understanding the
other-directed type:

> Relations with the outer world and with oneself are mediated by the flow of mass
> communication. For the other-directed types political events are likewise experi-
> enced through a *screen of words* by which the events are habitually atomized and
> personalized – or pseudo-personalized.[14] (emphasis added)

It is uncanny how accurately Riesman's 1950 remark applies to the obsession
with the emotional nuances of words in the politically correct 1990s. Thus other-
directed people look to their contemporaries as the source of direction, and

> the goals toward which the other-directed person strives shift with that guidance: it
> is only the process of striving itself and the process of paying close attention to the
> signals from others that remain unaltered throughout life.[15]

We learn from Riesman that unlike the mundane need for approval from others found in all societies and epochs, 'it is only the modern other-directed types who make this their chief source of direction and chief area of sensitivity.'[16] The other-directed type is cosmopolitan yet 'at home everywhere and nowhere, capable of a rapid if sometimes superficial intimacy with and response to everyone.'[17] Furthermore,

> The other-directed person must be able to receive signals from far and near; the sources are many, the changes are rapid. What can be internalized, then, is not a code of behavior but the elaborate equipment needed to attend to such messages and occasionally to participate in their circulation. . . . This control equipment, instead of being like a gyroscope, is like a radar.

Bill Clinton, whom I call the first postemotional President in US history, certainly exhibits other-directed traits. His Presidency is characterized by an obsessive sensitivity to various groups in the USA as well as the world, and a determined reluctance not to offend any of them. Thus, in his foreign policy toward Bosnia, he strove not to offend the Muslims or Serbs, as well as the French, British, and America's other allies. William Safire captures well this character trait in President Clinton, and explicitly uses the term 'other-directed':

> President Clinton told me 'the biggest single disappointment I've had as President' was the allies' refusal to lift the arms embargo that disadvantaged Bosnia; his reason for not leaning on Britain and France to adopt our idea was an *other-directed* 'We have a lot of fish to fry with the Europeans.'[18](emphasis added)

In addition, indicted war criminals in the 1990s fit Riesman's characterization of the other-directed type, as evidenced, for example, by Radovan Karadžić's smooth and easy manner on international television as he preached a new type of postemotional hate. For unlike the inner-directed, rigid, rough, and stereotypically hateful Hitler, Karadžić comes across as *likable*, even as he explained on the CBS program *60 Minutes* (aired on 17 September 1995) that he had to exterminate Muslims and Croats before they (in his view) resorted to genocide against Serbs. He frequently tuned into American fears of another Vietnam quagmire and warned Americans on their television screens – with apparent benevolence – that they should stay out of the Balkans if they did not want their sons and daughters to come home in bodybags. Even Karadžić's euphemism for the genocide committed by his troops and paramilitary units, 'ethnic cleansing,' has a 'nice' ring to it. A full analysis of Karadžić's other comments, made at crucial junctures in the development of the Balkan War, would undoubtedly reveal precisely the sensitivity but lack of rigid standards that Riesman calls other-directedness.

By contrast, the Croatian leader, President Franjo Tudjman, was invariably described by the media and Western diplomats as unsociable, unlikable, scowling, and as lacking charm.[19] His very lack of other-directed traits made him an easy target for diplomats, who insisted that he be brought up for war crime charges even though no factual basis for such charges could be found.[20] The media coverage of the Presidents of Serbia, Croatia, and Bosnia-Herzegovina

meeting in Dayton, Ohio, for peace talks in November 1995 used an emotional rhetoric that made Slobodan Milošević, President of Serbia, seem
angelic compared with his counterparts.[21] Even though Milošević is widely
accused of having started the Balkan War, he was described in the pages of the
New York Times as the 'best hope for peace', while the President of Bosnia-
Herzegovina, Alija Izetbegović, was described with the rhetoric of 'disoriented,'
possessing 'otherworldiness ill-suited to politics,' and as having 'zigzagged' in
policy, and Tudjman was described as a man of 'bigotry' who resorts to
'sometimes barbaric methods.'[22] Like Karadžić, Milošević is consistently
described in the American media in Riesman's other-directed terms:

> 'He [Milošević] is so easy to deal with compared to the Bosnian Government,' said
> one American official. 'He's charming and decisive. Sometimes we have to remind
> ourselves that with Milošević we are dealing with a compliant dictator, whereas in
> Bosnia we are dealing with a muddled, fledgling democracy.'[23]

During the peace talks held in Dayton, Ohio, in November 1995, Milošević
was again described by American diplomats as well as the media in other-
directed terms. Thus, in an article with the intriguing title 'In U.S. Eyes,
"Good" Muslims and "Bad" Serbs Did a Switch,' this is how Serbia's
Milošević was described: 'His taste for drink and hearty meals made him
accessible.'[24] In one instance of negotiation, 'Mr. Milošević downed a large
whiskey,' and the deal was consummated. 'It became known as "Scotch
Road."'[25] American diplomats commented on their 'remarkable rapport with
Mr. Milošević.'[26] Furthermore, 'Mr. Milošević, the man responsible for starting the war in the first place, sidled up to the piano in the Officer's Club to
sing tenderly.'[27] 'Tears came to his eyes' when the peace plan was completed.[28]

By contrast, American diplomats and media described Alija Izetbegović, in
inner-directed terms:

> Mr. Izetbegović, a devout man with a distant gaze . . . preferred to eat alone; he
> never talked of the future or economic reconstructions; and to American officials,
> he seemed strangely unmoved by the suffering of his people. . . . 'He's a very
> stubborn, very elusive man.'[29]

In terms of the present discussion, President Izetbegović was not charming,
he was a loner, and he clung to the rigid value of justice because of his belief
that Bosnia-Herzegovina was the victim of Serbian aggression. In a stereotypically other-directed fashion, the charming Serb delegation became 'good'
while the rigid Muslim delegation became 'bad,' even if facts would suggest a
contrary conclusion.

A similar tendency is to be found in the domestic arena. Thus, referring
back to the 'trial of the century,' O.J. Simpson was depicted as likable, and so
were his attorneys, who obviously knew how to work a crowd, and were
friendly, chatty, and gregarious. By contrast, the prosecution team was portrayed as steely and forbidding. The chief prosecutor, Marcia Clark, was not
friendly enough, according to many commentators, and especially unfriendly
toward the media as well as the jury. In fact, the entire Los Angeles Police
Department came across as unlikable.

Reading between the lines of Riesman's *The Lonely Crowd*, one gains the impression that an emotional shift is occurring in the transition from tradition through inner- to other-direction. It is a shift from a small set of basic emotions that are held passionately and rigidly in a group context, even if holding them meant offending others, to a vast array of superficial emotions that are as easy to slip on as off, depending upon circumstances, and that are managed, even staged. (Erving Goffman's writings on 'face-work' are worth noting in this regard as well.) Thus, Riesman wrote in a 1969 preface, 'the lessening of bigotries described in *The Lonely Crowd* has continued.'[30] To be sure, we saw in the O.J. Simpson trial that people expressed shock that a 1990s police officer (Mark Fuhrman) would use the word 'Nigger' (referred to euphemistically on television as the N-word, so as not to offend an audience otherwise jaded by sex and violence). But perhaps it is more accurate to state that the bigotries have been repressed. Repression in the present *fin de siècle* is centered on issues of gender and ethnicity in contrast to the repression of sexual issues in the previous *fin de siècle*. I agree with Riesman that in contrast to the rigid inner-directed type, the 'other-directed person wants to be loved rather than esteemed' and seeks mainly 'to relate to [others].'[31] He or she lives for 'being *emotionally* in tune with them. He lives in a glass house, not behind lace or velvet curtains' (emphasis added).[32] It is still true that the media presents 'an image of life as smiling, tolerant, urbane, and (save in sports and politics) relatively affectless.'[33] The trick is in getting more precision on the characterization of the other-directed as 'relatively affectless.' For it is clear that emotions are involved, but not the same type of emotions as in previous eras.

From Morality to Morale

There can be little doubt that, as Riesman shows, traditional and inner-directed types raised their children to hold rigid values and behavior patterns. Children were 'brought up' rather than 'loved up,'[34] in contrast to other-directed societies. In most middle-class American families, corporal punishment of previous generations has given way to the 'time out,' in which a misbehaving child is sent to his or her room or to a corner of a room as punishment. Note that the punishment consists of disapproval and of isolation from others (unbearable for the gregarious other-directed type). Moreover, the other-directed child's transgression these days is chiefly being rude, selfish, or hurting the feelings of others, not the old-fashioned transgressions of being too loud, failing to do well in school, or failing to meet parental expectations. Riesman is right that 'parents in our era can only equip the child to do his best, whatever that may turn out to be.'[35] For the 1990s child, it is still true, as Riesman wrote in 1950, that

> One makes good when one is approved of. Thus all power, not merely some power, is in the hands of the actual or imaginary approving group, and the child learns from his parents' reactions to him that nothing in his character, no possession he

owns, no inheritance of name or talent, no work he has done is valued for itself but only for its effect on others.[36]

The other-directed child manipulates his or her parents, and is in turn manipulated. Children negotiate 'deals' with their parents about bedtime and rewards. If the contemporary parent fails to take his or her child's emotional outbursts and needs seriously (what used to be called temper tantrums, which were either ignored or punished physically in previous eras), the other-directed parent is anxious about scarring the child emotionally for life. No other-directed parent would dream of breaking a child's will, but this was standard practice in inner-directed societies that resulted in characteristic adult psychopathologies centered on rebellion and submission to authority.

The ways that an inner-directed child used to be raised were rarely 'loving' and almost never tolerant of the child's personality and idiosyncrasies. The rough standards encountered in the inner-directed home were transferred to the school, where 'the focus is on an intellectual content that for most children has little emotional bite.'[37] The inner-directed teacher was socially and emotionally aloof from the child, and this distance 'affirms to the child that what matters is what he can accomplish, not how nice is his smile or how cooperative his attitude.'[38] The school system was as harsh as the family on the child.

But in other-directed schools, a completely new and different set of emotional trials is encountered by the child. Since seating is no longer pre-determined as it used to be in the old days, 'where to sit becomes problematical – a clue to one's location on the friendship chart.'[39] It is more true in the 1990s than it was in the 1950s that

> Whereas the inner-directed school child might well have hidden his stories and paintings under his bed . . . the other-directed child reads his stories to the group and puts his paintings on the wall. Play, which in the earlier epoch is often an extracurricular and private hobby, shared at most with a small group, now becomes part of the school enterprise itself, serving a 'realistic' purpose.[40]

If one were to update Riesman's observations, one would add that these days the child puts his or her paintings on the refrigerator. The bedroom wall is reserved for posters of the Little Mermaid, Beauty and the Beast, Pocahontas, the Power Rangers and other totems. Furthermore, the child is socialized early on to make 'friends' immediately at whatever playground he or she encounters, from McDonald's playgrounds to parks, schools, airports, and doctor's waiting rooms. (Moreover, it is worth noting that just about any middle-class site that involves waiting will now have a 'playground,' as if the other-directed child could not possibly tolerate what was expected of the inner-directed child, to wait in relative silence.) 'Friends' are instant, and interchangeable. But Riesman is undoubtedly correct that the teacher (and the teacher now includes the day care attendants who are paid minimum wage) is 'really asking simply that they [children] be nice.'[41]

It is more true than ever than in spatial as well as imaginative matters the other-directed types look for 'niceness,' as opposed to the frontiers sought by inner-directed types: 'That is, they look for nice neighborhoods in which their children will meet nice people.'[42] Being 'nice' is a fascinating emotion, a sort of hybrid between being polite but reserved to strangers from inner-directed days to the stereotypically American habit of being superficially cordial yet also distant. Being nice is an intricate act that involves the manipulation of self and others in highly predictable and deliberate ways, including: one's physical appearance, language, tone, eye contact, choice of clothing, smile, choice and length of conversation, among a myriad of other factors. The average middle-class child today knows the social formula for being 'nice' unconsciously, even if he or she could not necessarily recount all the factors if asked. And everyone today knows the importance of 'having to be nice to everybody' in every profession.[43] Note that 'niceness' is a synthetic, feigned, and ultimately insincere form of friendliness. The other-directed child is expected to have fun, and to never be lonely. By contrast, inner-directed children often encountered not-so-nice adults as well as peers who hazed them or otherwise mistreated them, but the children were expected to suffer in silence.

Riesman's discovery of other-directed niceness complements Herbert Marcuse's notion of the 'happy consciousness'[44] as an integral social trait in modern societies. The child's nice childhood, described by Riesman, prepared him or her for the happy adulthood found in Marcuse's writings. The nice and happy consciousness ensures that one will obey without thinking, join without hesitation, and be part of a society without opposition.

It really is amazing that Riesman could have foreseen so many years ago that parents would become 'the stage managers for the meetings of three- and four-year-olds, just as, in earlier eras, the adults managed marriages.'[45] Moreover, 'it is inconceivable to some supervising adults that a child might prefer his own company or that of just one other child.'[46] The only addition I would make is that the parent's job is made easier in this regard by the existence of 'pre-packaged' birthday parties and other sorts of parties available from restaurants, museums, zoos, and other institutions. One might call this new phenomenon the McDonaldization of childhood. For example, commercial chains of children's indoor playgrounds, such as the 'Discovery Zone,' have emerged in large US cities that offer pre-packaged birthday parties. Thus, even the parent's personal involvement in the child's emotional attachment to others is now commodified. For a flat fee, McDonald's restaurants will also provide the food, cake, balloons, and adult host-playmate for the child and child's friends on a birthday. Incidentally, such packaged fun is now available for adults as well on cruise ships, from travel agencies, and even locally in corporations that are set up to celebrate just about any occasion with pre-chosen cards, balloons, gifts, flowers, and so on. All this really constitutes the institutionalization of postemotionalism, the standardized, factory-like packaging of emotions pertaining to traditional events such as birthdays, weddings, anniversaries, and births, among others, which used to be more idiosyncratic, private, and personal. Social life has been modelled on the machine in ways that George Orwell and Henry Adams[47] could not have foreseen.

It is still true that, as Riesman observes, the other-directed peer group seeks to eliminate temper, jealousy, and moodiness. In fact, 'all knobby or idiosyncratic qualities and vices are more or less eliminated or repressed.'[48] Moreover,

> Judgments of others by peer-group members are so clearly matters of taste that their expression has to resort to the vaguest phrases, constantly changed: cute, lousy, square, darling, good guy, honey, swell, bitch (without precise meaning), etc.[49]

These terms still apply, for the most part, with the addition of 'cool,' 'sucks,' 'awesome,' and a few other new, albeit *standardized*, terms. But clearly Riesman's main observation holds: A social transformation has occurred from privately and passionately held rigid moral standards to a publicly and loosely held set of standardized feelings that are used in predictable ways depending upon social circumstances. This is evident from examining contemporary social interaction in the family, school, local and national political life, and also international affairs. Thus, the European who replies to the stereotypical American question 'How are you today?' with an honest answer receives an incredulous response. One is supposed to answer 'Fine,' no matter how one really feels. Similarly, Jimmy Carter's ostentatious touting of human rights has become a formula, and contrasts sharply with previous statesmen who exerted pressure *privately* on abusers of human rights. And, as I noted in chapter 1, Jimmy Carter is able to depict an indicted war criminal such as Radovan Karadžić as basically a 'good guy' and bring him flowers. In previous eras, the line dividing 'good guys' from 'bad guys' was rather clearly drawn, and one would never present a 'bad guy' with flowers. Clearly, other-directedness has set the stage for the easy transference and manipulation of emotional labels across cultural borders that our ancestors simply could not have imagined.

Changes in Storytelling

Tradition-directed societies made use of oral traditions, myths, legends, and songs to convey their values. The inner-directed child read fairy tales, which were essentially morality lessons on overcoming wickedness and temptation, or 'character-building' stories and biographies, such as *Robinson Crusoe* or the life of George Washington (who, as we all know, could not tell a lie). Riesman makes the important point that the inner-directed child read these stories primarily in isolation. But the other-directed child reads and listens in the company of others. Even when 'reading and listening are not communal in fact, they are apt to be so in feeling: one is almost always conscious of the brooding omnipresence of the peer-group.'[50] The comic book replaced the fairy tale with the new value of always winning, and with ease. 'Thus, whereas Jack of *Jack and the Beanstalk* gains magical assistance chiefly through his own daring, curiosity, and luck, a comic-book Jack would gain magical assistance chiefly through an all-powerful helper.'[51] Consequently, 'morality tends to become an inference from winning' and 'Winner take all' becomes a tautology.[52]

To update Riesman, one should note that the comic book has given way to the widespread consumption of children's films and television programs. What books and comic books are still read usually follow the most recent children's film (along with toys that inevitably follow every new Disney children's film). The fact that it is a 'children's film' means that it follows standardized formulas, for one must keep in mind that in previous eras children often consumed adult entertainment. Magical winning is more prominent than it was in the 1950s, but the new factor is that the most popular heroes in children's fantasies are now *groups*, as mentioned previously. The lone hero smacks too much of inner-direction, and had to be dropped. The inner-directed hero, Superman, for example, was recently killed and the comic book series was discontinued. The new children's role models are Barney *and* Friends, the Teenage Ninja Mutant Turtles, and the Power Rangers. All of these involve individuals working in groups and bent on tolerance. Thus, the eponymous character in Disney's film, *The Little Mermaid* operated with a group of friends, and was basically portrayed as an adolescent champion of women's rights who defied her father to marry the human of her choice. Similarly, the eponymous character in Disney's recent film *Pocahontas* represented all Native Americans, and nobody used tobacco in the film, neither the Native Americans nor white colonizers – smoking is politically incorrect today, even if it was the stuff of 'peace pipes' in the days of the real Pocahontas.[53] Contrast the postemotional film *Pocahontas* with the racist depiction of Native Americans in the inner-directed Disney film, *Peter Pan*, or the racist depiction of other minorities in Disney's *Dumbo*. (In fact, it would be a fascinating study to follow the progression of Disney films from inner-directed through other-directed to postemotional eras.) Without a doubt, the postemotional rule is that the nice heroes always win through the use of magic, and rather easily at that.

One would think that a theory as popular as Riesman's would have inspired many studies on how children's stories have changed from inner-directed times to our other-directed times. But in conducting a literature search by cross-listing Riesman and children's stories, I could not find a single article or study. In fact, there exist relatively few studies on children's stories at all. Most of the studies that do exist examine sex[54] and ethnic[55] differences in children's stories. This finding is in line with the general trend of other-directedness to promote fractured group-identities. Other studies examine the role of emotions in children's stories,[56] the role of plants in children's stories,[57] or the role of repetition,[58] among others that do not consider the role of social character as a whole.

Rather than examine a representative range of these children's story characters, I will focus on one program in the interest of space: *Barney and Friends*.[59] This is by far the most popular and the best selling children's program in the USA in the 1990s. Barney is a purple and green dinosaur who does not really exist, but is imagined into existence by a standardized group of multicultural and politically correct 'friends' of various ages. His main function is to sing happy songs with the children and to teach them that they can overcome any obstacle by using their imaginations. In one episode, for example, they want to experience igloos but are thwarted by living in a warm climate. It is important to note that in this episode, as in all others, the group immediately supports the wishes of one of its members. No child ever objects to another child's fantasy. In any event, the frustration is not a problem: Barney instantly imagines them into an arctic setting in which they sing a happy song. There is absolutely no obstacle in life that cannot be overcome by wishing in *Barney and Friends*.

But Barney and his friends speak through the television screen to tell their viewers that they, too, are their friends. 'I love you, you love me, we're a happy family' is how one of Barney's songs begins. It continues:

> With a great big hug and a kiss from me to you
> Won't you say you love me too?
> I love you, you love me
> We're best friends like friends should be
> With a great big hug and a kiss from me to you
> Won't you say you love me too?

While Barney occasionally teaches numbers, the alphabet, and colors, his lessons appear to be mostly emotional ones pertaining to multiculturalism and political correctness. Thus, one of his songs teaches that everyone's family is exactly right for him or her no matter how different it is from other families. One wonders how a child who is abused by his or her parents would react to such a message.

Adults are usually absent from *Barney and Friends*, or if they do appear, they are on camera for a few seconds. It is a strictly child-directed program. Barney's friends are regulars on the program, and are trained, paid actors and actresses. Missing is the spontaneity of previous children's programs such as *Captain Kangaroo* or even *Sesame Street* which had segments that featured ordinary, untrained children. Every song and dance sequence in *Barney and Friends* is carefully orchestrated and highly professional in appearance. One gets the sensation of carefully rehearsed emotions that are produced with perfect rhythm. The backgrounds and settings for the vignettes are impeccably 'nice,' middle-class, perfectly ordered environments. The result is a pre-packaged emotional experience in which there is no dissent and in which social life runs as if it were a well-maintained machine.

What do the children learn from *Barney and Friends*? They learn that they need never be frustrated by any obstacle. All obstacles to desire disappear magically with group wishing. They learn that adults are irrelevant to their lives, and they do *not* learn adult roles. They learn that they can hug each other and all will be well. But perhaps most significantly, they learn *postemotionalism*: Their private, idiosyncratic and perhaps dissenting emotions must succumb to the emotions of the group, and these group emotions are pre-determined and pre-packaged. There is absolutely no room in *Barney and Friends* for the child to explore his or her emotions. In Riesman's terms, there is no room in *Barney and Friends* for the child to learn the basis of autonomy, the ability to choose the extent to which one will conform or dissent from the group.

Language and Packaged Emotions

One of Riesman's most intriguing insights is that in other-directedness

> Language itself becomes a sort of consumer good. It is used neither to direct the work economy, nor to relate the self to others in any really intimate way, nor to recall the past, nor yet as sheer word play. Rather it is used in the peer-groups today much as popular tunes seem to be used: as a set of counters by which one establishes that one is 'in' and by which one participates in the peer-group's arduously self-socializing 'work.'[60]

Harking back to Thorstein Veblen, I interpret this insight as meaning that language itself becomes a 'useless' (in Veblen's sense) luxury item that bestows prestige upon the user precisely when it fails to serve a demonstrably useful purpose. In other words, this is the era of language for language's sake, the logical progression of the previous *fin de siècle*'s art for art's sake. Thus, other-directed types 'can afford, can technically provide, and have both the time and the need to receive a bounteous flow of imagery from urban centers of distribution.'[61] Baudrillard has also written extensively on this luxuriant growth of imagery in postmodern times, but he seems to argue that the imagery is rootless and random. It seems to be the case, instead, that the imagery is highly orchestrated and organized beforehand.

The new perspective that I would attach to the back of Riesman's insight is this: The language-as-consumer-good is no longer primarily the carrier of rationally intended meanings, but now carries standardized emotions as well. In addition, emotion itself becomes a luxury item exactly in Veblen's and Riesman's senses above. In previous eras, one expected that emotion could lead to action of some sort, but in today's postemotional society, this 'natural' relationship between emotion and action has been permanently severed. Emotions serve no appreciable purpose as such, and the more useless one's emotions are, the more one demonstrates to the peer group that one has attained the level of prestige that makes the owning of emotions a luxury that one can afford. Thus, Tolstoy made the often-cited depiction in one of his novels of an upper-class lady who wept for the wretched during a play while she continued to treat with contempt her wretched servant who was shivering in the cold outside the theater. She could afford to feel a useless pity. But, increasingly, the entire television-viewing middle class has taken on this privilege of the formerly leisure class.

For example, as I noted in chapter 1, most people in the world watched genocide in Bosnia on television, and, when interviewed, they expressed to the media their feelings of revulsion, so-called compassion (but in reality, pity), horror, and other emotions. But the genocide went on for many years despite these emotions, which clearly did not translate into actions that would have forced world leaders – who frequently expressed the same emotions – to put a stop to it. Thus, the new compassion has now become a luxury item, a consumer good that results in 'compassion fatigue,' on the same order of becoming bored with something one has purchased. Today's postemotional types know that they can experience the full range of emotions in any field, domestic or international, and never be called upon to demonstrate the authenticity of their emotions in *commitment* to appropriate action. Postemotional types are fundamentally uncommitted. If more prudish inner-directed types of a generation ago feared that pornography might lead to sex crimes, today's postemotional types do not believe it. Sex and violence on TV seem to increase with every passing year despite the respectable studies that suggest correlations with actual crimes. The public clearly does not respect these respectable findings or it would have resorted to actions to curb the sex and violence. Depending upon the television program or social context, one feels for rapists or rape victims, murderers and murder victims, adulterers or the victims of adultery, child molesters or the children who were molested, and so on. Today, everyone knows that emotions carry no burden, no responsibility to act, and, above all, that emotions of any sort are accessible to nearly everyone.

Thus, the average middle-class consumer of television programming received the cues from the media that he or she should be able to sympathize with both O.J. Simpson, the accused killer, and the victims, his former wife and Ron Goldman. It did not matter whether he was guilty or innocent. Simpson was a sympathetic figure because of his pleasant demeanor, because he rose from rags to riches, because he was African-American and therefore the possible target of a racist Los Angeles Police Department, because his wife was supposedly a drug user, and for other reasons carefully placed in the media coverage. His wife was a sympathetic figure because she was a woman, she was physically abused, she was the victim of jealousy, and so on. If one took sides, one lost one's status in middle-class neutrality. Thus, African-Americans who expressed the opinion in polls that Simpson was innocent were treated as biased along with white females who expressed the opinion that he was guilty. The most important factor in the postemotional consumption of emotions as luxury is to maintain one's neutrality at all times, one's ambivalent ability to sympathize with all sides. Any other reaction might lead to action.

Similarly, regarding the issue of taking sides in the Balkan War, the media made the indicted war criminals who led some Serbs to genocide seem sympathetic: Ratko Mladić's parents were killed by Ustasha in World War II; Radovan Karadžić feared for the fate of the Serbian people at the hands of the Croats and Muslims; Slobodan Milošević only wanted self-determination for the Serbs. But the Muslim victims of the Serbs were also worthy of sympathy: Innocent children were slaughtered in mortar attacks; male civilians were killed and buried in mass graves; and the Bosnian Muslims stood for multiculturalism. Again, the media as well as diplomats and spokespersons for the UN and NATO insisted on their neutrality. If one tried to justify

Serbian actions, one was dismissed as a Serb nationalist. If one insisted on the right of self-defense for the Bosnian Muslim victims, one was accused of forcing the West to take sides and therefore send its sons and daughters in harm's way – even though the Bosnian Muslims insisted they only sought weapons through the lifting of an illegal weapons embargo, not Western troops. Any emotion was tolerated so long as one's emotions did not possibly lead to action. Incidentally, the Croats present an interesting case of hardly ever seeming sympathetic in this conflict.[62] When Croats scored successful military victories against Serbs, the media quickly reminded the middle class that Croatia had a Nazi collaborationist regime in World War II. The Croats were labelled as intolerant – the supreme vice in other-directed ethics – and therefore could never be 'nice,' and could almost never earn sympathy. Of course, in order to maintain this emotional scenario, the media had to rigorously exclude discussion of Serbian Nazi collaboration, French Nazi collaboration, British appeasement of the Nazis and all other factors that might puncture the luxuriant emotions that were being entertained. The result is an 'incomprehensibility of politics.'[63]

Part of the problem is that in other-directed societies it is nearly impossible to tell truth from falsehood because, in Riesman's words, the individual 'is judged for his attitude toward the audience, an attitude which is either sincere or insincere, rather than by his relation to his craft, that is, his honesty and skill.'[64] But, 'just because such a premium is put on sincerity, a premium is put on faking it.'[65] Postemotional society has reached a phase in its development in which it values insincere sincerity, synthetic candor, feigned frankness, and affected openness. As illustration, simply consider the dozens of broken promises, failed peace plans, and dishonored truces over the course of four years in the Balkan War: Each instance of proven deceit was followed by another show of sincerity by the Bosnian Serb leader, Radovan Karadžić. So long as one is 'nice' in one's presentation, one can get away with just about any truth-claim.

Curdled Indignation

But indignation is the cardinal emotion that Riesman singles out for discussion. Other-directed curdled indignation is just as intricate as other-directed niceness and compassion. This is because contemporary indignation is also not linked to appropriate action, and is another luxury emotion. It is multidirectional and totally divorced from perceptibly fixed moral standards. Thus, as a CNN film crew told me recently, people called in to express indignation that CNN was covering the O.J. Simpson trial so extensively, thereby making it into a soap opera, while others called in to express indignation if CNN failed to cover the Simpson trial live for even a few hours due to other news.[66] Consider the wide range of phenomena which call forth indignation nowadays: coffee that is served too hot in a restaurant; service that is not friendly enough at a coffee shop; genocide; the fact that the Holocaust Museum would exhibit photographs that make it seem like the Croats and Muslims are victims of Serbian aggression; lines that are too long at a sporting event; President Clinton's apparent lack of conviction on any matter; the Republicans' very strong convictions on most matters; the media's coverage of a certain event; too many taxes; too little services when taxes are cut: and so on. The flip side of the fact that the USA has become a nation of victims is that it has become a nation of curdled indignants. Thus, to pick one example out of many, CNN reported on 22 September 1995 that Wal-Mart pulled T-shirts off its shelves in response to the indignation of one woman. The sentence on the T-shirt that offended her read: 'Someday a Woman Will be President.' The next day, women's organizations were offended that Wal-Mart pulled the shirt, and Wal-Mart put them back on its shelves.[67] Such back-and-forth indignation is the rule, not the exception.

In some cases, indignation has become a life-style. This is illustrated by the case of a woman in San Francisco who has terrorized her neighborhood by filing nearly fifty lawsuits 'against her neighbors, tenants, department stores – and others – for all manner of injury.'[68] In legal terms, she is considered a 'vexatious litigant.' In sociological terms, she seems to represent the *institutionalized indignation* that has resulted in numerous frivolous lawsuits clogging up the US judicial system.

Riesman's context for other-directed indignation must be kept in mind. Riesman feels that the other-directed type has concluded that he or she is fundamentally powerless to really change the government or any other social institution. The indignant can expect an occasional apology or financial compensation or some other specific reaction to a specific instance of feeling piqued, but, overall, other-directed indignants do not feel that they can really make an impact on the reified universe. (Keith Tester offers an interesting discussion of how humans come to feel that human creations in culture become inhuman forces.)[69] Hence, the other-directed type becomes the inside-dopester who wants to *know* the inside scoop on everything as a kind of compensation for being unable to do anything about it: 'The inside-dopester may be one who has concluded (with good reason) that since he can do nothing to change politics, he can only understand it.'[70] Since Riesman's prophetic assessment of the inside-dopester, the West in general and the USA in particular have witnessed an overwhelming institutionalization of inside-dopesterism: radio talk shows, television talk shows; gossip columns; yellow journalism; the in-between news and entertainment programs such as *Hard Copy*; on-line computer services; the Internet; even the availability of news twenty-four hours a day and the incredible success of CNN's *Headline News*, broadcast every thirty minutes. All these developments testify to the anomic thirst for news, opinion, gossip, and information that characterize the 1990s. Our age is drowning in information, but it is not at all evident that all this knowledge has contributed to autonomy, informed citizenry, increased democracy, or tolerance. On the contrary, various information outlets cater to particular groups which preach to the converted, such as Rush Limbaugh's programs aimed at conservatives. Hate is broadcast alongside tolerance on the airways. Pornography and recipes for making terrorist bombs can be found on the Internet alongside news. And even the news is so 'neutral' (in the sense discussed above) that the average citizen is left feeling confused, not enlightened, and suspects a slant or bias depending upon the source of the information. Thus, information becomes one more commodity to be consumed along predictable lines depending upon one's membership in a 'target audience.' The same is true for politics.

This incomprehensibility regarding domestic and international events has become so acute that even President Clinton, who is a lawyer by training, not a sociologist, made an astute sociological observation about the topic being discussed here:

> 'What makes people feel insecure is when they feel like they're lost in the fun house,' he [President Clinton] said. 'They're in a room where something can hit them from any direction at any time; they always feel that living life is like walking across a running river on slippery rocks and you can lose your footing any time' . . . 'I think in the information age,' he said, there can be 'too much exposure and too much information and too much sort of quasi-information. I mean, you guys [the media] have to compete with near-news too. It's like, you know, when we were kids, we'd drink near-beer.' He added: 'There's a danger that too much cramming in on people's minds is just as bad for them as too little, in terms of the ability to understand, to comprehend.'[71]

Riesman's treatment of contemporary versus traditional indignation is the most intricate of all discussions in *The Lonely Crowd*, and the most ambiguous. While such a claim might be construed as a reproach, I do not intend it in this way. On the contrary, Riesman's ambiguity regarding indignation is fruitful, in general, and especially regarding my attempts to delineate the parameters of postemotionalism.

Thus, Riesman begins his discussion with the broad claim that the movement from inner- to other-directedness can be generalized as a movement from indignation to tolerance and from moralizing to inside-dopesterism.[72] More importantly, it is also a movement toward the 'stylizing of political emotions.'[73] As soon as Riesman makes these generalizations, he adds, 'Having said this, I must immediately make certain qualifications.'[74] Both these types are contrasted with the tradition-directed types who were indifferent to politics simply because the bulk of the population had absolutely no say in the decisions of monarchs and other traditional leaders. Yet, writes Riesman, there crops up a new-style indifferent type among inner- and other-directed persons who are indifferent because they meet obstacles that will not bend to their will or are confused by the plethora of political alternatives: 'For the [other-directed] indifferents do not believe that, by virtue of anything they do, know, or believe, they can buy a *political package* that will substantially improve their lives' (emphasis added)[75] (one thinks immediately of widespread dissatisfaction in the USA with politicians on both ends of the ideological spectrum).

Clearly, other-directed types emulate inner-directed indignation and moralizing, and Riesman is well aware of this fact. He is explicit: 'Indeed, if influential men become moralizers, the other-directed person, because he is other-directed, will try to be a moralizer too.'[76] And 'even the tolerant other-directed person is often fascinated by the indignant's ire, not because it is compatible with his character structure but because it is not.'[77] If the inner-directed type wanted 'to improve all men and institutions,'[78] that applies equally to today's other-directed types who seek to make nearly utopian improvements via political correctness and multiculturalism. But the inner-directed moralizers wanted to improve humanity on the basis of conservative, rigid morals, whereas other-directed moralizers seek to do the same on the basis of tolerance. In both cases, indignation 'becomes *curdled* when lack of success reveals and renders intolerable his lack of understanding' (emphasis added).[79] The resultant apathy is such that, 'actually, the distinction between the inside-dopester and the [traditional] indifferent is often hard to draw.'[80] Even among other-directed types who are trained by the media to be tolerant, 'where they [the media] are moralizers in intention, the mood of the audience of peer-groupers will cause the indignant message to be received in an unindignant way.'[81] In this way one may account for the deadpan facial expressions and equally deadpan voice of newscasters who report indignation by every conceivable group from every point on the political spectrum in the same neutral way.

A surface reading of Riesman in these regards will lead to the conclusion that all of the character types being discussed may be considered equally as moralizers, indignants, cynics, enthusiasts, and indifferents. Riesman's thought is too complex to have assigned any of these conceptual categories to any one character type. This is one factor among many that makes his trea- tise a complex exercise in social inquiry rather than an ideological one. One must read between the lines to note that, first, all of these conceptual cate- gories are *qualitatively different* among tradition-, inner-, and other-directed types. It involves, clearly, a movement from rigidity to a certain degree of tol- erance and openness, yet this generalization can be second-guessed with the observation that, in some ways, contemporary other-directed types are *intol- erant in their tolerance* (the strict code of political correctness is one example) whereas the rigid tradition-directed types were remarkably tolerant in some respects with regard to raising children, for example.[82] An observation by Durkheim is worth pondering in this regard, namely, that corporal punish- ment in schools appeared with the Enlightenment (an inner-directed period for Riesman) and was relatively unknown in traditional societies.[83] Thus, I am not entirely satisfied with resolving the ambiguity in Riesman's argument *vis-à-vis* his theory of the development of social types. Second, and more importantly for the purposes of the present discussion, Riesman actually seems to posit that the progression of his types of social character *vis-à-vis* these conceptual categories *involves a diminution of emotion*. I turn next to this aspect of his discussion, which is not central to his argument, but is vital for my purposes.

The End of Emotion?

Consider the following claims made by Riesman, embedded in his larger discussion:

> So *loss of emotion* in politics leads to other-direction in character.[84] (emphasis added)

> The other-directed man possesses a rich store of social skills . . . one of these is his *ability to hold his emotional fire*.[85] (emphasis added)

> There are political newsmen and broadcasters who, after long training, have succeeded in *eliminating all emotional response* to politics and who pride themselves on achieving the inside-dopesters' goal: never to be taken in by any person, cause, or event.[86] (emphasis added)

I am of two minds concerning these assessments, as I indicated in the opening paragraphs of chapter 2. On the one hand, it seems to be true that journalists put on the appearance of being uninvolved emotionally in the stories they cover. Any speaker who wants to be taken seriously or respected in other-directed or postemotional societies must not show personal passion in the presentation of his or her topic (this is especially true in Britain, of course, where keeping one's cool is a mark of moral distinction). One must *appear* to be emotionally detached (as an interesting departure from Norbert Elias's discussion of detachment).[87] The entire twentieth century may be characterized as unemotional in its penchant for positivism, neutrality, focus on intelligence quotients (but not emotional quotients), standardized tests, federalism over nationalism, and rationalization, among many other phenomena. The twentieth century is the century of emotional cleansing. Even wars, which used to be the arena of powerful passions and hate, have been reduced to abstractions: The Vietnam War was ostensibly about containing Communism; the Gulf War was presented as a legalistic exercise in enforcing UN resolutions; and in the Balkan War of the 1990s, NATO insisted on its 'neutrality' even as it bombed Serbian targets. Consider President Clinton's remarks following one of these bombing raids against the Serbs: 'I would remind the Serbs that we have taken no action, none, through NATO and with the support of the UN, to try to win a military victory for their adversaries.'[88] Both apathy and cynicism are hallmarks of the current era, as numerous authors have argued.

On the other hand, it is just as easy to find emotion beneath the veneer of coolness. Journalists seem to 'go after' certain stories with a zeal and even malice that they do not show for other stories. An ideological position can be uncovered in the most coldly presented academic presentation. The underside of the overly rational twentieth century presents many instances of genocide, ethnic wars, anti-science movements, demagoguery, racism, and the cheapest of sentimentality, kitsch. The fact that the US lost the Vietnam War now influences the Vietnam Syndrome in which the American public refuses to support wars that are not short, winnable, and, above all, that guarantee minimal US casualties. If inner-directed types were willing to sacrifice their lives for democracy in the war against Hitler, other-directed types can find no cause worthy of this supreme sacrifice, because there are too many causes to choose from and each can be cynically debunked. The very fact that the USA was willing to lead a war against Muslims in the Gulf War but not willing to wage one against Christians to save Bosnian Muslims has not been lost on the Islamic world, and displays a certain kind of bigotry. At the same time that NATO leaders proclaimed their neutrality, they denounced the Serbs in passionate terms. Despite the documented apathy and cynical determination not to be taken in, it is well known that Americans 'rally around the flag' each and every predictable time that a US President holds one of his televised 'fireside chats' with them, no matter what opinion polls indicated the night before. Nationalism has emerged as one of the most powerful social forces in the world, and, it should be added, in the USA, France, Britain, and other Western countries that pride themselves on having eradicated nationalism, not just in Russia, Africa, the Balkans, and other places frequently dismissed as sub-civilized. One has only to recall the victory parades in the USA following the Gulf War, the crackdown on Muslims in France in 1995, and Britain's attitude toward Northern Ireland.

So how is one to reconcile these apparent contradictions? I propose that both sides of the argument are true. Postemotionalism can account for the emergence of a distinctly new and mechanized emotion-speak. Taking together all of Riesman's arguments in *The Lonely Crowd* – even the ones found between the lines – and adding a generous dose of Veblen's ideas, one arrives at the following assessment: Postemotionalism involves the use of 'dead' emotions from a nostalgicized tradition and inner-directed past that are almost always *vicarious* and *conspicuous* and are treated as objects to be *consumed*. The emotions do not disappear, but are socially transformed. Veblen wrote about vicarious leisure, vicarious consumption, conspicuous leisure, conspicuous consumption, and even implied hybrid combinations such as vicarious conspicuous leisure and consumption. I propose a vocabulary of vicarious emotions, vicarious indignation, conspicuous emotions, conspicuous indignation, vicarious conspicuous emotions, and vicarious conspicuous indignation. I shall take up each of these conceptions in turn.

Postemotionalism holds that contemporary emotions are 'dead' in the analogous senses that one speaks of a dead current versus a 'live wire,' or a 'dead nerve' in a limb or tooth. The current is still on, the nerve is still present anatomically, but neither is functioning as it was supposed to. The result is that all of the primal passions discussed from Aristotle to Hume to the present become shadows of their former selves. Anger becomes indignation. Envy – in the form of the traditional covetousness of a neighbor's cow, children, wife, or whatever – now becomes an objectless craving for something better. Hate is transformed into a subtle malice that is hidden in all sorts of intellectualizations. Heartfelt joy is now the bland happiness represented by the 'happy meal.' Loving really becomes liking. Sorrow, as the manifestation of affliction, anguish, grief, pain, remorse, trials, tribulations, and sadness, is magically transformed by the TV journalist's question 'How do you feel?'

(after a death of a loved one to a sniper, or a tornado, or other calamity) into the typical but vague answer 'I'm very upset.' Old-fashioned *caritas* or love of neighbor now becomes institutionalized tolerance. Thus, the shock at the Holocaust has given way to the Holocaust industry, and other instances of genocide in the world, from Cambodia and Rwanda to Bosnia, now become the equivalents of natural disasters, which in turn are treated according to the tenets of a pre-packaged humanitarianism. For example, the response to genocide in Bosnia was not an attempt to stop it, but involved the sending of *humanitarian aid* to the victims of genocide who survived, as if they had survived a hurricane.

These are all generalizations, to be sure, and as such are subject to exceptions, but, by and large, I think they hold, as the discussion up to now suggests. The notion of dead emotions helps to explain phenomena that many postmodernists find perplexing: our so-called museum culture (tolerance museums, Holocaust museums, wax museums, war museums, nostalgia museums, the Route 66 museum, the Liberace museum, and so on); the literal preoccupation with death that Chris Rojek discusses *vis-à-vis* tourism and JFK's assassination site, the cult of Marilyn Monroe, the sightings of Elvis, the cult that surrounds Jim Morrison's grave in Paris, and so on and the general obsession with recycling the dead past, already noted in chapter 1. Yet the dead or pale copies of emotions suggested above are part of a larger social framework of making emotional reactions conspicuous and vicarious in a standardized, neo-Orwellian manner.

I have made the claim that one of the most distinctive marks left by Veblen on the argument in *The Lonely Crowd* is that other-directed types are subject to public scrutiny, always with the understanding that their peers are their jury. Matters which used to be deemed private are now apparent to all, evident, marked by the media, noticed, obvious, and prominent in our judgements of people and events. Tune in to any talk show on television and you will find celebrities as well as non-celebrities discussing their sex lives, childhood traumas, favorite foods, exercise routines, and other intimate things.[89] Whereas President John F. Kennedy's sexual affairs were kept private by journalists – under a 'gentleman's honor' code that still operated – President Bill Clinton's love affairs are public knowledge. Senator Robert Packwood was forced to resign because of public charges of sexual impropriety with his office staff, but such charges are becoming increasingly common regarding politicians and celebrities. Since most people have sex lives, increasingly, it seems, most people's sex lives are subject to public inspection. Such public disclosures are the staple of tabloid journalism. If President Truman's decision to drop the atomic bomb on Japan was not discussed much before or after the fact, current wars are packaged by the Pentagon such that the TV viewer can follow the 'smart bomb' right into the explosion. 'You are there.' If humanitarianism used to involve private and anonymous donations, this is quite different from today's public displays of humanitarianism for the victims in Sarajevo, of AIDS, or any other calamity. Jimmy Carter, for example, wears his humanitarianism on his sleeve for all to see.

But each and every post-emotion holds the potential for such public display, whether it involves one's immediate peer group or the larger television-viewing public. Indignants want to be noticed. And the ingredients of indignation have become pre-packaged: One knows how to be provocative (for example, smear all Croats as Nazis); one offends in a stereotypical way (for example, the entire Los Angeles Police Department is racist); one is incensed using a standardized list of transgressions (lookism, using the politically incorrect vocabulary, and so on). All emotions displayed on television are necessarily at least partly staged. Even secret romances in the office or classroom are virtually impossible given the heightened monitoring of affection, gossip, and the habit of disclosing one's secrets to friends and colleagues.

Finally, post-emotions are vicarious in at least three senses. The first is that, as Riesman notes, the other-directed type is keenly aware of the peer group even when the other-directed person is physically alone. This is because, mentally, other-directed types are anxious about the opinions and receptions of their peers regarding all their thoughts, actions, and feelings. Clearly, this was not the case with the tradition- and inner-directed types, who were relatively less sensitive to the feelings and opinions of others. By contrast, the other-directed postemotional type in all professions automatically *rehearses in advance* the imaginary emotional reaction of others, and thereby lives the emotion vicariously before it is allowed to be expressed. (This is not the same as George Herbert Mead's empathetic taking the role of the other.) Thus, today's university professor must wonder if a particular lecture will offend standards of multiculturalism and political correctness. Authors have to worry about the *image* of themselves that they are presenting in addition to the usual concerns of writing a book. In a sense, everyone becomes a politician (but not in the sense of the inner-directed politician, who expected that some if not many people would dislike him or her for a particular stand), and thinks ahead to the opinion poll, review, and other manifestations of the peer group's verdict. Curiously, even indicted war criminals such as Radovan Karadžić think ahead about how to manage their images with the right haircut, the right spokesperson, the right interview, and so on – this is a relatively new way to commit genocide, in contrast to the straightforwardly brutal and secretive Hitler and Stalin. In general, old-fashioned spontaneous emotion is now processed ahead of time through vicarious participation in the reactions of the proposed audience.

The other direction of vicariousness is backward to history and even the not-so-distant past. Precisely because the present cannot be a source of spontaneous emotion, for all the reasons discussed thus far, the emotional inspiration must come from the past. Hence, the cult of recycling with which I began this book. Most emotions borrow from the historical past or some other past context such that the other-directed type feels vicariously through the past even as he or she lives in the present. President Clinton's frequent borrowings from the emotional imagery surrounding John F. Kennedy are just one example among many.

But the most distinctive, and ominous, form of vicariousness is the one that does not allow the other-directed person to live fully in the present. The postemotional type is simply incapable of being taken in by the present event, of reacting with spontaneous emotions. He or she must not only borrow from the past, and rehearse for the future, but must also *process* the appropriate emotions for the present. Unlike the process of historical revisionism, which analyzes and refurbishes the past, this is a revisionism in *status nascendi*, literally a revision of emotions as they are being born to make sure that they are appropriate to the peer group. Hence, opinion-makers tell us what to think, and feel, as an event is unfolding. Then there are the commentators on television who package the event for us emotionally, live, as it happens. Again, nearly all the professions partake in this political opinion-making, even though it is disguised as neutrality. Physicians, lawyers, professors, and others tell us how to feel about abortion or the day's events in the O.J. Simpson trial or the Los Angeles riots and so on. The other-directed type thereby lives his or her own emotions vicariously, in the present, through other opinion-makers, and nearly everyone is an opinion-maker in some capacity or other.

Perhaps the finest model of this vicariousness from literature is Dostoevsky's underground man. Dostoevsky makes it clear on the opening page of *Notes From the Underground* that his quasi-fictional character, the underground man, is the modern type: Although 'the author of these *Notes* and the *Notes* themselves are, of course, fictional . . . such persons as [their] composer . . . not only exist in our society, but indeed must exist.'[90] The underground man 'was bound to appear in our midst.'[91] Riesman's other-directed type and my postemotional types are, in some significant ways, refinements of Dostoevsky's underground man. This is because the underground man, due to his heightened consciousness of self *and others*, ruminates upon his every emotion and thereby becomes a retort. He takes two years to plan his revenge and still can't go through with it, because he worries about the reaction of others. How is that different from, let us say, NATO taking three years to plan its punishment against the Serbs in the Balkan War, and in the end being unable to go through with it fully because of concerns of how the 'international community' will react? (By contrast, Truman seemed to care very little about how the international community would react to the dropping of the atomic bomb, for example.) Is the underground man really different from President Clinton, whose tortured shifts in position on all issues, domestic and political, have been the focus of discussion throughout his Presidency? The more important point, of course, is that political leaders most often reflect the collective consciousness that elected them, so that we are all underground men. Lives have become endless crises, not because life has become more complex, but because men and women cannot decide upon what they really feel and are forced to live without real conviction, always ill-at-ease, constantly waiting for tomorrow to 'start living life.'

Conclusions

David Riesman has written in retrospect on the innocence of *The Lonely Crowd*, and, in a sense, he is right.[92] The nascent other-directed type that he delineated so many years ago is innocent relative to today's cynical and indignant yet also 'nice' and 'happy' postemotional type who knows so much, but is able to feel, genuinely, so little. The always generous and fundamentally optimistic Riesman concludes *The Lonely Crowd* with the hope that autonomy is always an option to conformity: 'In each society, those who do not conform to the characterological pattern of the adjusted may be either anomic or autonomous' and 'the "autonomous" are those who on the whole are capable of conforming to the behavioral norms of their society – a capacity the anomics usually lack – but are free to choose whether to conform or not.'[93] But I confess that I am unable to see how the other-directed, or, by extension, postemotional, types can achieve autonomy to any appreciable extent, despite Riesman's admonition that 'we must remember that social character is not all of character.'[94] Traditional and inner-directed societies always allowed enough privacy to the individual so that he or she could go through the motions of the traditions and rigid values yet maintain a reservoir of strictly private and authentically personal emotional reactions to these behaviors. Perhaps even in the 1950s, the other-directed type could still find ways to escape the scrutiny of the peer group. For all the reasons examined above, I conclude that such autonomy is nearly impossible for the other-directed type who has become the postemotional type. The escape routes have been blocked. Who can mobilize resistance against nice and happy villains? In the society without opposition (from Marcuse), the group's surveillance has become too sophisticated, the camera is omnipresent, the packaging of emotions has become too standardized, and everyone must become a politician and must navigate the opinion-makers as he or she goes through life. The possibility of autonomy seems to be closed.

Thus, I disagree with David Riesman that other-directedness has 'opened up hitherto undreamed-of possibilities for autonomy'[95] because 'the autonomous at all times have been questioners,'[96] and questioning is the norm in other-directed societies. The questioning has now reached an institutionally pathological stage in which it is nearly impossible to ascertain what one truly feels, as I suggested above with the reference to Dostoevsky's underground man. I disagree especially with Riesman's concluding paragraph in the chapter on autonomy:

> We already discern on the horizon a new polarization between those who cling to a compulsive adjustment via other-direction and those who will strive to overcome this milieu by autonomy. . . . [There is] the possibility of an organic development of autonomy out of other-direction.[97]

Clearly, my position is that postemotionalism, not autonomy, is the organic development out of other-direction. I do not think it is true any longer that 'many currents of change in America escape the notice of the reporters of this best-reported nation on earth.'[98] There are simply too many reporters and news networks in the 1990s in contrast to the relatively innocent 1950s. I do not think it is true any longer, as it was in the 1950s, that 'America is not only big and rich, it is mysterious.'[99] The former mysteries, in the realm of culture as well as physical locations, have been tracked down and packaged by the culture industry. The notion of mystery itself has been pre-packaged, as in the TV program *Unsolved Mysteries.*

The deadness of feeling that Riesman at times ascribes to anomic other-directed types I hold to be the norm in postemotional society. Riesman writes:

> The anomics . . . [may be] those who are overadjusted, who listen too assiduously to the signals from within or without. . . . We have seen, for example, the effort of the other-directed person to achieve a political and personal style of tolerance, *drained of emotion, temper, and moodiness.* But obviously, this can go so far that *deadness comes to resemble a clinical symptom.* . . . Taken all together, the anomics – ranging from overt outlaws to catatonic types who lack even the spark for living, let alone for rebellion – constitute a sizable number in America.[100] (emphasis added)

Since Riesman wrote these lines, tolerance has been institutionalized by the political Left, and is inescapable. In the USA in the 1990s a person who as the result of a bad day or a bad mood delivers a politically incorrect look or utterance or touch faces the possibility of a lawsuit or dismissal or other threatening reaction from the peer group jury. No event is covered by the media or academia or any other institution unless it is filtered first through the multicultural, politically correct gauntlet. The anomic deadness of emotion has become the normative postemotionalism, while those few who defy the norms, the autonomous, meet the fate of the formerly anomic type. (Here I would point out that even Durkheim, who coined the term 'anomie', feared that it had become institutionalized.)[101]

Of course, as a social theorist I am aware that social change is always relatively open-ended, and that the most seemingly authoritarian social systems eventually crumble as the result of revolution or rebellion, or that they might just crumble under their own weight. Logically, postemotional society, too, ought to be vulnerable to change. But in this regard, the most important insight to be gleaned from Riesman (and Marcuse) is that postemotional authoritarianism of the peer group presents such a 'nice,' friendly, happy, and tolerant face that it prevents traditional types of rebellion. It was easy to oppose Nazi ideology because it was so offensive, or even Communism, which, as Veblen noted, threatened the capitalist's pocketbook. But who could justify an attack on 'tolerance,' even if it is intolerant?

I have not shared these conclusions during class discussions of *The Lonely Crowd*, partly because such pessimism is disconcerting, and partly to allow the students to express their views. Nevertheless, it is interesting that my students do not put much stock in autonomy. Instead, two common reactions to Riesman's book emerge. One is the 'escape from tolerance' position, in which students fantasize about escaping to Alaska or a Vermont cabin and wish not to deal with society any longer. And I should add that my politically correct students seem to abhor political correctness even as they embrace it, in a sort of schizophrenia that makes genuine rebellion difficult. The other reaction is a yearning for the 'good ol' days' of inner-directedness. I remind them that Riesman never intended for inner-directedness to serve as a model for them, and that the inner-directed types were frequently ruthless, bigoted, cruel to their children, unyielding, and so on. Far from dissuading them, however, these reproaches seem attractive to them. They are drawn by the inner-directed type's imperfections and passion. Many of them express the view that Speaker of the US House of Representatives Newt Gingrich's Republican revolution is a move back into inner-direction, a move that many students, as so many US citizens, seemed to endorse, at least for a short time. But when Gingrich's program came to be perceived as not-nice, he became the object of widespread indignation in the USA.

But I do not think that Gingrich or the Republicans or the other exemplars of the political Right have escaped the forces of postemotionalism or other-directedness. The political Right uses the same other-directed and postemotional technology (the media) and cultural forms that are omnipresent in society as a whole. They try to appear 'nice' for the most part; they try to extend the mantle of tolerance to white males rather than promote open bigotry; they are adept at using indignation; and their references to the past are still pre-packaged emotional distortions of the past. The good old days were not all that good, after all.

In precluding the possibility of autonomy, at least in the foreseeable future, I do not preclude the possibility of far-reaching revolution, however. But it will not be the postmodern revolution of tolerance that many postmodernists think has already been achieved. Rather, it is more likely to be the old-fashioned, violent type of revolution. As I have argued in my *The Balkanization of the West*, the O.J. Simpson trial and the war in Bosnia would not be the first and second most-covered media events of the present *fin de siècle*, respectively, unless their themes of racism, suspicion of the US government, and Balkanization did not hit an unconscious chord in the other-directed, television-viewing public. Ethnic cleansing has already become a metaphor for our times, clearly visible not only in Bosnia but in the ethnic partition in many Western cities from Washington, DC, to London and Paris.[102] And if such an assessment seems extreme, one has only to recall Alexis de Tocqueville's gloomier prediction in *Democracy in America*[103] that the ethnic groups who comprise the USA will never truly mingle. Rodney King, the victim of a notorious and televised beating by the Los Angeles Police Department, asked the question 'Can't we all just get along?' 'Getting along' is a postemotional, other-directed phrase, a move away from the old-fashioned melting pot and assimilation models of social relations, but also a move away from the postmodern 'salad bowl' model of tolerating. Getting along is the minimal amount of tolerance, and it has become problematic. It has become a question.

Notes

1. See, for example, Patrick M. Reilly, 'Nothing Stings Like A Spurned Employer With a Printing Press,' *Wall Street Journal*, 29 September 1995, p. A1:

Should newspapers report on intimate details of private lives? Time and time again, journalist Geneva Overholser has advocated precisely that . . . [she urged] rape victims to tell their stories in public. When a reader came forward with her story, Ms. Overholser led the Register to a Pulitzer Prize for recounting it. . . . But all that talk about honesty came before another private life was put on display: Ms. Overholser's own.

2. David Riesman, *The Lonely Crowd* (New Haven, CT: Yale University Press, [1950] 1961), p. xl.

3. One of the best appraisals of David Riesman's theoretical eclecticism was made by Bernard Rosenberg, *Analyses of Contemporary Society* (New York: Thomas Crowell, 1966), p. 1:

In the pages presented here will be found a typical representation of Riesman's intellectual antecedents. Among them are many of the great precursors and founders of sociology. Amateurs, one and all! In this excerpt alone figures . . . Tocqueville . . . Simmel (1858–1918), a German philosopher of Jewish ancestry, and therefore academically unacceptable in his homeland, who gave public lectures on human interaction so beautifully wrought that today we sit and ponder them word by word; Max Weber . . . Émile Durkheim . . . [who] received his doctorate as an Agrégé de Philosophie with the greatest difficulty, spent years teaching philosophy in provincial high schools, finally reached the university of Bordeaux as a professor of both sociology and pedagogy, a combination he was obliged to bear, in later years, even at the Sorbonne; and Thorstein Veblen (1857–1929), the American iconoclast best known as an economist despite his Ph.D. in philosophy, author of more than one ironic masterpiece about contemporary society, who always lived only on the periphery of our culture and in its interstices. . . . These men provide Riesman with the rich legacy that he puts to such good use.

4. Riesman, *The Lonely Crowd*, p. 79.

5. Riesman (ibid., p. 138), writes:

Instead of referring himself to the great men of the past and matching himself against his stars, the other-directed person moves in the midst of a veritable Milky Way of almost but not quite indistinguishable contemporaries. . . . To outdistance these competitors, to shine alone, seems hopeless, and also dangerous.

6. Douglas Kellner, *Jean Baudrillard: From Marxism to Postmodernism and Beyond* (Stanford: Stanford University Press, 1989).

7. Mike Gane, *Baudrillard: Critical and Fatal Theory* (London: Routledge, 1991).

8. Chris Rojek and Bryan S. Turner (eds), *Forget Baudrillard?* (London: Routledge, 1993). The contributors are Roy Porter, Zygmunt Bauman, Barry Smart, Bryan S. Turner, Sadie Plant, Chris Rojek, Dean MacCannell, and Juliet Flower MacCannell.

9. See especially Stjepan G. Meštrović, *The Barbarian Temperament* (London: Routledge, 1993).

10. Riesman, *The Lonely Crowd*, p. 14.

11. Émile Durkheim, *The Evolution of Educational Thought* (London: Routledge & Kegan Paul, [1938] 1977).

12. Riesman, *The Lonely Crowd*, p. 19.

13. Ibid.

14. Ibid., p. 21.

15. Ibid.

16. Ibid., p. 22.

17. Ibid., p. 25.

18. William Safire, 'The Politics of Bosnia,' *New York Times*, 30 November 1995, p. A19.

19. See especially Warren Zimmermann, 'Origins of a Catastrophe: Memoirs of the Last American Ambassador to Yugoslavia,' *Foreign Affairs*, 74 (1995), pp. 2–20. Zimmermann clearly

depicts Milošević and Karadžić as evildoers, but he is just as clearly taken by their charming manners, whereas he depicts the Croats and the Slovenes, as well as their leaders, Tudjman and Kučan, as surly nationalists. He holds that nationalism is an abomination, and, curiously, does *not* regard Milošević as a nationalist. For an interesting rebuttal to Zimmermann, see Slaven Letica, 'West Side Story,' in Thomas Cushman and Stjepan G. Meštrović (eds), *This Time We Knew* (New York: New York University Press, 1996), pp. 163–86.

20. Carl Bildt, the European Union mediator, called for Tudjman to be indicted as a war criminal. See Elaine Sciolino, '3 Balkan Presidents Meet in Ohio to Seek End of the Bosnian War,' *New York Times*, 2 November 1995, p. A1.

21. See, for example, the analysis by Georgie Anne Geyer, 'West's Calibrated Response to Serbs Won't Work,' Universal Press Syndicate, 7 September 1995:

The Western alliance and the UN have now totally accepted Serbian President Slobodan Milošević as their bargaining partner . . . He has been accepted as such almost with gratitude – the Balkans' man who can! But we put our principles in grave danger by forgetting that Milošević is the man who started it all, that the blood of Bosnia is mostly on his hands. And so the Western leaders who march dutifully in lockstep to Belgrade to gain his acquiescence ought to ask somewhere along the way: If this ends, are we going to graciously accept Milošević at the United Nations? Perhaps for one of those September speeches at the General Assembly, where he can speak nostalgically of his 'Greater Serbia,' that began this manslaughter? At a state dinner at the White House?

22. Roger Cohen, 'Balkan Leaders Face an Hour for Painful Choices,' *New York Times*, 1 November 1995, p. A1.

23. Roger Cohen, 'Peace in the Balkans Now Relies on Man Who Fanned Its Wars,' *New York Times*, 31 October 1995, p. A1.

24. Elaine Sciolino, Roger Cohen, and Stephen Engelberg, 'In U.S. Eyes, "Good" Muslims and "Bad" Serbs Did a Switch,' *New York Times*, 23 November 1995, p. A1.

25. Ibid.

26. Ibid.

27. Ibid.

28. Ibid.

29. Ibid.

30. Riesman, *The Lonely Crowd*, p. xii.

31. Ibid., p. xxxii.

32. Ibid.

33. Ibid., p. liii.

34. Ibid., p. 44.

35. Ibid., p. 47.

36. Ibid., p. 48.

37. Ibid., p. 59.

38. Ibid.

39. Ibid., p. 61.

40. Ibid., p. 63.

41. Ibid., p. 64.

42. Ibid., p. 67.

43. Ibid., p. 137.

44. Herbert Marcuse, *One-Dimensional Man* (Boston: Beacon Press, [1964] 1991).

45. Riesman, *The Lonely Crowd*, p. 71.

46. Ibid.

47. Henry Adams, 'The Dynamo and the Virgin,' in Henry Adams (ed.), *The Education of Henry Adams* (New York: Viking, [1900] 1983), pp. 1068–75.

48. Riesman, *The Lonely Crowd*, p. 72.

49. Ibid.

50. Ibid., p. 99.

51. Ibid., p. 100.

52. Ibid., p. 104.

53. See Simon Schama, 'The Princess of Eco-Kitsch,' *New York Times*, 30 June 1995, p. A1.

54. For example, Marion N. Libby and Elizabeth Ariès, 'Gender Differences in Preschool Children's Narrative Fantasy,' *Psychology of Women Quarterly*, 13 (1989), pp. 293–306.

55. For example, Walter Dean Myers, 'Telling Our Children the Stories of Their Lives,' *American Visions*, 6 (1991), pp. 30–2.

56. Nicholas B. Allen and Benjamin S. Bradley, 'The Place of Emotion in Stories Told by Children: An Exploratory Study,' *The Journal of Genetic Psychology*, 154 (1993), pp. 397–406.

57. Candace Miller, 'Storytelling,' *American Horticulturist*, 73 (1994), pp. 12–13.

58. Harriet Waters, Fung-ting Hou and Yuh-shiow Lee, 'Organization and Elaboration in Children's Repeated Production of Prose,' *Journal of Experimental Child Psychology*, 55 (1993), pp. 31–55.

59. Let me note that in addition to watching seemingly endless hours of *Barney and Friends* with my daughter, Ivy, I benefited from reading a term paper by Dianne Sykes, a graduate student in one of my seminars on postmodernism. Her paper is entitled 'Finding Ourselves in Each Other: Barney and the Other-Directed Child,' in *Free Inquiry in Creative Sociology*, 24, 1 (May, 1996), pp. 85–93.

60. Riesman, *The Lonely Crowd*, p. 83.

61. Ibid., p. 85.

62. One of the few exceptions to this rule is to be found in Georgie Anne Geyer, 'Croats Have the Right to Defend Themselves,' United Press International, 8 August 1995.

63. Riesman, *The Lonely Crowd*, p. 176.

64. Ibid., p. 194.

65. Ibid., p. 196.

66. Comment made to me by a member of a CNN film crew in College Station, Texas, on 7 September 1995.

67. 'Wal-Mart Stops Sale of T-Shirt,' *Houston Chronicle*, 24 September 1995, p. 7A.

68. Richard B. Schmitt, 'One Thing to Say About Ms. McColm Is: She Sues People,' *Wall Street Journal*, 26 September 1995, p. A1.

69. Keith Tester, *The Inhuman Condition* (London: Routledge, 1995).

70. Riesman, *The Lonely Crowd*, p. 181.

71. Todd S. Purdum, 'Clinton Plans to Lift Public Out of "Funk",' *New York Times*, 24 September 1995, p. A1.

72. Riesman, *The Lonely Crowd*, p. 163.

73. Ibid., p. 164.

74. Ibid., p. 163.

75. Ibid., p. 171.

76. Ibid., p. 180.

77. Ibid., p. 202.

78. Ibid., p. 172.

79. Ibid., p. 177.

80. Ibid., p. 185.

81. Ibid., p. 189.

82. I elaborate on both points in *The Balkanization of the West* (London: Routledge, 1993).

83. Riesman, *The Lonely Crowd*.

84. Ibid., p. 180.

85. Ibid., p. 181.

86. Ibid.

87. Norbert Elias, *Involvement and Detachment* (Oxford: Basil Blackwell, 1987).

88. Roger Cohen, 'US Seeks to Persuade Serbs NATO and UN are Neutral,' *New York Times*, 15 April 1994, p. A23.

89. CNN reported on 17 November 1995 on a study that found that 50 percent of the content on television talk shows was sexual in content.

90. Fyodor Dostoevsky, *Notes From the Underground* (Lanham, MD: University Press of America, [1864] 1982), p. 1.

91. Ibid.

92. David Ricsman, 'Innocence of the *Lonely Crowd*,' *Society*, 27, 2 (1990), pp. 76–9.

93. Riesman, *The Lonely Crowd*, p. 242.

94. Ibid., p. 241.

95. Ibid., p. 257.

96. Ibid., p. 256.

97. Ibid., p. 260.

98. Ibid., p. 307.

99. Ibid.

100. Ibid., pp. 244–5.

101. Discussed in Stjepan G. Meštrović, *Durkheim and Postmodern Culture* (Hawthorne, NY: Aldine de Gruyter, 1992).

102. Akbar Ahmed, 'Ethnic Cleansing: A Metaphor for Our Time?' *Ethnic and Racial Studies*, 18, 1 (1995), pp. 2–25.

103. Alexis de Tocqueville, *Democracy in America* (New York: Vintage Books, [1845] 1945).

4

The Authenticity Industry

Clearly, the claims put forth in this book concerning postemotional theory invite the retort, 'What, then, is authentic?' In some ways, a similar question was asked on a mass scale in the 1960 counter-culture movement. The very fact that this concern with authenticity was part of a self-conscious mass movement makes it suspect. A more academic precursor to the concern with authenticity is to be found in the works of the Frankfurt School, particularly in the work of Walter Benjamin on aura and Herbert Marcuse on 'happy consciousness.'[1] The previous *fin de siècle* was also concerned with spontaneous, genuine emotion as opposed to the modernist rationalization of feelings, and this concern is reflected in the works of Dostoevsky, Henry Adams, T.S. Eliot, Joseph Conrad, Thorstein Veblen, Friedrich Nietzsche, Georg Simmel, Sigmund Freud, Émile Durkheim, Ferdinand Tönnies, and many other writers.[2] Some of these writers were writing in the early twentieth century rather than the *fin de siècle* strictly speaking, but were still influenced by its spirit. Thus, Dostoevsky's underground man has been interpreted by many humanists as being the honest 'anti-hero' because he refuses to feign sociability and, instead, he constantly and cynically debunks and analyzes every rationalization for action, including his own. Henry Adams expressed his contempt for the mechanical dynamo, which he saw as the model for social as well as industrial life, and yearned for a restoration of the emotional life symbolized by the cult of the Virgin Mary.[3] Eliot's poem 'The Waste Land' has been interpreted widely as an indictment of the over-regimentation of spontaneity in modernity. Eliot took some cues from Nietzsche, Durkheim, and Freud in positing that modern persons need mythology as an escape valve into an authentic domain of passion from the aridity of civilization.[4] Simmel's writings were dormant until David Frisby's[5] and Michael Kaern's[6] recent revitalizations of his thought, but Simmel clearly portrayed modern culture as a suffocating system of 'forms' that always seek to strangle the passionate 'will,' a term he takes directly from Schopenhauer and Nietzsche. In *Community and Society*, Ferdinand Tönnies labelled *Gemeinschaft* as authentic and the modern *Gesellschaft* as artificial.[7] I have demonstrated in *The Coming Fin de Siècle* that a century ago most writers followed Schopenhauer to conclude that authentic passions would eventually break through forms, representations, and other modernist categories.

Things are not so clear in the present *fin de siècle*. A return to the cult of the Virgin, as envisioned by Adams, seems out of the question. Contemporary mythologies and rituals seem unable to offer an escape from

Eliot's waste land. It is no longer evident that, as Simmel hoped, life can
break through forms. George Orwell noted that even if one sought to rebel
against the culture of the machine by destroying all machines, new ones
would immediately replace them: Machines have become a modernist habit of
the mind.[8] Most relevant of all to the present discussion is the dawning that
a post-*Gesellschaft* society (a post-society society) has emerged in which *the
authentic (community) is mass-produced artificially*. The notion of an artificially authentic community seems to be an oxymoron at first glance, but
appears to be the meaning of Disneyland culture, the McDonaldization of
society, Internet 'communities,' and other anomalies that postmodernists
have already uncovered. It is no longer Adorno's culture industry, but a new
authenticity industry that seems to characterize postemotional societies.

David Riesman's *The Lonely Crowd* makes one wonder whether authenticity – in any of the senses used a century ago – is possible to achieve any
longer. As noted previously, Chris Rojek is right to conclude that for postmodernism authenticity is no longer an important issue. De-differentiation
and the triumph of simulation have made it seem absurd to ask again, so
many years after the 1960s concern with authenticity, 'What is genuine versus
phony?' The public concerns of writers in the current *fin de siècle* are not with
authenticity but with cyberspace, the 'information superhighway,' the end of
history, virtual reality, simulation, and completing the Enlightenment 'project.' (One should pay particular attention to the modernist overtones of the
word 'project,' as opposed to characterizing the Enlightenment as the emotional 'cult' of Reason.) I take issue with the postmodernists, not with Chris
Rojek's assessment. To the extent that the problem of authenticity enters
contemporary discourse, it is phrased in *cognitive* terms of ascertaining the
true, real, or original. Not surprisingly, I shall recast this problem in terms
of the *emotions* and, in the subsequent chapter especially, in terms of group
rituals and collective effervescence.

Specifically, in this chapter I shall explore large conceptual areas in which
emotion is routinely manufactured. I shall be pursuing several aims simultaneously: (1) I shall be extending the argument that emotion, not just cognitive
representations, is the object of contemporary simulation, virtual reality, and
recycling. (2) I shall be exposing the irony that in the obsession with manufacturing 'real feelings,' the contemporary era is betraying a repressed longing for
the authentic that is presumed to be as unknowable as the thing-in-itself was for
Immanuel Kant. (3) I shall be broadening the Frankfurt School's concept of
the culture industry (by which they referred to the mass reproduction of music,
popular literature, film, and other artefacts for mass consumption) to include
taken-for-granted ideas that are saturated with emotions. That is, I shall argue
that one should admit into discourses of this sort the possibility that the often-
cited Enlightenment project itself is really a counterfeit Enlightenment project;
that the nationalism that is the object of derision by so many contemporary
writers is a counterfeit nationalism; that Philip Rieff's 'therapeutic society' is a
counterfeit or post-therapeutic society; that Norbert Elias gives us a counterfeit
civilizing process; that the so-called postmodern community formed through

information technology is a fake community: and so on. My allusions to the authentic versions of these and other phenomena shall be necessarily brief, but shall be treated more extensively in the subsequent chapter. Nevertheless, my allusions are meant to be sufficiently suggestive to warrant future empirical corroboration and theoretical expansion.

Before I begin this segment of the discussion in earnest, let me give two general illustrations of the overall point that I made above. The authentic has not been completely eclipsed in contemporary times. Pockets of authenticity have survived despite postmodernism, other-directedness, postemotionalism, and other trends that seem to work against it. Consider, for example, a fairly typical scene in church in which a four-year-old child's voice penetrates the service with the piercing line, 'Daddy, I have to go potty.' The routine response by the embarrassed parents is to ask the child to hush, and wait until the service is over. But the child just as typically is found to respond, louder than before, 'I have to go right *now!*' Most of the other parents smile as the child's parents look around sheepishly and take the child to a bathroom. The entire sequence of events resembles a collective *ritual* that is familiar to most persons, yet the ritual is spontaneous. This is an example of authenticity that has survived into contemporary times, as so many children's behaviors are. Even though this example is mundane, it is worth pondering, 'What makes the child's behavior authentic?' One obvious reply is that the child is not staging his or her emotions for the benefit of others. He or she is a miniature underground man (from Dostoevsky). Note that the issue of authenticity here is *not* the cognitive one whether the child 'really' has to go potty or not – any parent can recall the false alarms in situations like these. It is not the 'reality' question that determines authenticity, but the spontaneous emotion that works seemingly *through* the child in apparent defiance of social conventions at the same time that society cooperates with this defiance. The other, less obvious response is that the group is clearly unified in its collective belief that children, as the future bearers of civilization, are thereby exempt from certain social norms at certain times. Authenticity presupposes a community. While most group identities still coalesce in such instances and the group smiles knowingly, one can envision a future time in which the larger group will not tolerate such behaviors, much as contemporary groups no longer tolerate public breast-feeding. The issue of authenticity stems from a complex social interaction between the child and larger social group in which the group finds a social space for the child's emotional rebellion. To be sure, such space is getting increasingly crowded, for children and adults alike.

The other broad point I wish to make is that the role of emotions is mysteriously overlooked in the existing scholarly discourse concerning various aspects of the culture industry. Consider the existing literature on Disneyland and Disney World as one example among many that could be drawn from contemporary cultural interests (and recall Baudrillard's often-cited claim that all of America is a Disneyland simulation of reality).[9] Chris Rojek is right to claim that 'the twentieth century has been the Disney century,' and that the Disneyesque refers to a general modernist tendency to seek escape.[10]

(I would add that it should refer to the postemotional tendency to seek a perfectly manipulated community, complete with artificial emotions.) Disney has become ubiquitous, as illustrated, for example, by Vice-President Al Gore's use of a Disney costume for a Halloween party:

> The Walt Disney Co. has sent Vice President Al Gore for those nifty *Beauty and the Beast* costumes he and wife Tipper wore at their annual Halloween party for the news media and their *enfants terribles*. And how much did Disney charge for the outfits, custom-made to the Gores' measurements? A beastly $8,365.00, thank you very much.[11]

In the existing scholarly literature on the Disney phenomenon, one reads that Disney World is America's pilgrimage site; that Marxism explains the class divisions in the consumption of Disney imagery; that Walt Disney's family background explains the curious family interactions in the fictional lives of Disney characters; that Disney World represents the utopia of American values such as the desire for eternal childhood and the freedom from responsibility; that Disney World represents a New Right utopia of an all-heterosexual world and traditional views of male/female relationships: and so on.[12] Horkheimer and Adorno write that Disney cartoons

> hammer into every brain the old lesson that . . . the breaking down of individual resistance is the condition of life in this society. Donald Duck in the cartoons and the unfortunate in real life get their thrashing so that the audience can learn to take their punishment.[13]

All this is well and fine, but the most obvious aspect of the Disney experience is missing in these analyses: Disneyland, Disney World, and the Disney industry attempt to manufacture *emotions*. More particularly, Disney World is an attempt to create an artificial community.

This claim is literally true when one considers Disney Corporation's plans to build Celebration near Disney World, a 'true planned community including a downtown, health center, school, post office, town hall, golf course, single family homes, townhouses and apartments.'[14] 'Restrictive covenants will dictate what homeowners can and cannot do in Celebration.'[15] There will be six approved design styles for homes: 'Classical, Victorian, Colonial Revival, Coastal, Mediterranean, French.'[16] The advertising for Celebration reads, in part:

> Imagine a town with tree-lined streets flanked by traditional houses with big front porches and neighbors who keep an eye out for you. A town that's 'on-line' with high-quality communications technology and a downtown business and shopping center that is alive and bustling. . . . The company known for its fantasy communities such as Walt Disney World's Magic Kingdom or EPCOT Center is now taking the planning expertise it lavished on theme parks and using it to produce our collective vision of small-town America, a place where people will want to come to live.[17]

Apart from this literal Disneyfication of community, the metaphorical Disneyfication of America includes some of the following characteristics. One boards the Disney World Steamboat ostensibly to 'experience' how it felt to take a ride on such a boat a hundred years ago. Something similar is true for other theme parks. At Six Flags theme parks, one is strapped into a virtual reality seat to *feel* what it's like to fly in a military jet airplane, not just to know what it's like. Indeed, one could not 'know' what it was like from merely watching the film shot from the cockpit without the emotions generated by the violent movements in the seat that is technically designed to move in tandem with the cognitive imagery. One experiences 'flight' viscerally without leaving one's seat. Something similar is true for all the other attractions in other theme parks: One is supposed to experience the 'authentic' emotions of the Western frontier, travelling in outer space, taking a journey in a submarine, visiting a 1950s drive-in restaurant, and so on. But note also that none of these artificial emotional experiences is achieved by a solitary individual. This important point, too, is overlooked by contemporary analysts. The inner-directed type of a generation ago might have been able to imagine artificial emotional experiences in solitary confinement, so to speak. But in line with Riesman's analysis, the postemotional type must consume such experiences in a group. Can one imagine Disneyland designed for private consumption by hooking into individualized virtual reality machines? The obvious reply is negative. And that is precisely the important point: The entire setting of Disneyland as well as Disney World is group-oriented and is meant to serve as an artificial community. This is evident from the 'town square' that one encounters immediately upon entering the park to the impeccable cleanliness in the park, the uniform friendliness of all the attendants, and other finishing touches that contribute to an overall atmosphere of the perfect community. This insight helps to explain also why Eurodisney in Paris had a difficult time drawing American tourists initially: The local French attendants were simply not friendly enough by American standards. And of course, traditional French men and women could not understand why anyone would prefer Eurodisney to traditional Parisian tourist draws such as the Eiffel Tower and the Latin Quarter, which *can* be consumed privately. The difference between the Eiffel Tower and Eurodisney, culturally speaking, is really the difference between inner-directedness and other-directedness or, more precisely, postemotionalism.

Comparative studies with precursors to Disneyland would also be instructive. Consider, for example, the closest Dutch equivalent to Disneyland, Efteling. Efteling reproduces traditional and inner-directed fairy tales such as Hansel and Gretel. For many years, it did not have the rides, atmosphere of group fun, and virtual reality exhibits characteristic of Disneyland. But in recent years, Efteling had to add such Disneyesque attractions in order to keep drawing Dutch families, who are becoming increasingly other-directed. A study of how Efteling is becoming Disneyesque would illustrate the cultural war that accompanies the Americanization of Europe.

Of course, something similar is true with regard to the McDonaldization of Paris. Traditional Parisian cafés are closing in record numbers because their inner-directed cultural milieu can no longer compete with increasing other-directedness in France. In the traditional Parisian café, one sipped coffee for hours on end, usually *alone* or in a small company of others. The attraction was solitary, inner-directed reverie or old-fashioned European conversation with an intimate friend. But, clearly, other-directed and postemotional types find such isolation unbearable, and also object to the undependability or even rudeness of service at such cafés. McDonald's promises the postemotional utopia of foolproof, friendly service in a 'nice' atmosphere in which one is in the midst of a throng.

This focus on the centrality of emotions *vis-à-vis* an artificially created community deepens the meaning of current assessments that are found in the postmodernist discourse. Thus, if America is Disneyland, as Baudrillard suggests, it means that the emotional lives of Americans are being manipulated on a mass and highly organized scale. Its real meaning is that Americans are duped and dupe themselves into believing that they live in the perfect community, free of racism, ethnic cleansing, and other uncivil phenomena relegated to the rest of the world. If Disneyland has become the contemporary pilgrimage site for contemporaries, one must inquire into the emotional yearning and needs of contemporaries in contrast to the emotional needs met by traditional pilgrimages. Why would Americans and pilgrims from other Western industrialized nations seek out sites in which their emotions are manipulated such that they 'experience' the perfect family life, the perfect community, the perfect Enlightenment ideal and other unreal emotional utopias? These are among the new questions that the concept of postemotionalism exposes.

The Two Modernisms and the Two Postmodernisms

I had suggested earlier that post-emotions are quasi-emotions in that they partake of the passion–idea dualism simultaneously. Chris Rojek offers the most promising point of departure for deepening this insight by arguing that, first, 'some aspects of modernity are evident in postmodernity,'[18] and, second, that 'there are indeed contradictory forces in modernity which simultaneously pull in the direction of greater unity and greater disunity, more standardization and more diversity, further centralization and further de-centralization.'[19] More precisely, Rojek distinguishes between Modernity 1 as the force of order and Modernity 2 as the force of disorder. He correctly points out that most theorists since the previous *fin de siècle* have taken one position or the other whereas the true picture of things today clearly must involve some aspect of both. Thus, the Modernity 1 position is found in the works of the functionalists, positivists, pluralists, Max Weber's famous Protestant Ethic thesis, Norbert Elias's work on the civilizing process, and the works of Thorstein Veblen, among others. Modernity 1 seeks to control both nature and society. It is an extension of the modernist's love of progress and machinery in that social life itself is made to run as if it were a machine. Modernity 1 is necessarily artificial. In terms of social theory, it resonates with Ritzer's notion of the McDonaldization of Society, George Orwell's cult of the machine, Henry Adams's culture based on the dynamo, and Zygmunt Bauman's notion of the modernist as the perfect gardener.

Modernity 2 is the focus on constant change found in Baudelaire's often-quoted depiction of the modern as 'the ephemeral, the fugitive, the contingent.'[20] Rojek uses Nietzsche's distinction between Apollo and Dionysus to reinforce his own distinction between Modernity 1 and Modernity 2. Rojek argues that Baudrillard and Simmel are two important thinkers who clearly take up the themes of circulation, repetition, the dreamworlds of consumption and the carnivalesque as aspects of Modernity 2. Modernity 2 is the refuge of all those who, seeking to escape or criticize the controlling aspects of Modernity 1, point to chaos, nihilism, and all sorts of disarray in society. Although Rojek does not mention community, it seems to be the case that community may be conceptualized in terms of Modernity 2 as the realm of authentic community, which was spontaneous and disorderly *vis-à-vis* emotional life, as well as in terms of Modernity 1, illustrated by the attempts of many contemporary communitarians to *construct* 'communities' rationally.

I agree with Rojek overall and believe that his focus on the contradictory pushes and pulls of modernity – and, by extension, postmodernity – is fruitful. It is a more realistic appraisal of the current situation than either Habermas's dreary call to complete the Enlightenment project (Modernity 1) or the naive optimism a century ago that Modernity 2 or the will would eventually triumph over the artificiality and hardness of a highly mechanized, organized, and bureaucratic world. The Enlightenment project is clearly in disarray and one is hard pressed to believe that authentic myth or authentic community or authentic anything will save humankind. I would add only that for Nietzsche, the Dionysian realm is more than the other side of the Apollonian: The Dionysian is the authentic. And it should be kept in mind that Nietzsche derives the notion of the Dionysian from his teacher, Arthur Schopenhauer's notion of the passionate and unruly will to life.[21] Nevertheless, Rojek's distinction serves as a warning that modernity and postmodernity cannot be grasped with one generalization. It allows the theorist more freedom to maneuver in discussions of this sort and to avoid premature allegiance to one type of modernity versus the other. But clearly, the present discussion is not about modernity or postmodernity *per se*, but about postemotionalism as an alternative to them. And Rojek does not take up the role of emotions or what I call post-emotions *vis-à-vis* these seemingly contradictory social currents.

What I intend to do in this chapter is to use Rojek's distinction as a springboard for elaborating on the following ideas: (1) Modernity 1 has entered a new phase in which it seeks to order and control an aspect of Modernity 2 that has always been seen as the most autonomous and unruly aspect of human social life, namely, the emotions. (2) Ultimately, Modernity 2 'wins' in the battle with Modernity 1 (much as Simmel argued that 'will' always triumphs over 'forms') by giving the seemingly rational and orderly forms an emotional appeal and allegiance that runs counter to what Modernity 1 is all about. The end result is the postemotional social world that is the subject of the present discussion. (3) The most important illustration of how Modernity

1 and Modernity 2 interact is the creation of artificial (Modernity 1) communities (Modernity 2). The confluence of these two social forces is responsible for the dawning of artificially contrived authenticity, or what I call the authenticity industry.

Counterfeit Enlightenment

Critical theory's role as a harbinger of certain forms of postmodernism have been discussed so many times that I shall not add anything new on this connection. Nor will I add directly to the criticisms of Theodor Adorno as an elitist, of the concept of mass society, or the lack of empirical support for concepts such as the authoritarian personality.[22] All this is *passé*. The new perspectives on critical theory that postemotionalism brings to this discussion include the following: Critical theorists have neglected the role of the emotions; their focus on mechanical reproduction as the phenomenon that destroys authentic aura is unintelligible; and their implicit as well as explicit emotional sanctification of the Enlightenment – renamed the Enlightenment 'project' by their contemporary successor, Jürgen Habermas – constitutes a paradoxically irrational overestimation of rationality. In the end, critical theory offers a *counterfeit vision of the Enlightenment* that has become the unexamined staple of many if not most contemporary social theories.

Let us note immediately that the Enlightenment was not a 'project' in its inception. As Keith Tester[23] and others have demonstrated, the original Enlightenment philosophers were 'strangers' in their cultures who had to 'keep under cover,' so to speak, or flatter political leaders, or keep their views secret. The fact that Habermas and others can now refer openly to a project means that the assumptions of the Enlightenment are no longer considered dangerous, and have become reified. These assumptions are now amenable to postemotional manipulation. Moreover, contemporary disciples of the Enlightenment are often able to turn the state and the polity to their own interests. This is an amazingly different situation from that of the real, historical Enlightenment! More importantly, Durkheim has a point when he observed that the Enlightenment really made a religion out of rationality; that it erected a veritable cult of Reason. Critical theorists never delve into the emotional underpinnings of worshipping Reason, and betray their uncritical stance by assuming that the Enlightenment can be made into a project, that is, mechanized, synthesized, artificially constructed. Finally, one should not forget that the Enlightenment had to deal with cultural resistance, some of it formidable. Rousseau and Jonathan Swift expressed a radical distrust of science, for example.

Critical theorists have written on the commodification and mass reproduction of music, information, art, popular music, and all sorts of other phenomena *except* emotion. It is true, as Adorno claims, that culture has been 'pre-digested,' pre-handled by hundreds of thousands of others before it reaches the consumer, such that it becomes cultural 'baby-food.'[24] But it is not only, let us say, listening to music that follows a formula and comes to the consumer second-hand. *Feeling* also frequently follows a formula and arrives stale in contemporary cultures. Curiously, even in his discussion of fascism, Adorno offers no insights into this important domain beyond noting that authoritarian leaders have 'to mobilize irrational, unconscious, regressive processes.'[25] The more important point is that fascist leaders must manipulate standardized feelings. Hitler was the prototype of Barney and Friends: Nearly everyone must experience the same feelings and there is almost no room for dissent. Let me repeat that Herbert Marcuse's notion of the 'happy consciousness,' found in *One-Dimensional Man*, is still remarkably relevant in this regard.

But even critical theory's notions of commodification and mass society are problematic. It is a paradox of contemporary cultures that they simultaneously promote individualism as well as automatized reactions. Since Adorno's time, advertisers have perfected the skill of appealing to tastes, not of a whole strata of society, but a particular neighborhood, block, life-style, and other very narrow categories. The contemporary consumer is not just a mass society automaton, as Adorno claimed, but an agent convinced that he or she possesses some degree of freedom to choose group identities, and this belief makes the agent a target of manipulation by corporations who pitch advertisements in relation to specific subgroup versions of emotional reality. And heightened consciousness of this fact will *not* alter matters. As noted previously, contemporary advertisements sell feelings, moods, and emotions that are synthetically attached to a given product. Billions of dollars are spent on achieving and maintaining consumer 'loyalty' to a particular emotional experience. Thus, consumers allow themselves to be manipulated in associating the feeling of rugged individualism with the Marlboro Man, for example, or with the happy feelings of family life that McDonald's promotes with its playgrounds and happy meals. In addition to actual, material products, contemporary politicians know how to put an emotional 'spin' on a particular issue so as to appeal to Jews, women, Hispanics, Poles, and various subgroups and permutations of these and other group categories. This results in a postemotionally complex 'mass society' of competing groups in which people believe that they are individualists. This is a much more dangerous state of affairs than Adorno envisioned because the masses are too happy to know that they are being manipulated.

To be sure, Herbert Marcuse comes close to making a similar argument. In *One-Dimensional Man*, he posits the existence of a 'happy consciousness':

> Loss of conscience due to the satisfactory liberties granted by an unfree society makes for a *happy consciousness* which facilitates acceptance of the misdeeds of this society. It is the token of declining autonomy and comprehension.[26]

Happy consciousness is commensurate with Riesman's focus on the other-directed type's obsession with niceness, and, of course, culminates in the McDonald's happy meal. Marcuse elaborates:

> The Happy Consciousness – the belief that the real is rational and that the system delivers the goods – reflects the new conformism which is a facet of

technological rationality translated into social behavior. It is new because it is rational to an unprecedented degree. It sustains a society which has reduced – and in its most advanced areas eliminated – the more primitive irrationality of the preceding stages, which prolongs and improves life more regularly than before. The war of annihilation has not yet occurred; the Nazi extermination camps have been abolished. The Happy Consciousness repels the connection. Torture has been introduced as a normal affair, but in a colonial war which takes place at the margin of the civilized world. And there it is practiced with good conscience for war is war. . . . Otherwise, peace reigns . . . 'the Community is too well off to care!'[27]

Marcuse's observations have an important ring of truth to them, but the sound is muffled. Looking at the modern world through his eyes reveals an important insight, yet one's vision is blurred. This is because Marcuse, like other critical theorists, paradoxically pursued a rational solution to the problem of over-rationalization. The irrational for him amounts to little more than barbarism. He assumes uncritically that Nazism was an irrational phenomenon, whereas one could argue that it involved a meticulously rational program of controlling emotions. One could update his observations to include the tragedy of Bosnia in the 1990s: the comfortably well-off still don't care. But Bosnia, too, represents more than irrationalism. It illustrates Belgrade's crafty, *rational* creation of 'community' and mythology bent on genocide. The Belgrade regime consists of inner-directed types who have mastered the skill of coming across as other-directed.

Marcuse concludes his book with a call for liberation from the false consciousness of one-dimensional society. This liberation is to be achieved, vaguely, by grasping some magical form of authentic rationality to offset the false consciousness wrought by capitalist and technical systems of rationality. In this regard, Marcuse's conclusion does not differ from Max Horkheimer's *The Eclipse of Reason*,[28] wherein Horkheimer also seeks a 'pure' rationality as salvation from the 'false' rationality of modernity.

It seems high time to conclude that Marcuse and the other critical theorists begged the question of what constitutes pure or authentic rationality. To keep pursuing their Holy Grail amounts to a new form of mysticism that requires faith, not any sort of rationality. I contend that this pursuit of an illusory, perfect rationality is itself postemotional. It constitutes Enlightenment fundamentalism, not enlightenment.

Another acclaimed member of the Frankfurt School is Walter Benjamin, whose essay 'The Work of Art in the Age of Mechanical Reproduction'[29] is obsessively covered in most graduate seminars on social theory. Its central thesis is well known: Mechanical reproduction destroys the 'aura' of an object and thereby makes fascism possible. But Rojek is right to point out that Benjamin begs the question of what constitutes aura.[30] The implicit answer seems to be that the 'original' is the auratic. Moreover, Benjamin seems to share Adorno's disdain for reproduction as the phenomenon most responsible for mass society. But the more serious problem with this assessment is that even when an 'original' is involved, the so-called aura is subject to emotional manipulation. What Benjamin as well as Adorno and the other critical theorists overlook is this: Other-directed and postemotional types could not care less whether they are consuming the real thing or an artificial reproduction. Aura really presupposes an authentic community context which is no longer possible. Critical theorists have neglected this Durkheimian angle on the authentic and auratic. Their theory presupposes an inner-directed social world that no longer exists.

For example, consider the plans to build a Cold War theme park in Florida. Its promoters boast that they will use *authentic* uniforms, weapons, watch-towers, and concrete that the East Germans actually used to sustain the Berlin Wall. The theme park 'will give visitors the feeling of living on the east side and the west side' of the Berlin Wall and 'it would recreate the feelings of the Cold War.'[31] A real piece of the Berlin Wall was brought to the United States for similar reasons to inaugurate the George Bush Library in College Station, Texas, and to create the image of former President Bush as the states-man who ended the Cold War. But does this use of 'authentic' material objects, as opposed to their re-creation in other museums and parks, really create aura? It is more likely that it creates the emotional illusion of authen-ticity. This is because the overall context of converting the Berlin Wall into a group-oriented theme park or ideological statement (in the case of the Bush Library) bespeaks the rational manipulation of emotions. The visitor will never be able to feel what it was like to seek to escape through the Berlin Wall because one knows that one will be able to leave this site for the comfort of one's home at the end of the experience. And the thoughtful visitor to the Bush Library will be able to discern that he or she is being had: One could argue that the Soviet Union collapsed of its own accord, or because of the collective effervescence of dissent in the Soviet Union, not because of George Bush.

Similarly, albeit somewhat cynically, one could argue that the visitors who crowd around the *Mona Lisa* in the Louvre in Paris are not experiencing aura, even though that is presumably the original painting, but are experi-encing what Baudrillard calls the 'I did it' feeling. In a typically other-directed way, one wants to tell one's friends that one was there, for the same reasons that one buys T-shirts that read 'I survived Hurricane Opal,' or 'I survived Waco,' or that one 'survived' any other commodified spectacle. The experi-ence is an other-directed token of participation that the jury of peers finds acceptable. In sum, when one examines Benjamin's celebrated essay critically, one concludes that it is a faithful extension of Adorno's diatribes against reproduction and commodification, but that it does not stand up to scrutiny. Originals can be and often are manipulated emotionally and in group settings quite apart from the process of mechanical reproduction. Conversely, mass-produced kitsch can and often does produce spontaneous emotions in children that deserve to be called authentic. A four-year-old who tears open a 'happy meal' toy does not know and does not care that he or she is the object of mass commodification, mass consumerism, and mass production. The child's joy is real enough, so long as parents and peers reinforce the 'happy' experience.

The supreme irony in critical theory is that in its venting of rage at capitalist mass commodification as a criticism of one aspect of
Enlightenment-based modernity, it commodifies the Enlightenment. To be
fair, Horkheimer and Adorno's *Dialectic of Enlightenment* does expose the
duality of the Enlightenment legacy as being capable of producing high culture as well as fascism. As I have already noted, Zygmunt Bauman, in
particular, has elaborated on this dark side of the Enlightenment legacy as
being responsible in significant ways for the Holocaust, Communism, and
fascism. Nevertheless, Bauman and Jürgen Habermas follow the critical theorists in concluding that next time the 'right' manipulation of the
Enlightenment project will yield positive results, including an ethic of tolerance, and that the negative results can be avoided. Adorno's elitism amounts
to a similar, high-handed faith that if he and his followers could have controlled the Enlightenment project, they could have made it work. I submit
that this assessment constitutes a postemotional attachment to a distorted
vision of the Enlightenment.

This is because the Enlightenment was about more than individualism,
human rights, science, rationality, and other phenomena that are glorified by
modernists. The Enlightenment was also about civil and religious wars, mass
executions, witch hunts, colonialism, slavery, and other unsavory phenomena.
It is worth repeating that Émile Durkheim characterized both the
Renaissance and the Enlightenment as periods of excessive anomie, and
pointed to the Scholastic period or so-called 'Dark Ages' as a more preferable
period of moral balance.[32] Note that I am not criticizing the Enlightenment
per se but am treating it objectively as one would analyze any other period of
history, namely, as a mixture of benign as well as negative characteristics. I
am not raising cognitive issues of historical revisionism, but emotional issues.
The Enlightenment was a period characteristic of Modernity 2, one of
tremendous collective effervescence, in addition to being a period characteristic of Modernity 1, marked by the pursuit of reason, science, and order. But
critical theorists and their successors have tried to make the Enlightenment
seem as if it were an exclusive example of Modernity 1. They have given us a
Disneyland version of the Enlightenment. They have McDonaldized it. To be
sure, *Dialectic of the Enlightenment* exposes some negative aspects of the
Enlightenment, but these are not seen as fundamental flaws, just blemishes
that can be corrected with the right social engineering.

The critical theorists and their successors are just as simplistic in their portraits of the role of the Enlightenment legacy in twentieth-century fascisms
and Communism. They blame the dehumanization, bureaucracy, and other
overly rational aspects of modernity for these evils and neglect the role of culture. I have argued, with Miroslav Goreta and Slaven Letica, in *Habits of the
Balkan Heart*,[33] for example, that Communism was a modernist system, as
Bauman argues, but it was more than that: It was the successor to autocratic
but quite anti-modern, traditional habits of the heart in specific regions of
the former Soviet Union, the former Yugoslavia, and other formerly
Communist states. Even with regard to studies of Nazism, the role of the

habits of the heart in Prussia, which produced most of Hitler's general staff, is severely neglected. In other words, critical theorists and others have neglected the role of Modernity 2 in their assessment of the Enlightenment.

This caricature of the Enlightenment as a historical period as well as of the Enlightenment project is even more pronounced in the current *fin de siècle*. Francis Fukuyama's celebrated concept of the 'end of history'[34] is a gross oversimplification of the meaning of Western culture that conveniently over- looks the racism, nationalism, and other irrationalisms (Modernity 2) in Western countries and ascribes them all to the non-Western world. Leah Greenfeld's[35] distinction between 'our' Western, 'good' nationalism based on civic nationalism versus 'their' non-Western, 'bad' nationalism based on eth- nicity follows Fukuyama's tack, but really constitutes the fundamental assumption found in scores of contemporary political writers. Following the end of the Cold War, Western analysts sought to export an idealized version of pure capitalism to formerly Communist countries that never existed in his- tory and that does not exist in contemporary capitalist countries. *If Communism suffered and eventually failed because it was too ideological, the efforts to make capitalism into an ideology that can be exported is inevitably suspect.* To be sure, capitalism and the free market have many uses. But cap- italism and democracy *per se* do not suffice for a good society. (It is worth noting that in his *Democracy in America* Alexis de Tocqueville offers a much more thoughtful appraisal of the limitations, faults, and weaknesses of democracy as well as its strengths.) This is because capitalism is a mixture of rational phenomena associated with Modernity 1 as well as irrational phe- nomena associated with Modernity 2 such as greed, anomie, and conspicuous consumption. Now that the exportation of pure 'free market' economic sys- tems – so pure, so Disneyesque that they never existed even in the capitalist West in their pure forms, because of socialist safety nets – has failed in for- merly Communist countries, Western pundits are trying to export 'pure' democracy, much like the critical theorists tried to find 'pure' rationality. The newest line of thinking is that the democratization of the formerly Communist countries must precede their transformation into capitalism. Against these Disneyesque fantasies, let us face the facts: The West never had 'pure' democracy. The history of every Western, democratic nation is replete with racism, inequality, oppression, and other undemocratic phenomena that co-existed, and continue to exist, with respect to human rights, individualism, freedom of the press, and other democratic phenomena. The West is bent on selling an artificially contrived image of itself to other countries, and is bound to fail. The countries that are supposed to be importing this Disneyesque postemotional dogma are reacting in much the same way that formerly colo- nized peoples responded: They perceive Americanization and Westernization to be new forms of *cultural imperialism*, and are developing Americaphobia and Westophobia. This is especially true in the former Soviet Union, but is evident in many Western European countries as well. Thus, the French and the Dutch, for example, are attempting to offer 'cultural resistance' to the onslaught of American cultural icons such as McDonald's and Disney.

Moreover, Western analysts did not bother to do fieldwork in Communist and formerly Communist nations to discover their habits of the heart. Had they conducted such investigations, they might have been able to modify the tenets of the West's Enlightenment project to suit the existing cultures in postcommunist lands. This would have been a workable project involving a blend of Modernity 1 and Modernity 2 (because habits of the heart are irrational). Instead, Western analysts assumed that formerly Communist nations were a clean slate, a 'dead garden' in Keith Tester's[36] words, in which they could be the supreme gardeners who would create the perfect garden. In this regard, the arrogance of Western analysts was no different from the arrogance of the Bolsheviks who made the same assumption about the lands that became the Soviet Empire. Not only is the Western plan to make formerly Communist nations a perfect capitalist garden failing, ironically, the West is Balkanizing.

Thus, the so-called Enlightenment project is really a postemotional counterfeit of the Enlightenment. Contemporary devotees of the Enlightenment live emotionally in an idealized past. The dead emotional relics of the Enlightenment animate their reveries, and blind them to the chaos, disarray, and evils all around them, in the West as well as the non-West. When they confront these unwelcome realities, their reaction is stereotypical. Francis Fukuyama dismisses the ethnic hatred in the former Yugoslavia as being contained within the borders of that former country. Leah Greenfeld concludes that the Balkan War holds no meaning for analyses of the West. Ethnic hatred in the West, when it erupts, is rationalized away as an aberration. The solution offered for the suffering caused by unbridled capitalism in formerly Communist nations has been to offer still more 'pure' capitalism. The end result really is the attitude uncovered by Baudrillard: 'We' will live in our Disneyesque utopia, and all the others 'must exit.' Pluralism and tolerance for 'us' in the West, and ethnic hatred for 'them.' The West in general and the USA in particular betray an ironic provincialism in these regards: The Enlightenment project, which is supposed to be universalizing, ends up being a postemotional filter through which the West views the rest of the world and keeps it out of its 'civil societies.' Thus, the Enlightenment project does not lead to real multiculturalism. In the USA, it is an American multiculturalism that so often fails to make contact with reality, internationally or domestically. All this amounts to a gross vulgarization of Max Weber's famous Protestant Ethic thesis such that 'we' in the West become the 'elect' and everyone else is 'damned' to live in the hell of Modernity 2.

It is not difficult to discern the alternative outlines of an authentic Enlightenment project. The Enlightenment was an important period of history in a small corner of Western Europe whose legacy is mixed: science and irrationalism, human rights as well as the brutal oppression of human rights, cosmopolitanism and nationalism, and so on. Such an honest appraisal would promote dialogue with non-Enlightenment traditions and seek to find accommodation and common ground, not the imposition of yet another ideology, albeit, this time, a postemotional ideology based on the dead past.

The Post-Therapeutic Society

Philip Rieff's writings on Freud and his legacy are representative of a larger intellectual movement to reread Freud as a 'doctor of the mind.'[37] For example, Erich Fromm,[38] the psychoanalyst, critical theorist, and Marxist interpreter of culture, reads both Freud and Marx as fundamentalist rationalists who sought to liberate humankind from irrational illusions. Allan Bloom[39] also sought to cast Freud along the lines of a caricatured Enlightenment legacy. These and other misinterpreters of Freud omit his gloomy pronouncements on the strength of the id, the inevitability of civilization and its discontents, the impossibility of being completely free of neurosis, and the desirability of some forms of illusion.[40] In other words, they misread Freud as an exclusive promulgator of Modernity 1 and neglect those aspects of his thought that fall under the rubric of Modernity 2. It is easy to forget in the present *fin de siècle* that Freud lived in the previous *fin de siècle* and was influenced by Schopenhauer's and Nietzsche's beliefs that myth or illusion is a necessary component of human life. Thus, Freud, along with his contemporaries Durkheim and Simmel, found a place for the irrationalities of religion alongside science.

But Rieff and others have taken their postemotional reading of Freud to its logical conclusion: the therapeutic society. If therapy can be analyzed logically into its rational components, why should it be restricted to the analyst's couch? Therapy is ubiquitous in contemporary societies: Alcoholics Anonymous, rape counselling hotlines, child abuse hotlines, overeating hotlines, dieter's programs, drug rehabilitation therapies, and so on. One can join therapeutic groups to quit smoking, quit abusing one's spouse, quit codependency relationships, and to quit just about any vice that one's reference group decides is unwanted – one can even join groups designed to help one stop joining groups. In addition, and as noted in chapter 3, all societal institutions have quasi-therapeutic mechanisms by which celebrities as well as non-celebrities can disclose intimacies that used to be confined to the analyst's couch or the confessional. Almost every hour of every day, Americans and other Westerners can tune into a television program that either offers some sort of self-help therapy or presents someone confessing how they engaged in or overcame drug abuse, rape, adultery, obsessions, psychotic symptoms, or whatever. President Clinton, the postemotional President, frequently confesses his weaknesses, confusion, and other foibles in public. Inner-directed types are put off by his apparent 'weakness' in making such confessions, but other-directed and postemotional types probably find vicarious therapy in them.

For example, David Binder's interview with the indicted war criminal and Serbian General Ratko Mladić was essentially an exercise in therapy.[41] General Mladić disclosed some of the private reasons that led him to commit what many regard as genocidal acts against Bosnian Muslims, including the fact that his father was killed by Croatian Ustasha in World War II. This interview is hardly atypical when one considers the many other interviews with alleged or convicted murderers and other sorts of criminals that one finds in contemporary Western societies. Thus, following his acquittal on murder charges, O.J. Simpson sought to 'tell his story' such that his disclosures would be therapeutic for him and for others who are in the role in which his ex-wife found herself, namely, the battered wife: Simpson 'said he was now willing to meet with "battered women" to "talk about my relationship."'[42] The institutionalization of such disclosures can be read as other-directed disavowal of privacy or exhibitionism or as due to any number of motives, but most certainly as therapy in its broadest sense. The public has acted as a jury of sorts in the past, but nowadays the public has also taken the place of the analyst. Interviews now put a psychological spin on the disclosures such that the audience not only judges and 'understands' cognitively, but empathizes with the subject and joins with the interviewer vicariously to probe into the childhood traumas that caused anti-social behaviors.

But several crucial aspects of Freudian therapy are missing from this new and postemotional spin on therapy. One is Freud's insistence that the patient attains insight into his or her symptoms and subsequently controls them to some extent. Freud perceived himself as following Socrates by engaging in 'talking cures' that change the 'soul' of the analysand. But Ratko Mladić did not seem healed following his disclosures for he was later implicated in the mass slaughter of innocents at Srebrenica.[43]

Perhaps the most crucial missing ingredient is Freud's gloomy assessment of the discontents caused by civilization. Let me be clear that I do not intend to resuscitate Freud's work, but intend to use it as a springboard for apprehending post-therapy as an aspect of postemotionalism. And I shall analyze portions of one essay by Freud, 'On the Psychical Mechanism of Hysterical Phenomena,' published in 1893, to make my points. This essay not only foreshadows Freud's *Civilization and Its Discontents*, it makes a more succinct argument, and foreshadows what I call postemotionalism. I shall argue that humanity in Western, industrialized nations has entered a phase in which the mechanisms that Freud thought would lead to catharsis in civilized countries are less available than they were in the times in which he lived and wrote. The end result is a widespread, albeit postemotional, tendency toward pseudo-therapy.

Freud begins, 'Let us suppose that a man is insulted, is given a blow or something of that kind. This psychical trauma is linked with an increase in the sum of excitation in his nervous system.'[44] Fair enough. I would add that an insult is a specifically human phenomenon – an animal cannot be insulted. Furthermore, the occasions for and receptivity to insults have increased dramatically in the present *fin de siècle*. In chapter 3, I have analyzed David Riesman's claim that other-directed, curdled *indignation* is a central emotional reaction in contemporary times. Let us continue with Freud's example. He writes:

> There then instinctively arises an inclination to diminish this increased excitation immediately. He hits back, and then feels easier.[45]

Freud claims that in traditional societies, the insulted person might have run a spear through the offender's chest, but that such a reaction is clearly prohibited in civilized societies. I would add that in contemporary societies such traditional reactions persist nevertheless and may account for some of the generally perceived high crime rates, like the case of a teenager who beat a 78-year-old woman to death and then set her body on fire because she complained about the obscene lyrics in the music he played.[46] Freud continues:

> Now this reaction may take various forms. For quite slight increases in excitation, alterations in his own body may perhaps be enough: weeping, abusing, raging, and so on. The more intense the trauma, the greater is the adequate reaction. The most adequate reaction, however, is always a deed. But as an English writer has wittily remarked, the man who first flung a word of abuse at his enemy instead of a spear was the founder of civilization.[47]

In searching for a contemporary illustration of Freud's point, one can scarcely avoid referring to the Unabomber's promise that he would stop killing people if only his manifesto were published. Reading his manifesto, one notices that he is personally indignant at the discontents caused by civilization, and he demands an outlet for his indignation. But, he notes in his manifesto, the publishing world is so restrictive that he concluded that he stood no chance of having his words of abuse published unless he killed people first. If the traditional insulted man with a spear is Freud's metaphor for the trauma process, the Unabomber is the postemotional metaphor: a person highly skilled in using words but also highly cognizant that words hardly matter any longer, and that the most adequate reaction is always a deed.

Two related points need to be made: Weeping, abusing, raging, and words are no longer adequate routes for channelling emotions and all of these reactions are more tightly regulated than they ever were in history. This is a neo-Orwellian consequence of extending the love of the machine to social life. In the modernist desire to make social life function as smoothly as a machine, there is no emotional space for traditional and inner-directed idiosyncrasies such as rage and abuse. Thus, in an other-directed world of curdled indignation, what is the meaning of one more fit of weeping, cursing, defamation, and hostile speech? Such reactions are drowned out in a culture of rampant indignation and self-pity for one's perceived status as victim. Simultaneously, contemporary culture restricts these reactions severely: Billboards advertise that one should stamp out hate, hateful speech is monitored and punished, and 'politically correct' speech attempts to ensure that the words one uses do not offend others even inadvertently. A fit of rage resulting in hateful words might have made both parties feel that they had 'cleared the air' in Freud's time, but nowadays it is likely to result in a costly lawsuit. One result of this double-bind is the proliferation of discontented persons, such as 'disgruntled postal workers,' whose tendency to murder each other on the job has become the butt of jokes. Another, more serious consequence is that an important channel for catharsis has been blocked. Freud continues:

Thus words are substitutes for deeds, and in some circumstances (e.g. in Confession) the only substitutes. Accordingly alongside the adequate reaction there is one that is less adequate. If, however, there is no reaction whatsoever to a psychical trauma, the memory of it retains the *affect* which it originally had. So that if someone who has been insulted cannot avenge the insult either by a retaliatory blow or by a word of abuse, the possibility arises that the memory of the event may call up in him once more the *affect* which was originally present.[48] (emphasis added)

The present discussion of postemotionalism suggests that words are no longer adequate substitutes for deeds. Returning to the case of Ratko Mladić, could it be that this indicted war criminal turned to genocide in part because in Communist Yugoslavia – which was run on modernist principles, after all – he and others could not vent their anger at Croats and Muslims adequately? One must keep in mind that following World War II Tito imposed a 'politically correct' system in Yugoslavia such that it was depicted as the land of brotherhood and unity. Anyone who brought up historical emotional wounds was liable to be imprisoned – and many people were imprisoned for precisely such offenses. Perhaps if Croats, Muslims, and Serbs in the former Yugoslavia could have wept, raged, and expressed their psychic wounds to and at each other, the result might have been generalized catharsis and even mutual forgiveness. One can do no more than speculate on such a course of events as an alternative to genocide in Europe in the 1990s. But if this conjecture holds any merit, it serves as an ominous warning to the industrialized West and its current institutionalization of 'politically correct,' non-hateful speech. The end result may not be the desired climate of tolerance, but a potentially dangerous condition of repressed hate that makes ethnic cleansing a metaphor for our times.

I do not agree with Freud that an *affect* which was originally present is called up when an adequate reaction is blocked. It would be more precise to claim that a *post-affect* is called up, because it had been embellished with rationalizations, intellectualizations, and other products of mental rumination that occurred with the passage of time. Thus, in the case of Mladić, he recalls the evils committed in history by Croats and Muslims, but fails to recall or chooses to ignore the evils committed by Serbs. In other words, the post-emotion is partially contrived and artificial. This possibility seems not to have occurred to Freud, who believed that such mental rumination might serve as a cathartic reaction, albeit the least adequate form of catharsis:

An insult that has been repaid, even if only in words, is recollected quite differently from one that has had to be accepted; and linguistic usage characteristically describes an insult that has been suffered in silence as 'mortification.' . . . Incidentally, a healthy psychical mechanism has other methods of dealing with the affect of a psychical trauma even if motor reaction and reaction by words are denied to it – namely by working it over associatively and by producing contrasting ideas. Even if the person who has been insulted neither hits back nor replies with abuse, he can nevertheless reduce the affect attaching to the insult by calling up such contrasting ideas as those of his own worthiness, of his enemy's worthlessness, and so on.[49]

Freud's assessment here seems naive. A postemotional possibility he neglects to pursue is that the person who works over an affect mentally when other modes of catharsis are blocked will develop precisely those hybrids of rationality and emotion that I call post-emotions. In contemporary times, when persons are unable to hurt each other through words or deeds to avenge an insult, they resort to lawsuits using the tenets of 'political correctness' as weapons: Calling someone a racist, anti-Semite, sexist, or bigot is often sufficient to ruin someone's reputation even if he or she is none of these things. To go to court and prove that one is not a bigot is frequently too costly a proposition, and an impossible one, because almost everyone has experienced a thought or uttered a word that could indict one. For example, the president of Rutgers University, Francis Lawrence, was accused of racism – despite a formidable record of making it easier for African-Americans to succeed at his university – on the basis of one remark concerning standardized tests. The editors of the *Wall Street Journal* suggested that the real motive behind the accusation was that some faculty at his university felt disgruntled at his policies toward them.[50] The cunning of reason is such that when traditional words of abuse no longer seem to count, one resorts to the use of emotionally charged labels based on the very system of hate-free speech that prohibits such abuse in the first place. And of course, such use of sensitive labels makes it harder to find real bigots, racists, sexists, and anti-Semites.

Freud concludes his discussion as follows:

> Whether a healthy man deals with an insult in one way or the other, he always succeeds in achieving the result that the affect which was originally strong in his memory eventually loses intensity and that finally the recollection, having lost its affect, falls a victim to forgetfulness and the process of wearing away.[51]

I maintain that in the postemotional age emotions are not forgotten and are not 'worn away.' Because catharsis is often blocked due to the over-rationalization of social life, it seems that postemotional types remain traumatized for life. How else can one explain the sudden revivifications of distant collective memories in the postemotional 1990s? The Serbs still remember their defeat at Kosovo in 1389. African-Americans are increasingly revivifying the memories of slavery. Feminists cannot let go of the memory of patriarchy. And so on. Of course, most of these are not real memories in any case, because their bearers never experienced the original event. These are carefully, rationally, artificially crafted post-memories.

In sum, the idealized vision of the therapeutic society turns out to be as Disneyesque and artificial as many other aspects of postemotional society. Authentic therapy was often rough and presupposed traditional and inner-directed forms of catharsis that were not 'nice.' In other-directed and postemotional societies, where everyone is expected to be 'nice,' and in which speech and behavior has been codified by political correctness, all forms of catharsis have actually been blocked. It is not surprising that the postemotional consciousness has coined the phrase 'walking time bombs' to refer to people who could potentially 'blow up' at any time due to repressed traumas that have not been and cannot be abreacted.

The Postemotional or Counterfeit Civilizing Process

In *The Civilizing Process*,[52] Norbert Elias argues that with the progress of civilization, certain behaviors and actions come to be labelled as disgusting and are systematically removed from the sphere of public life. Manners are invented in order to control and regulate emotion and unrestrained excitability in social interaction. To the extent that such phenomena intrude into the public sphere, they are tightly regulated. Examples include bodily functions such as belching, passing gas, and spitting, as well as executions, bloodletting in sports, butchering animals, and so on. Chris Rojek is right to characterize Elias as a Modernity 1 thinker, and has already reviewed praise for and criticisms of Elias by others.

Postemotionalism offers a new perspective on the theory of the civilizing process. Why should the civilizing process be associated with Modernity 1 rather than Modernity 2? Social control is not always or unequivocally a civilizing tendency. Many episodes of modernist barbarism have been performed in the guise of highly polished manners. An interesting illustration is the scene in the film *Schindler's List* which depicts a Nazi officer playing classical music on the piano as his colleagues are engaging in brutal killing of Jews in the background. The flip side of this observation is that Modernity 2 might serve a civilizing function even if it appears disorderly or chaotic. In overemphasizing the Modernity 1 aspects of the civilizing process, Elias gives us a McDonaldized, Disneyesque version of this process. Elias's distinction between the state of being civilized versus the civilizing process might be regarded as a rhetorical device that deflects criticism, but is not substantive. Elias can never be accused of defending the present state of civilization, only the civilizing process.

There can be no doubt that the phenomena Elias uncovers as disgusting are no longer normative in contemporary Western societies, even though they used to be accepted as a matter of course in the past. But it is just as true that phenomena that he excludes from the civilizing process form the staple of contemporary and extremely graphic cinematic style. I am referring, of course, to graphic violence and sex, cursing, and the standardized use of belching, passing gas, and other disgusting habits in film. Thus, the postemotional public participates vicariously in behaviors, thoughts, fantasies and emotions that are forbidden in everyday life in societies that are purportedly civilizing through books, film, magazines, and even the Internet. Modernity 2 comes in through the back door of fantasies that preoccupy persons whose manners are in keeping with Modernity 1. Of course, in his *Quest for Excitement*, Elias seems to account for this seemingly sublimated excitement in popular culture (especially in sports) as the controlled and enjoyable decontrolling of restraints on emotions.[53] I am suggesting a different interpretation. Despite the rules, regulations, and other controls put on sports events and television programs, there is an uncivilizing process at work that reduces these 'controls' to nothing more than a postemotional contrivance for appearance's sake. For example, any parent in the 1990s knows that he or she

cannot protect a child from hearing obscenities on television. Sexual sugges-
tiveness permeates advertisements as well as programs. The important point
is that Elias holds an overly felicitous view of how excitement is allegedly
'controlled' in postemotional societies.

In the interest of space, let me focus on just one more phenomenon as illustration: executions. It is true and in keeping with Elias's work that in most
civilizing countries the spectacle of public executions no longer exists. But it
is just as true that, increasingly, journalists and selected persons have been
demanding and have won the right to witness and even film executions.[54] In
the state of Texas, the victim's family members will soon be able to demand
the right to witness executions. It seems that it is just a matter of time before
executions will be broadcast live from prisons, to become postemotional par-
odies of the television program *This Is Your Life*, perhaps renamed *This Is
Your Death*.[55] Similarly, a book entitled *Pictures at an Execution* deals with
Western culture's insatiable fascination with the depiction of murder in law,
morality, and art despite the so-called civilizing process.[56]

Postemotionalism alerts one to the possibility that an uncivilizing process
runs concurrently with the civilizing process. The perversion, disgusting
habits, explicit violence, and other barbaric phenomena that have been
banned from public life in Western, industrialized nations not only reappear
but seem to grow stronger with time in the private realm of fantasy. 'Other
people's' barbaric reality – such as murders, rapes, and genocide – are
watched on television by voyeurs bent on the civilizing process. This voyeuristic, vicarious aspect of contemporary social life seems to have escaped Elias
completely.

But the most serious flaw in Elias's theory is that he relies too much on the
control and regulation of barbaric habits as the hallmark of the civilizing
process. To the extent that these many years of the civilizing process have
achieved some degree of civilization – and despite Elias's claims that there
will be reversals and downward spirals – genuine civilizing traits are a matter
not of specific habits, but of certain attitudes that are compassionate and that
otherwise seek to overcome the brutality that was extant in the past. Everyone
knows that a person can have the most polished manners, never utter a hateful word in public, and exhibit refinement in his or her every movement, yet
can secretly harbor the most cruel indifference to the suffering of others, the
most hateful prejudices, and the most cleverly disguised brutality. The contemporary explosion of litigation is perhaps the best illustration of such
civilized barbarism. When persons sue one another in place of either the
overt anger or attempts at accommodations that existed before the widespread use of litigation, they are destroying someone's life every bit as
effectively as the traditionalist who ran a spear through his opponent's chest.
This new barbarism is dressed up in the refined use of language that characterizes all court proceedings, but this civilized gloss cannot obscure the hostile
intent. In foreign affairs, too, seemingly cultured euphemisms are often used
to disguise motives that should never qualify as civilized. Thus, 'humanitarian aid' to the victims of genocide in Bosnia camouflages the West's cruel

indifference, even the dereliction of its duty to stop the genocide, as required by the UN Charter. 'Economic sanctions' on whole peoples conceal the fact that they are a barbaric recourse to the pre-Enlightenment doctrine of collective guilt in which children and other innocents are forced to suffer or even die because of the faults of leaders of the countries in which they live. (The most recent example involves sanctions against Iraq.) 'Friendly fire' is a civilized-sounding term that obscures the negligence that led to death at the hands of one's own military. Even 'ethnic cleansing' carries incredible connotations of civilizations: pure, clean, sanitary, wholesome, decent, tidy. But it has often been used to obfuscate the most evil crime that humans can commit, genocide.

When persons who live in countries designated as civilized or as 'civil societies' exhibit such wanton indifference to the suffering of others in countries designated as sub-civilized, it no longer makes sense to conceptualize the civilizing process in the manner that Elias does. It seems more appropriate to point out the irony that Western, so-called civilized nations take on the characteristics of the Balkans, which have, in this century, been designated as the barbaric backdoor of Europe. The cool contemplation of other people's suffering while one exhibits polished manners in a society that is deemed civil is only a shade less immoral than the direct infliction of suffering. Thus, civilization, as it is often practiced today, is really manufactured, inauthentic civilization.

Postemotional Communities

According to Alvin and Heidi Toffler, information networks will bypass nation-states to create a cosmopolitan community of interactors: 'Nations will wither, knowledge will triumph.'[57] Neither of these predictions has been actualized. The so-called community of Internet users is not a real community because one can enter and leave the interaction in cyberspace at will. One does not have such freedom in real communities. Nations are proliferating as the twentieth century draws to a close, and nationalism is arguably the most powerful social force in the world today. Finally, knowledge alone is insufficient for establishing community, because communities are held together by sentiments, not cognition. At the end of the twentieth century, one might well exclaim: 'We have reasoned so much! We know so much more information in contrast to our ancestors.' But is the world really a better place, actually or potentially, as the result of so much information? On the contrary, the proliferation of information has caused widespread confusion and isolation among postemotional types. The confusion stems from the fact that individuals are unable to internalize, assimilate, or contextualize the massive amounts of information. For example, despite extensive knowledge about the genocide in Bosnia, AIDS, cancer, pollution, and other phenomena, most persons seem confused about the appropriate actions to take with regard to the social problems they represent. The various 'spins' put on all this knowledge by competing groups serve to Balkanize societies and to make individuals feel isolated from neighboring communities. Knowledge does not automatically translate into communal action.

Nevertheless, it is of sociological interest that communitarianism is a highly popular concept at the end of the twentieth century. The theme of the 1995 American Sociological Association was 'Community of Communities.' This pleasant characterization overlooks the fission, nationalism, secessionism, and group hatred in much of the world today. Politicians as well as scholars write of community as an unqualified good without taking into account its cancerous aspects. An especially strong sense of community can mutate easily into overt communal aggression against neighboring communities.

In his classic *Community and Society*,[58] Ferdinand Tönnies claimed that a community preserves a sense of unity despite differences and forces that seek to splinter it, while a society fosters disunity despite efforts to promote unity. The concept of 'society' was a pejorative term for Tönnies. He described *Gesellschaft* with the following rhetoric: artificial, mechanical, hard, cold, superficial, and evil. *Gesellschaft* was the domain of the 'rational will,' as opposed to the 'natural will' of communities. And regarding rational will, Tönnies wrote:

> The forms of rational will set the individual as giving and receiving against the whole of nature. Man tries to control nature and to receive from it more than he himself is giving. But within nature he is confronted with another rational will which aspires to do the same, i.e., with another individual who is to gain by his loss.[59]

Although his bias in favor of communities was evident, he conceded that traditional communities were authoritarian, restricted freedom, and were often cruel to women and children. Anyone who reads this nearly forgotten work will no doubt conclude that traditional communities are increasingly becoming extinct while contemporary societies are still characterized by traits he ascribed to *Gesellschaft*. Tönnies's accurate vision of community would be intolerable to the freedom-loving and democratic postemotional types. For example, postemotional children no longer subscribe to the old dictum that children are to be seen but not heard. Nowadays, children are seen *and* heard, and they intrude into the lives of their parents except when they are at day care. Few contemporary parents would wish to reverse this democratization process in which children have been emancipated from the yoke of authority that resided in the traditional role of parenthood. In sum, community should not be idealized or viewed nostalgically: It bound peoples together, but at a heavy cost of human freedom.

Note also that Tönnies's rhetoric of mechanization in describing *Gesellschaft* is similar to the rhetoric used by George Orwell, Chris Rojek, George Ritzer, Henry Adams, Zygmunt Bauman, and other theorists whose works have been discussed *vis-à-vis* modernity. But note also that contemporary communitarians tend to neglect Tönnies in their analyses. Communitarians seek to promote an idealized vision of community, minus its negative characteristics, that can supposedly exist alongside an increasingly bureaucratized, rational-legal, artificial, cold, and individualistic society. For those who take Tönnies seriously, this is an impossible state of affairs, and constitutes postemotional magical thinking. Contemporary individuals confront more paperwork, red tape, and other characteristics of bureaucracy than Max Weber could have imagined in his writings on bureaucracy, yet they seem to accept the gloss of community that is painted on this state of hyper-*Gesellschaft*.

To be sure, some communitarians are aware of the objections that are made to contemporary communitarianism. Amitai Etzioni, for example, reviews many such objections, and concludes:

> While responsive communitarians seem to have reasonably sound responses to many of the criticisms raised against them recently, the standing of community values is the one that needs the most attention and, so far, has received the least. More broadly speaking, communitarians and their critics must break out of the debate about the social embedded self and instead deal with numerous subsequent issues that have been raised. As I see it, none of these issues challenges the basic communitarian thesis, which is that communities, properly constructed, are of great value.[60]

No one would argue against the proposition that communities can be of great value. But note that Etzioni writes of a 'properly constructed' community. Such a notion is again in line with the cult of the machine uncovered by thinkers from Tönnies through Henry Adams to George Orwell, and is one of the most problematic aspects of communitarianism. One finds Anthony Giddens making a similar claim, that post-traditional societies must construct artificial traditions.[61] In traditional societies, one did not self-consciously construct communities: They sprang up spontaneously. But to construct a community, 'properly' no less, is to apply the Modernity 1 principle to one of the last frontiers of nature. For one must recall that for Tönnies communities were natural. One could no more construct a community than one could construct a forest. Of course, adherents of Modernity 1 feel that any aspect of nature can be created and controlled, from gardens and forests to communities. If modernists can flavor penicillin to taste like bubble gum and have a pink color so that children will ingest it, why not 'flavor' bureaucracy with selected, nice elements of community so that the masses will consume it? It is my contention that a 'properly constructed' community can never be genuine.

Unlike the Tofflers, Etzioni is also aware that communities require emotion:

> Communities require a web of affect-laden relations among a group of individuals (rather than merely one-on-one relations or chains of individual relations), relations that often crisscross and reinforce one another. And being a community entails having a measure of commitment to a set of shared values, norms, and meanings.[62]

It is interesting that Etzioni's understanding of community does not involve the German notion of group consciousness, found in the works of thinkers ranging from Hegel and Lazarus and Steinthal to Tönnies and Durkheim. Etzioni attempts to derive a sense of community from individualism. It is doubtful whether individual self-interest is up to this task. The affect that is typically cited by communitarians is compassion.[63] Liberal communitarians tend to write in terms of compassion for gays, women, the poor, minorities, and other specific groups designated as disadvantaged or victimized. But as stated previously, it seems to be the case that the contemporary use of 'compassion' is really pity. Genuine compassion or *caritas* would make no distinction between the elites and those who require pity. Compassion would not be withheld from a suffering individual if he or she happened to belong to a wrong or unaccounted for group. Compassion should be the emotional glue that holds together all members of a society on the basis of a common humanity.[64] But traditional philosophers, from Plato through Schopenhauer to Durkheim, held that compassion could never be taught.[65]

Conclusions

Postmodernism has not triumphed over the question of authenticity. The daily diet of phoniness in postemotional societies cannot help but impact society profoundly at every level. On television talk shows, people disclose what seem to be their most intimate sexual secrets, but in the back of their minds the viewers know that these disclosures were made with the camera rolling. Inevitably, every disaster, from tornados and hurricanes to genocide in Bosnia, brings the television journalist who protrudes a microphone into the face of the distraught victim and asks, 'How does it feel?' to have had your son killed by a sniper's bullet, to have been raped, to have lost your wife in a car crash, and so on. Once the private domain of individuals reacting to personal losses, emotions such as grief and rage are now broadcast around the world, often live and on the spot. But something seems to be missing in these seemingly heartfelt disclosures of apparent authenticity. Part of what is missing is an authentic sense of community.

It is difficult to ascertain whether government officials and politicians are more corrupt today than they were in previous generations. Yet it is certain that stories of government as well as corporate corruption fill the airwaves more than they did in the past. Postemotional types cannot escape the gnawing feeling that authority figures lie to them and manipulate their emotions on a host of issues, from the reasons why the Allies got involved in the Gulf War to what really happened at Waco, Texas, to the supposed needs to change the health care system in the USA. Postemotional types have been had so many times, their underlying reaction to government overtures of any sort is cynicism.

Contemporary times are characterized by lofty talk of completing the Enlightenment project, constructing communitarianism, and increasing the level of civilization, but the average postemotional type knows too much to fall completely for this emotionally laden rhetoric. In the USA, everyone knows that race relations have deteriorated since Martin Luther King Jr. Trade wars, military campaigns, and genocidal wars intrude upon the postemotional consciousness every day on television news. And the pervasive fear of crime, of taking a stroll through Central Park in New York City, even the fear of getting off the subway train at 125th street in New York, make the rhetoric of increased civilization seem fake.

Most importantly, the rhetoric of constructing idealized communities and havens of civilization is the same rhetoric that was used by Communists and is still used to promote progress based on machinery. The habits of the mind instilled in the masses for over a century regarding mechanical progress have now been extended to the last frontier left in social life, the realm of the emotions. The McDonaldization of emotions has been an attempt to make the Enlightenment project, therapy, civilization, and communities all seem predictably 'nice' and to create Disneyesque, artificial realms of the authentic.

Notes

1. Herbert Marcuse, *One-Dimensional Man* (Boston: Beacon Press, [1964] 1991).

2. See my treatment of these and other intellectuals in *The Coming Fin de Siècle* (London: Routledge, 1991), *Durkheim and Postmodern Culture* (Hawthorne, NY: Aldine de Gruyter, 1992), and, with Miroslav Goreta and Slaven Letica *Habits of the Balkan Heart* (College Station, TX: Texas A&M University Press, 1993).

3. Henry Adams, 'The Dynamo and the Virgin,' in *The Education of Henry Adams* (New York: Viking, [1900] 1983), pp. 1068–75.

4. Discussed in Meštrović, *The Coming Fin de Siècle*.

5. David Frisby, *Simmel and Since: Essays on Georg Simmel's Social Theory* (London: Routledge, 1992), *Sociological Impressionism: A Reassessment of Georg Simmel's Social Theory* (London: Routledge, 1992), *Fragments of Modernity: Theories of Modernity in the Work of Simmel, Kracauer and Benjamin* (Cambridge, MA: MIT Press, 1986).

6. Michael Kaern, *Georg Simmel and Contemporary Sociology* (Boston: Kluwer Academic Publishers, 1990).

7. Ferdinand Tönnies, *Community and Society* (New York: Harper and Row, [1887] 1963).

8. George Orwell, *The Road to Wigan Pier* (New York: Harcourt Brace, [1937] 1958).

9. Jean Baudrillard, *America* (London: Verso, 1986), p. 55.

10. Chris Rojek, 'Disney Culture,' *Leisure Studies*, 12, 1 (1993), pp. 121–35.

11. Al Kamen, 'Gores Had a Beauty of a Party and a Beast of a Bill,' *Houston Chronicle*, 30 November 1995, p. 2A.

12. See, for example, Alexander Moore, 'Walt Disney World: Bounded Ritual Space and the Playful Pilgrimage Center,' *Anthropological Quarterly*, 53, 4 (1980), pp. 207–18; M. Gottdiener, 'Disneyland: A Utopian Urban Space,' *Urban Life*, 11, 2, (1982), pp. 139–62; Hernan Vera and Gerald R. Leslie, 'The World of Disney: Notes on the American Family From a Sociology of Knowledge Perspective,' *Sociological Symposium*, 28 (1979), pp. 71–86; Jack C. Wolf, 'Disney World: America's Vision of Utopia,' *Alternative Futures*, 2, 2 (1979), pp. 72–7; Christine Holmlund, 'Tots to Tanks: Walt Disney Presents Feminism for the Family,' *Social Text*, 2 (1979), pp. 122–32; Margaret J. King, 'Empires of Popular Culture: McDonald's and Disney,' *Journal of American Culture*, 1 (1978), pp. 424–37.

13. Max Horkheimer and Theodor Adorno, *The Dialectic of Enlightenment* (New York: Continuum, [1944] 1972), p. 138.

14. http://home.ptd.net/"glisman/cele2.htm#WHAT, p. 2.

15. Ibid., p. 3.

16. Ibid.

17. http://www.nortel.com/english/navigator/navigate395/Disney.html, p. 1.

18. Chris Rojek, *Decentring Leisure* (London: Sage, 1995), p. 6.

19. Ibid., p. 101.

20. Ibid., p. 79.

21. Nietzsche makes his intellectual debts to Schopenhauer clear in *Schopenhauer as Educator* (South Bend, IN: Gateway Press, [1874] 1965).

22. An excellent analysis of Adorno is to be found in Keith Tester, *The Two Sovereigns: Social Contradictions of European Modernity* (London: Routledge, 1992).

23. Ibid.

24. Theodor W. Adorno, *The Culture Industry* (London: Routledge, 1991).

25. Ibid., p. 129.

26. Marcuse, *One-Dimensional Man*, p. 76.

27. Ibid., p. 84.

28. Max Horkheimer, *The Eclipse of Reason* (New York: Oxford University Press, 1947).

29. Walter Benjamin, 'The Work of Art in the Age of Mechanical Reproduction,' in *Illuminations*, ed. Hannah Arendt (New York: Harcourt, Brace and World, 1968), pp. 219–66.

30. Chris Rojek, 'Indexing, Dragging and the Social Construction of Tourist Sights,' in Chris Rojek and John Urry (eds), *Touring Cultures: Transformations in Travel and Theory* (London: Routledge, 1996).

31. Reuters News Service, 'Cold War Theme Park Planned for Florida,' *The Boston Globe*, 8 May 1995, p. A10.

32. I document these claims by Durkheim in Stjepan G. Meštrović, *Émile Durkheim and the Reformation of Sociology* (Tottowa, NJ: Rowman and Littlefield, 1988).

33. Meštrović et al., *Habits of the Balkan Heart*.

34. Francis Fukuyama, *The End of History and the Last Man* (New York: Free Press, 1992).

35. Leah Greenfeld, *Nationalism: Five Roads to Modernity* (Cambridge, MA: Cambridge University Press, 1992).

36. Tester, *The Two Sovereigns*.

37. See especially Philip Rieff, *The Triumph of the Therapeutic: Uses of Faith After Freud* (New York: Harper and Row, 1966).

38. Erich Fromm, *Beyond the Chains of Illusion: My Encounter With Marx and Freud* (New York: Simon and Schuster, 1962).

39. Allan Bloom, *The Closing of the American Mind* (New York: Simon and Schuster, 1987).

40. The interested reader will find documentation of these claims in my *The Barbarian Temperament* (London: Routledge, 1993).

41. David Binder, 'Ratko Mladić, Pariah as Patriot,' *New York Times Magazine*, 4 September 1994, pp. 26–42.

42. Bill Carter, 'Simpson Cancels TV Interview, But Talks of Life Since Verdict,' *New York Times*, 12 October 1995, p. A1.

43. Elaine Sciolino, 'Fate of 2 Bosnian Serb Leaders, Facing New Charges, Snags Talks,' *New York Times*, 17 November 1995, p. A1.

44. Sigmund Freud, 'On the Psychical Mechanism of Hysterical Phenomena: A Lecture,' in James Strachey (ed.), *The Standard Edition of the Complete Psychological Works of Sigmund Freud*, vol. 3 (London: Hogarth, [1893] 1974), p. 37.

45. Ibid.

46. Story broadcast on CNN on 11 October 1995.

47. Freud, 'On the Psychical Mechanism', p. 37.

48. Ibid.

49. Ibid., p. 38.

50. 'Riled at Rutgers,' *Wall Street Journal*, 13 February 1995, p. A14.

51. Freud, 'On the Psychical Mechanism', p. 38.

52. Norbert Elias, *The Civilizing Process: Vol. 1* (Oxford: Basil Blackwell, 1978).

53. Nobert Elias, *Quest for Excitement: Sport and Leisure in the Civilizing Process* (Oxford: Basil Blackwell, 1985).

54. See, for example, 'Ban on Reporters Lifted: Media Can Cover Executions, But Judge Says No Cameras,' *The Fourth Estate*, 15 June 1991, p. 52; Cynthia Barnett, 'Covering Executions,' *American Journalism Review*, May 1995, pp. 26–31; Thomas Mallon, 'The

Executioner's Encore,' *Gentlemen's Quarterly*, June 1994, p. 86; Steve McClellan, 'Stations Seek Tape of Harris Execution,' *Broadcasting*, 4 May 1992, p. 33; Carl Mellor, 'Final Moments,' *The Progressive*, December 1992, p. 14.

55. Jacob Weisberg, 'This is Your Death,' *The New Republic*, 1 July 1991, p. 23; Frances Elizabeth, 'Gentlemen, I Have One More Thing to Say: Women on Scaffolds in England, 1563–1680,' *Modern Philology*, November 1994, pp. 157–78; Tipton C. Kindel, 'Live From San Quentin: Planning is the Key to Handling Media Interest in an Execution,' *Corrections Today*, July 1993, p. 65; John S. Detweiler, 'Three Newsgathering Perspectives for Covering an Execution,' *Journalism Quarterly*, Summer/Autumn 1987, pp. 454–62; 'Videotape of a California Execution is Destroyed,' *New York Times*, 13 February 1994, p. 35.

56. Wendy Lesser, *Pictures at an Execution* (Cambridge, MA: Harvard University Press, 1995).

57. Alvin Toffler and Heidi Toffler, 'Societies at Hyper-Speed,' *New York Times*, 31 October 1993, p. E17.

58. Tönnies, *Community and Society* (see note 7 above).

59. Ibid., p. 140.

60. Amitai Etzioni, 'The Attack on Community: The Grooved Debate,' *Society*, 32, 5 (1995), pp. 12–17.

61. Anthony Giddens, *Beyond Right and Left* (Stanford: Stanford University Press, 1994).

62. Etzioni, 'The Attack on Community', p. 14.

63. See Christopher Lasch, *The Revolt of the Elites and the Betrayal of Deomocracy* (New York: Norton, 1995).

64. Arthur Schopenhauer, *On the Basis of Morality* (Indianapolis: Bobbs-Merrill, [1841] 1965).

65. Discussed in Meštrović, *The Barbarian Temperament*.

5

The Disappearance of the Sacred

I raised the question early in chapter 1: How are postmodern and postemotional recycling of culture and simulation of historical phenomena different from the ritualized simulation of the past found in traditional societies? This is a decisive question. If there is no fundamental difference between, let us say, a contemporary 'pilgrimage' to Disneyland and a traditional pilgrimage to the Himalaya Mountains, then the terms 'postmodernism' and 'postemotionalism' amount to little more than rhetoric. On the other hand, if there are important differences to traditional rituals, then one is in a better position to argue that a decisive break with the past has occurred in Western societies. In this chapter, I will attempt to examine a possible reply to this question through a recontextualized reading of Émile Durkheim's classic work *The Elementary Forms of the Religious Life*. As with my rereading of Riesman's work, I am concerned not with an exegesis of Durkheim's work, but with finding its relevance to contemporary times and, more specifically, postemotional issues. It is possible that Durkheim's work is not even an accurate ethnography of aborigine social life, and that his portrait of traditional rituals is not accurate either. While such matters might be important in an exegetical treatment of Durkheim, they are largely irrelevant here. Let us accept from the outset that any and all ethnographies of traditional social life are filtered through the collective as well as private representations of the ethnographer, reader, and culture in which he or she lives. There can be no doubt that Durkheim was making a reading of traditional social life based on his cultural heritage, cultural context, and philosophical assumptions, which have already been discussed. Nevertheless, he thereby transformed an apparent ethnography into a cultural reading that can be used as a springboard for further discussion on the topic of this book. There is no way to tell if Durkheim was right or wrong. But his insights can be used to assess and discuss pertinent issues that are important to contemporary times. T.S. Eliot commented on this book by Durkheim: 'It is perhaps the most significant, and one of the most fascinating, of books on the subject of religion which have been published during the present century.'[1] But Durkheim's understanding of religion transcends the standardized boundaries for such discussions as found in the subdiscipline of the sociology of religion. In line with the overall theme of the present discussion, I will argue that Durkheim locates the emotions in collective effervescence and the notion of the sacred. Postemotionalism must therefore involve some sort of diminution of emotional life or pathology in the collective consciousness.

I will tip my hand from the outset and summarize my reply to the question posed at the beginning of this chapter: Durkheim anticipated the postmodernists by claiming that society is a system of representations that he characterizes as 'hallucinations' or 'delirium.' In this regard, he comes close to Baudrillard's characterization of the postmodern social world as a heap of circulating fictions. Yet Durkheim also argued that this representational delirium is grounded in *emotional* (not cognitive) reality: the 'hallucinations' are based on explosions of emotional life created in *assembled groups* through 'collective effervescence.' Because postmodernism has failed to take into account the emotional side of humanity, I think it is more rhetoric than solid theory. As for postemotionalism, a decisive break with traditional ritualization seems to have occurred in the following ways: Televised collective effervescence cannot fulfill the same function that Durkheim ascribed to the spontaneity of assembled groups. Television adds another level of hallucination to collective hallucinations. Thus, the emotional experience of contemporary consumers of media images constitutes a vicarious emotional experience that has already passed through cognitive filters. We have seen in chapter 3 that other-directedness leads to a splintering of group identities and reference groups. Thus, the collective consciousness has been Balkanized, which is something that Durkheim anticipated. The result is that postemotional humans try desperately to recapture the emotional energy that used to be achieved through collective effervescence, yet fail more often than they succeed.

Harking back to the controversy surrounding Daniel Bell's comments on religion, it is worth noting that Durkheim's assessment is more extreme than Bell's. Specifically, Durkheim depicts something that might be called the primal sacral complex in which religion is conceived to be the womb from which almost all other social and cultural phenomena are born. Durkheim would have one seek out the religious origins of culture itself, as well as art, dance, music, language, ideas, beliefs, ethics, economic arrangements (the idea of private property, the contract), the state, kinship, family, marriage, education, philosophy, metaphysics, and, finally, even science. All of these institutions were religion at first, and continue to be imbued with a religious character even in contemporary societies.

In chapter 2, I have already suggested that Durkheim did not think of religion in contemporary terms as church attendance, belief in deities, or subscription to dogma. In this chapter, I will deepen Durkheim's understanding of religion as involving sacred and profane representations primarily by exposing his linkage between the sacred and emotions. But before proceeding on this path, it is necessary to sketch briefly the social, personal, and cultural context for Durkheim's momentous claims. This is warranted because Durkheim has been misappropriated as having been solely a French positivist writing in the traditions of the Enlightenment and of Auguste Comte. While these two influences are undeniable, there were others: Durkheim's rabbinical heritage; the influence of Fustel de Coulanges's *Ancient City*,[2] which stresses the central role of religion, particularly ancestor cults in Greece and Rome, and the importance of sacredness; the ethical foundations of the Third Republic in France, which sought a secular foundation for morals and therefore exposed the need to find a role for religion; the influence upon Durkheim of Herbert Spencer's writings and of Jean-Marie Guyau's *The Non-religion of the Future*,[3] whose themes include religion as a social phenomenon and the claim that law, morality, and religion all have an obligatory character; the general refraction of Arthur Schopenhauer's philosophy in the previous *fin de siècle* as found in literature, art, philosophy, and a fledgling social science, all centered on the thesis that the will or passions are more important and stronger than the mind or rationality; Durkheim's trip to Germany in 1885 and 1886, and the influence of Wilhelm Wundt's[4] version of *Völkerpsychologie*, which was established by Lazarus and Steinthal (who were among Georg Simmel's teachers). Wundt taught that religion is one of the determining factors in morality and that in traditional societies law, morality, and religion formed an indistinguishable synthesis. One should also note that Durkheim's themes in *The Elementary Forms of the Religious Life*[5] are reflected most strongly in his neglected book *Professional Ethics and Civic Morals*,[6] especially with regard to the sacred character of private property, the state, and the contract. He also foreshadowed his arguments in *Elementary Forms* in his *The Division of Labor in Society*,[7] in which he had already claimed that law, morality, political institutions, and philosophy emerge out of religion, and also in his *Suicide*,[8] wherein he argued that religion is the system of symbols by which society becomes conscious of itself.

Several other factors must be considered in order to appreciate Durkheim's originality *vis-à-vis* the sociology of religion. In 1895, he read Robertson Smith's book *Lectures on the Religion of the Semites*,[9] which is noteworthy in several respects: Its main theme is that religion must be accounted for in social terms. Durkheim claimed that he 'discovered' religion after reading Robertson Smith's book. In 1896, Durkheim initiated the organization of *L'Année Sociologique*, and the first volume of this celebrated journal, published in 1898, included Durkheim's essay on the prohibition of incest.[10] (I have already drawn parallels between this essay and Freud's theory of religion in my *Émile Durkheim and the Reformation of Sociology*.)[11] From 1898 to 1900, Durkheim was profoundly shaken by the Dreyfus Affair, and in 1899 wrote an essay on anti-Semitism, in which he argued that anti-Semitism is endemic and traditional in Germany and Russia but is only acute in France, where it is a response to specific crises. The preface to the second volume of *L'Année Sociologique* is essentially a manifesto for the sociology of religion. Durkheim's 1898 essay 'Individual and Collective Representations,' published in a collection of essays entitled *Sociology and Philosophy*,[12] also foreshadows an important theme in *Elementary Forms*: Social life is defined by its hyper-spirituality. Ideas are social products of the second degree which have a life of their own and are subject to the yet unknown laws of collective ideation. But this collective ideation is born in explosions of 'collective effervescence' that are primarily emotional, collective experiences. The important point is that

social life of the first degree is emotional, while social life of the second
degree is cognitive.

These contextual remarks are important for appreciating Durkheim's passion for religion and his continued relevance for the current *fin de siècle* and
especially for the present discussion on postemotionalism. He was clearly
not writing in the manner of many detached scholars of today who pick a
topic for study primarily to further their careers. Durkheim was emotional,
not postemotional, in his concern with the religious origins of society. Let us
now turn to the new reading of his *Elementary Forms* that I am proposing,
and especially the linkage between the sacred and the emotions.

The Sacred as Emotional

Durkheim makes it clear from the beginning of his *Elementary Forms* that he
is not writing an ethnography of aborigines but is searching for what is universal in all societies, including modern societies. Thus, religion responds to
something 'essential and permanent' in reality.[13] Religion is a concrete reality
and not an artificial construct.[14] Far from religion being an intellectual construct, it has contributed to the forming of the intellect itself.[15] Durkheim
adds that the categories of understanding are born in and of religion: time,
space, class, number, cause, and others.[16] I have argued elsewhere that these
incredible claims are more in line with Arthur Schopenhauer's anti-
Enlightenment philosophy than the Enlightenment-based belief in the
supremacy of the intellect over passion.[17]

The cornerstone of Durkheim's understanding of religion is that it
involves the absolute heterogeneity of the categories sacred and profane.[18]
For Durkheim, an object is sacred because it inspires 'a collective sentiment' of respect which removes it from the profane or the pedestrian.[19]
Various Durkheimian scholars have objected to the fact that Durkheim
imposes only two categories, reasoning logically that there might exist three
or more categories, including the category of the mundane.[20] Scholars also
tend to read Durkheim's discourse on the sacred and the profane from the
vantage point of a sociology of knowledge, as strictly cognitive categories.
Most scholars seem to miss completely Durkheim's point that the sacred is
the site of society's emotional effervescence so that the profane is the mundane, the dreary and unemotional. Scholars also object to Durkheim's claim
that there is a need to distinguish religion from magic[21] such that there can
be no religion without a church and there can be no church of magic.[22] A
magician can have a clientele, but never a church.[23] For Durkheim, there can
be no private religions. Magical faith is derived from religious faith arising
from collective effervescence.[24] Magic is full of religious elements because it
was born of religion.[25] Psychologists as well as some sociologists have
objected to this claim by Durkheim as part of his alleged sociologism and
alleged anti-psychologism.[26] All these objections are *passé* by now, and are
beside the more important point that if Durkheim is correct, then society's

collective effervescence is the real source of emotion and postemotionalism is located in the private, magical efforts to imitate this authentic emotion. Durkheim's original formulation is useful for postemotional theory, and is worth pursuing despite the now standard objections that it engenders. Let me add also that I agree with Daniel O'Keefe's extension of Durkheim's use of 'church' to include many societal institutions, not just religious ones, and 'magic' to include many private efforts to emulate the social, including self-help books.[27] I will elaborate on this point later.

Durkheim also claims that religion must involve 'delirious imagination'[28] and that religion and myth are inseparable. This sounds like Nietzsche's central thesis in *The Birth of Tragedy*, even the theme in T.S. Eliot's 'The Waste Land,' except that Durkheim claims that the *sacred is the real*: Religion cannot be built on an illusion even if it does involve delirium.[29] According to Durkheim, religion may be *emotionally* a delirium, but it is a well-founded one because it is based on emotional realities created by the group.[30] All social thought, like all religious thought, is in a sense delirious, that is, based on socially agreed upon sentiments, feelings, ideas, and values (for example, the flag, postage stamps, blood, emblems, and so on). This passage by Durkheim is worth quoting extensively:

> If we give the name delirious to every state in which the mind adds to the immediate data given by the senses and projects its own sentiments and feelings into things, then *nearly every collective representation is in a sense delirious*; religious beliefs are only one particular case of a very general law. Our whole social environment seems to us to be *filled with forces which really exist only in our own minds*. We know what the flag is for the soldier; in itself, it is only a piece of cloth. Human blood is only an organic liquid, but even today we cannot see it flowing without *feeling* a *violent emotion* which its physio-chemical properties cannot explain. . . . A canceled postage stamp may be worth a fortune; but surely this value is in no way implied in its natural properties. In a sense, *our representations of the external world are undoubtedly a mere fabric of hallucinations*. . . . However they [representations] continue to correspond to certain objective states of the things represented; they express in their way the properties.[31] (emphasis added)

At least two things are worth noting about Durkheim's claim for the purposes of the present discussion. One is that unlike the postmodernists, who posit the circulation of rootless fictions (or hallucinations), Durkheim feels that they are rooted in reality. The other is that in making this decisive epistemological move, Durkheim is following Schopenhauer's momentous claim that the representation is the other side of the will.

Thus, let us examine Durkheim's rhetoric in his long-winded discussion of the clan, totem, and other sacred categories. According to Durkheim, these sites of the sacred involve 'collective enthusiasms,' 'collective passions,' 'collective sentiments,' the 'reinforcement of common faith,' 'energy,' 'sensations,' 'respect,' 'passionate energies,' 'effervescence,' 'transports of enthusiasm,' 'social life,' and 'religious life.'[32] The sacred involves the 'enthusiastic,' the 'emotional,' the 'concentrated,' and 'ceremonies,' while the profane involves the 'uniform,' the 'languishing,' and the 'dull.'[33] In fact, according to Durkheim, all social life involves the social periodicity of sacred transports of enthusiasm with the ordinary, profane, routine. This is why societies establish holy calendars, feast days, holidays, and all sorts of celebrations. One can hardly resist the generalization that the sacred is the site of the emotional.

When the aborigine or another traditionalist engages in totemism, he or she is really participating *emotionally* in collective representations, or, more accurately, representations of the collectivity. One must keep in mind that the representation is not only a cognitive category for Durkheim, but involves *homo duplex*, passion and idea, as I have demonstrated in *The Barbarian Temperament*[34] and elsewhere. Thus, totems are engraved on woodwork and walls, totem poles, even on bodies, but in all cases the totem as name or emblem is also a sacred thing.[35] Sanctuaries are established; totems are kept in sacred places; there are collective treasuries, sacred oak trees, and so on. The totem is treated with the emotions of devotion, respect, and awe.[36] By extension, the totemic believer is also sacred: He or she bears the totemic mark and thereby partakes in the sacredness of the totemic mark.[37]

Totemic mythology and other mythologies weave genealogical connections between humans and nature.[38] Traditional religions teach a 'mystic sympathy'[39] between humans and things. There is nothing that does not receive to some degree something of a religious character in this complex and systematic representation of the world.[40] The domain of totemic religion extends to the final limits of the known universe.[41] But there are private totems too, which deliberately select acts of hallucination and super-excitation in a magical effort to imitate the religious.[42] Another type of private totemism is sexual totemism, in which men and women have separate totems regardless of the tribe to which they belong.[43] According to Durkheim, by examining totemism we shall probably discover the causes that give rise to the religious 'sentiment' in humanity.[44] Again, as an irritant to those who claim that Durkheim is anti-psychological, Durkheim claims that religion is too complex and the needs to which it responds are too many to originate in a 'premeditated act of the will.'[45] Which came first, the individual or the collective totem? For Durkheim, the answer is tied to the issue of whether religion is born in the individual or the collective consciousness, and his reply is unequivocal.[46] Individual totemism presupposes collective totemism,[47] and is a collective cult adapted to personal needs.[48]

The Breakdown of the Sacred

Thus, totemism is a vast system of sacred things,[49] and the religion of an anonymous and impersonal force, an impersonal god without name or history, is immanent in the world and diffused in a number of things.[50] Durkheim makes the incredible conceptual leap from traditional totemism to modern societies by claiming that civic religions spring up by 'deifying' human or societal objects and representations.

> This aptitude of society for setting itself up as a god or for creating gods was never more apparent than during the first years of the French Revolution. At this time,

in fact, under the influence of the general *enthusiasm*, things purely laical by nature were transformed by public opinion into sacred things: these were the Fatherland, Liberty, Reason. *A religion tended to become established which had its dogmas, symbols, altars, and feasts.* It was to these *spontaneous* aspirations that the *cult of Reason* and the Supreme Being attempted to give a sort of official satisfaction. . . . This experiment, though short-lived, keeps all its sociological interest. It remains true that in one determined case we have seen society and its essential ideas become, directly and with no transfiguration of any sort, the object of a verifiable cult.[51] (emphasis added)

I agree with Durkheim that the worship of reason that arose with the French Revolution deserves to be called a cult of Reason, and not an exemplar of the Enlightenment 'project' as so many contemporary theorists believe. A project is dull and rational, bound by duty; a cult is emotional and irrational. In general, civic religions celebrate some great event in national life or the promulgation of a new moral or legal system.[52] Robert N. Bellah extended Durkheim's insight to invent the concept of 'American Civil Religion.'[53] But curiously, instead of identifying and studying civil religions in contemporary non-American societies,[54] sociologists reacted to Bellah mainly with so much scorn that he finally abandoned the concept.[55] And Bellah fails to distinguish between the spontaneous, emotional celebrations of the cult of America from the pre-packaged, rationally planned allusions to American Civil Religion that are used to convince Americans to support the actions of the Commander-in-Chief. This is a crucial distinction. Nevertheless, there can be no doubt that both Durkheim and Bellah are correct: Contemporary societies still attempt to at least *imitate* the collective emotional excitement of traditional societies by bestowing a contagious sanctity on money, emblems, celebrities, dates, battles, places, and ideas. Recent examples include the celebrity status of Pope John Paul II even among non-Catholics and actress Sharon Stone's receiving an award for culture by the French government. Contemporary rock stars and television celebrities have become gods in postemotional societies. On the other hand, the fact that Bellah and Durkheim have so many critics in this regard may be an indication that contemporary intellectuals cannot really relate to their claims that modernists need to engage in wholesale and irrational deification of non-religious persons and things: Modern societies find it increasingly difficult to sustain emotional life. The sacred may well have dried up with modernity, giving rise to postemotionalism.

Are modern societies capable of what Durkheim called 'collective effervescence'? These are period of heightened social *feelings* of confidence, courage, boldness, and other emotions.[56] Durkheim regarded the French Revolution as one such example of collective effervescence, but a more recent one might be America's collective celebration of victory in the Gulf War. But again, one wonders if this was true collective effervescence or a desperate act of postemotional imitation, given that American confidence, courage, and boldness evaporated so quickly and returned to the collective neuroses that stem from the Vietnam War, and that precluded a forceful response to Serbian genocidal aggression in the Balkan War that began in 1991.

Durkheim gives us a 'big bang' theory of religion as born out of such periods of collective effervescence.[57] It may well be the case that, as with the physical 'big bang' of the universe, in which the remnants of the original explosion have cooled off and are slowing down, the emotional life of modern societies is cooling off and slowly but surely dying.

Consider, for example, the celebration of Thanksgiving in the United States. Durkheim would have one consider the integrative and emotional aspects of celebrating this holiday in the USA. Bellah regards Thanksgiving as one of the holidays of American Civil Religion. But in line with Riesman's claim that other-directedness leads to splintered group-identifications, Americans can no longer agree on a general meaning to Thanksgiving. Thus,

> Thanksgiving is getting a makeover, as teachers recast the Pilgrim-and-Indian story to reflect the political and cultural sensibilities of the 1990s. . . . [They] cast the European settlers as selfish trespassers. . . . Pilgrims have been likened to tree-cutting aliens, or émigrés from oppressive countries.[58]

Instead of there being an American meaning to Thanksgiving, there is a Native-American meaning (which views the Pilgrims as oppressors), an African-American meaning (which likens the oppression of Indians to slavery), a female-American meaning (which exposes the sexism of the Pilgrims), a white-American meaning (which interprets Thanksgiving as a celebration of Americanism), and so on. Durkheim's assumption of a collective consciousness no longer seems to hold.

Because of his reliance on the idea of collective effervescence, Durkheim claims that the *sentiments* that form the basis of all religions are 'happy confidence.'[59] Note that 'happy confidence' is supposed to be genuine, and far removed from Marcuse's 'happy consciousness.' But happy confidence is not the most prevalent sentiment in contemporary societies. An anxious cynicism might be a more accurate description of how most modernists feel collectively.

For Durkheim, collective effervescence cools into symbols, which are emotionally charged and express social unity. He does not seem to be even a bit concerned with the discussion of the rupture between the signifier and the signified that occupies so many intellectuals who are engaged in the postmodernist debate. Instead, Durkheim claims that symbols are 'a constituent element' of society[60] so that, without symbols, 'social sentiments can have only a precarious existence.'[61] Let us note carefully that contemporary intellectuals generally fail to account for the emotional import of symbols. Instead, they treat the world primarily as a cognitive text. But for Durkheim, symbols are essential for social origins and continuity.[62] These are arresting claims. Modern and so-called postmodern societies certainly have their symbols, but the process of de-differentiation has destroyed in large measure their power to convey meaning. Postmodernists such as Jean Baudrillard have written extensively on this loss of meaning in a world dominated by simulations, not symbols, but Durkheim alerts us to the non-cognitive consequence of de-differentiation: The modern world may be losing its capability to produce and sustain emotions. This is an important, albeit depressing, step in the movement toward postemotionalism.

Social life is made possible only by a vast symbolism, in Durkheim's sense of the symbol as the integral component of the emotions that hold society together.[63] It seems to follow that postmodern de-differentiation must therefore lead to Balkanization and other processes of social fission. Further evidence that this conclusion flows from Durkheim's analysis is to be found in his discussion of the internationalization of totemism. Durkheim held that the totemic god came to be perceived as the creator-father of humanity and the benefactor of all humanity such that supreme gods warranted international recognition.[64] Amazingly, Durkheim found the origins of internationalism and cosmopolitanism in traditional totemic religions. He felt that the international aspect of religion reflects the international aspect of society.[65] One must conjoin this aspect of his discussion with other discussions, such as the one in his *Moral Education*, wherein he argues that love of family, love of intermediate groups, love of nation, and love of cosmopolitan humanity are not incongruous but co-exist harmoniously:

> Family, nation, and humanity represent different phases of our social and moral evolution, stages that prepare for, and build upon, one another. Consequently, these groups may be superimposed without excluding one another. . . . The problem of whether humanity ought to be subordinate to the state, cosmopolitanism to nationalism, is . . . one of those that arouses the greatest controversy today. There could not be a graver issue, since the orientation of moral activity will be altogether different and moral education understood in almost contrary fashion, depending on the group to which priority is accorded.[66]

This is still a grave issue in the 1990s. In contemporary times, it seems that Durkheim's felicitous conclusion that these varieties of communitarianism can harmonize has become problematic. Increasingly, and despite the ostentatious rhetoric of a united Europe or even a world supposedly united by information technology, the world is becoming Balkanized.[67] Nationalism has emerged unexpectedly as arguably the most powerful social force in the world today, and it is the sort of nationalism that does *not* lead to internationalism or cosmopolitanism. On the contrary, the contemporary scene is one of protectionist trade policies, tough anti-immigration laws, ethnic cleansing, and chauvinistic nationalism. One important Durkheimian reason for this state of affairs seems to be that the symbol has become de-differentiated, thereby robbing humanity of the integrative function of social sentiments. As I have argued throughout this book, Balkanization and postemotionalism seem to run together.

The Disappearance of the Collective Consciousness

Sociologists already seem to agree that in the conclusion of his *The Division of Labor in Society*, Durkheim argues that the concept of collective consciousness applies primarily to traditional, not modern, societies. The significance of this claim for the purposes of the present discussion emerges in light of the foregoing: If collective consciousness is disappearing, then (1) the emotional life associated with it is also disappearing, thereby leading to postemotionalism as a nostalgic quest to try to regain what modernists perceive unconsciously that they have lost, and (2) modern social life is characterized by splintered, fractured group mini-consciences which promote divisiveness, not unity.

Thus, modernists are still able to entertain a compassionate attitude toward Dutch flood victims if they are Dutch, or American hurricane victims if they are Americans, and so on. But as social as well as geographical distance increases, modernists increasingly complain of compassion fatigue. One of the most powerful pieces of evidence for this transition lay in the West's inability to feel sufficient compassion for the victims of genocide in Bosnia, despite the massive media coverage of this event, to put a decisive end to it. And Balkanization accompanies this diminution of the collective consciousness such that Western allies such as France, Britain, the USA, and the Netherlands argued publicly with each other at conferences and meetings of NATO, the UN, the CSCE, and other ostensibly cosmopolitan organizations about what should be done. This is a far cry from Durkheim's descriptions in *The Division of Labor in Society* of the function of punishment as a response to crime that thereby strengthens cosmopolitan norms and standards of justice. Each and every time that domestic or international crime is not punished, the collective conscience is weakened further.

This postemotional splintering of collective consciousness is also illustrated by contrasting Louis Farrakhan's march on Washington, DC – the largest in US history – with Martin Luther King Jr's march. Farrakhan attempted a postemotional copying of the collective effervescence that King galvanized, though with a radically different agenda, and with only a male constituency. As I noted in chapter 1, the response to Farrakhan involved further fission as Jews, females, whites, and others responded negatively to Farrakhan's imitation collective effervescence. Harking back to the discussion of David Riesman's theory of other-directedness, one may conclude that Farrakhan's attempt at postemotionalism is the rule, not the exception, in contemporary modernist societies.

For those who take this line of inquiry seriously, it would seem that the task for postemotional society is to achieve Durkheim's vision of integrating splintered mini-consciences into a cosmopolitan collective consciousness such that the smaller collective consciences based on ethnicity, nation, family, and so on, would work together harmoniously. It is beyond the scope of the present discussion to speculate on how such a goal might be achieved.

Nevertheless, for the sake of scholarly completeness, it is worth speculating briefly on possible alternatives to Durkheim's sociological explanation. Suppose, for the sake of argument, that his critics are correct to charge him with anti-psychologism. Suppose that the symbols which he claims are essential for collective emotional life need not originate in society. Where would they come from? One source might be the archetypes that Carl Gustav Jung claimed are collective but carried within individuals. Archetypes are very much like Durkheim's symbols, even regarding the emotional effervescence that surrounds both. Abraham Maslow and Erik Erikson are among the other psychologists who posited that the seeds of self-actualization lie within the individual, not in society.

These alternatives to Durkheim might be worth pursuing, yet the same postemotional and Balkanized barriers that stem from Durkheim's analysis will have to be overcome first. Jung is widely regarded as a Nazi of sorts in psychological circles. This label has divided psychologists trying to integrate his theories into general psychology, not to mention the more difficult task of reconciling him with sociology. Maslow and Erikson were popular in the 1960s, but are mostly *passé* in the 1990s. The general thrust of both psychology and sociology today is to complete the postemotional project of a distorted vision of the Enlightenment in which analyses of cognition and behavior using positivistic methodology take precedence over emotion and the integration of the personality. I leave the Herculean project of finding a common ground between Durkheim and Jung, Maslow, and Erikson for others to pursue.

But I will note that there is one promising psychological theory that purports to involve the body, self, and culture in ways that are commensurate with Durkheim's approach. It is the theory of the 'dialogical self,' proposed by Hubert J. Hermans and Harry J.G. Kempen.[68] This theory proposes that body, self, and cultural relations must be de-reified and treated simultaneously in order to understand how social meanings are created and maintained. Such a psychological theory seems very close to what Durkheim intended with his concept of collective effervescence.

Postemotional Rituals

I began this book with the observation that postmodern recycling and imitation of the past must be compared and contrasted with traditional re-enactments of the past through ritual. Let me return to Durkheim's *Elementary Forms* to clarify the similarities and differences by re-examining his complex discussion of various types of ritual with an eye toward their relevance to postemotional societies. The main difference between traditional rituals and postemotional rituals seems to be that traditional ones serve as tools to bring out spontaneous emotions as part of collective effervescence while postemotional rituals are mechanical, routinized attempts to simulate authentic collective effervescence. But this difference, if it exists, is an intricate one.

For Durkheim, negative rituals are those whose function is to separate the sacred from the profane through abstentions, taboos, and interdictions.[69] Consistent with his earlier claims that religion is fundamentally different from magic, he argues that there are no interdictions in magic: There is no sin in magic, and magic lives in profanations.[70] If one accepts Durkheim's claim for the sake of argument, one is led to the conclusion that modern societies revel in what he calls magic, and have abandoned religion. Consider the common religious interdictions as depicted by Durkheim, interdictions of contact (the profane should never touch the sacred), eating, sight, word (certain words and sounds are sacred), breath, clothing, ordinary everyday life (for example, days of rest, occupations), space (temples, sanctuaries) and time (holy days), and so on. All of these are routinely de-differentiated and profaned in modern and postmodern societies. Celebrities try to show that they are like the rest of us by disclosing publicly their traumas from childhood, divorces, abusive parents, and so on. Interdictions regarding food are practiced primarily by some Jews and Muslims with little impact on others. With regard to sight, the television camera has profaned the sanctity and mystery of just about any phenomenon known or imagined by humanity. The backlash of the information revolution is that almost nothing is sacred any more. Postemotional types can peer into the recesses of the vagina, or travel with a 'smart bomb' as it explodes into a target, or 'visit' exotic tourist sites without leaving their living rooms, or 'be there' when a mother weeps for her dead child in Sarajevo right after he or she had been shot by a Serbian sniper's bullet.

What words are sacred anymore? It is practically impossible for old-fashioned types to teach their children that saying 'God damn it' is naughty when they are exposed to such profanations daily on television. The child's interdiction of 'naughty' or forbidden words is practically non-existent today. Even children's programs and channels, such as the Disney Channel, use 'naughty' words. (Anyone who doubts this needs only to consult a four-year-old child.) In general, adulthood is no longer a mystery for children. They are routinely exposed to adult topics that used to be forbidden, such as AIDS, cocaine use, condoms, and so on. Entire families, consisting of mother, father, and children, are found filing past the glass prostitute booths in Amsterdam. Prostitution has now become a tourist attraction, even for small children. Adulthood has collapsed into childhood, minus the coming-of-age rituals that characterized this rite of passage in traditional societies.

There are no 'days of rest' for most Westerners: Middle-class persons in Western countries are likely to mow their lawns on Sunday because they have a few hours of private free time on this day. Holidays in the USA are spent mainly on shopping, not reflecting collectively on the cultural meaning of the holiday. Advertisements make sure that there is a Labor Day Sale, Thanksgiving Sale, 4th of July Sale, and so on. As for interdictions against profaning sacred places, tourists routinely storm into sanctuaries in foreign lands as if they were any other place on their itinerary. One finds churches in Holland that are surrounded by pubs and brothels, and are usually locked in any event. The very act of making any 'shrine' to this or that open to the public, such as the Alamo, in San Antonio, Texas, means that it is no longer extraordinary but banal, hence profane.

The commonly heard expression 'Nothing is sacred anymore' contains an important germ of truth. Defenders of desacralization might argue that it has made the West more democratic by making previously forbidden words, places, sights, sounds, and other phenomena accessible to almost everybody and anybody. This may be true, but the flip side of this democratization is that it has emptied the social world of the sacred and therefore of emotion. Increasingly, all that is left is the post-emotion that Baudrillard observed, 'I did it.' I went to the Alamo, I saw the prostitutes in Amsterdam, I survived Sarajevo, and so on.

Durkheim wrote that if there is no notion of the sacred, then there is no religion, and, consequently, no society.[71] By the term 'society,' clearly he meant more than a collection of atomized individuals, and referred to society as an emotional complex with its own collective consciousness.

Durkheim also analyzed 'negative rituals,' those that give one ritualized access to the sacred. These include initiation ceremonies, asceticism, hazing, and other ritual cruelties.[72] All of these rituals involved some degree of pain and suffering that had to be endured in order to prove that one was worthy of membership in a cult deemed to be sacred: fasts, vigils, retreats, silence, renunciation, abnegation, detachment from the self, endurance, and so on. It is interesting to observe in this regard that modernity tends to eliminate or tone down hazing and other rites of passage into universities, corporations, the military service, and other societal institutions. For example, Shannon Faulkner apparently was not prepared for the hazing that went along with her admission to the all-male military academy at the Citadel in South Carolina. But unlike the near-total collapse of the rituals of interdiction discussed above, it seems to be the case that hazing and rites of passage are staging something of a comeback in contemporary life.

For example, Texas A&M University is replete with elaborate hazing rituals for male as well as female students, who seem to participate in them with considerable relish. Increasingly, one finds private schools cropping up in Western countries that imitate the severe hazing practices of private schools from a century ago. The students will tell you immediately why they participate: They feel that the hazing sets them apart from other schools and makes them feel special. An empirical study would have to determine whether these contemporary students are really experiencing the emotions that Durkheim had in mind or if they are merely aping, postemotionally, the initiation rites from traditional societies. Either way, the fact that secular, middle-class Western youth often chooses to undergo ritual cruelties is worth pondering. This phenomenon could indicate an unconscious desire to compensate for the emotional vacuum left by the nearly total profaning of the rest of social life.

According to Durkheim, interdictions are logically implied in the notion of sacredness,[73] but one must also consider the extraordinary contagiousness of the sacred.[74] Contagiousness itself is explained by the notion that the 'force' in sacred things lies outside them. In fact, these are collective forces, hypostatized ideas and *sentiments* awakened in us by the 'spectacle of society,' not sensations coming from the physical world.[75] The 'existence' of sacred things depends on the beliefs and actions of those who sustain them as sacred. Hence, there is the requirement of renewal.[76] Rituals must be carried out in *assembled groups* in order to renew the sense of the sacred:

If these sacred beings, when once conceived, are to have no need of men to continue, it would be necessary that the representations expressing them always remain the same. But this stability is impossible. In fact, it is in the communal life that they are formed, and this communal life is essentially intermittent. So they necessarily partake of this same intermittency. They attain their greatest intensity at the moment when the men *are assembled together and are in immediate relations with one another, when they all partake of the same idea and the same sentiment.* But when the assembly has broken up and each man has returned to his own peculiar life, they progressively lose their original *energy.* Being covered over little by little by the rising flood of daily experiences, they would soon fall into the unconscious, if we did not find some means of calling them back into consciousness and revivifying them. *The only way of renewing the collective representations which relate to sacred beings is to retemper them in the very source of the religious life, that is to say, in the assembled groups.*[77] (emphasis added)

One wonders whether television or other forms of information technology are able to act as substitutes for these acts of collective renewal. Do President Clinton's televised 'town hall meetings,' for example, really serve the same function as traditional town hall meetings, or is this another example of postemotionalism? This is a very important question that needs to be investigated empirically.

Beyond the empirical issue, theoretical issues remain. Globalization and the coalescing of nationalities into larger federations have made it impossible for human agents to renew collective life in assembled groups. The groups that would be required for such revivification would simply be too large. Thus, most members of the group must experience the revivification vicariously, through the information medium. But this means that their experience will already be rationalized and pre-processed cognitively. Additionally, and because of the trend toward other-directedness, each person automatically experiences collective effervescence through the filters of his or her own private life or small reference group. For this reason, the emotional meaning of any contemporary rite of collective effervescence will be splintered immediately into a myriad of competing meanings.

Durkheim seems to have been right in believing that such collective emotional renewal is essential for societies, yet his optimism concerning the possibility of such renewal in modern societies seems naive. Again, it is worth quoting an extended passage from Durkheim in this regard:

There can be no society which does not feel the need of upholding and reaffirming at regular intervals the collective sentiments and the collective ideas which make its unity and personality. *Now this moral remaking cannot be achieved except by the means of reunions, assemblies and meetings where the individuals, being closely united to one another, reaffirm in common their common sentiments; hence come ceremonies which do not differ from regular religious ceremonies . . .* what essential difference is there between an assembly of Christians celebrating the principal dates of the life of Christ, or of Jews remembering the exodus from Egypt or the promulgation of the decalogue, and a reunion of citizens commemorating the promulgation of a new moral or legal system or some great event in the national life?

If we find a little difficulty today in imagining what these feasts and ceremonies *of the future* could consist in, it is because we are going through a stage of transition

and moral mediocrity. The great things of the past which filled our fathers with
enthusiasm do not excite the same ardor in us. . . . In a word, the old gods are growing old or already dead, and others are not yet born . . . but this state of incertitude
and confused agitation cannot last forever. A day will come when our societies will
know again those hours of creative effervescence, in the course of which new ideas
arise and new formulae are found which serve for a while as a guide to humanity;
and when these hours shall have been passed through once, men will *spontaneously*
feel the need of reliving them from time to time in thought, that is to say, of keeping alive their memory by means of celebrations which regularly reproduce their
fruits.[78] (emphasis added)

The future which Durkheim tried to imagine in 1912 is quite different from
his fantasy. In an age of induced childbirth, induced peace treaties, and most
things induced rationally, collective effervescence is also induced. But for this
reason, it is not spontaneous. When the President of the United States
addresses the American public with new ideas for guiding humanity, he reads
a speech that has been prepared by an army of speech-writers, consultants,
opinion-makers, and opinion-takers. One simply cannot avoid the cynical
appraisal that much of contemporary collective effervescence comes to the
masses pre-planned and pre-packaged. This process of synthetically inducing
emotions is integral to the existence of postemotional societies.

Imitative rites are those that reproduce some aspect or behavior of the
totem.[79] Resemblance to gods is sought for the same reason that later believers try to resemble God – to communicate with the sacred being, that is, the
collective ideal it symbolizes.[80] The imitative rite renews *faith*.[81] For
Durkheim, faith must be affirmed collectively: A philosophy may be elaborated in the silence of the interior imagination, but not so a faith.[82] The
closest contemporary example of what Durkheim meant by imitative rites
seems to be the behavior of football fans, who often affix the 'totemic' symbols of their football team to their bodies, cars, homes, and other personal
things. The behavior of football fans often seems to resemble a collective
effervescence. The difference with traditional imitative rites, however, is that
even the most fanatical football fan does not leave the rite with a renewed
sense of faith, and the allegiance to a football team is a postemotional release
from the dreariness of the rest of social life. Football fanaticism may well
constitute a postemotional imitation of imitation rites. Nevertheless, its widespread popularity bespeaks the emotional hunger in postemotional societies.

Representative or commemorative rites are those that remain faithful to the
past. These types of rites represent the role of ancestors and mythical events
and have the function of *revivifying* the memory of the essential elements of
collective consciousness.[83] Ceremonies attach the present to the past, and
the individual to the group.[84] These representational rites have a recreative
element by involving games as well as an aesthetic element. Durkheim makes
the important claim that games and the principal forms of art were born in
religion and for a long time retained a religious character.[85]

Without a doubt, Durkheim's discussion of these types of rites is the most
relevant to contemporary times. We have seen in chapter 1 that recycling history and the simulation of history are so prevalent that postmodernists have

already discussed both phenomena extensively. But are postmodern recycling and simulation what Durkheim had in mind? Probably not. In the first place, contemporary commemorative rites fracture communities more than unify them, as we have seen in the discussion of the controversy surrounding Auschwitz. Instead of bringing Jews and Poles closer, the Auschwitz commemorative rites in 1995 drove them further apart. Similarly, the controversy surrounding the meaning of the Alamo as the site of Texas democracy for whites versus the site of Texan imperialism against Mexico for Hispanics served to Balkanize these two groups in Texas.[86] Second, no one is quite certain *which* aspect of a collective memory should be commemorated. Thus, the Smithsonian Institution planned an exhibit of the *Enola Gay*, the airplane that was used to drop an atomic bomb on Hiroshima. Indignants appeared who objected to the Smithsonian portrayal of the USA as the aggressors and racists in the war against Japan.[87] The Smithsonian backed down, with this explanation offered by its secretary, I. Michael Heyman:

> In this important anniversary year, veterans and their families were expecting, and rightly so, that the nation would honor and commemorate their valor and sacrifice. They were not looking for analysis and, frankly, we did not give enough thought to the intense feelings such analysis would evoke.[88]

Third, the postemotional interpretation of 'games' and 'play' is far removed from the spontaneous play in commemorative and representative rites that Durkheim describes. Consider the proposal to turn the Martin Luther King Jr memorial in Atlanta, Georgia, into a Disneyesque theme park: "'I have a dreamland" . . . would include attractions like a "time machine" filled with holograms of Dr. King and simulated encounters with "firehoses and police dogs."'[89] The purposeful simulation of authenticity cannot be authentic, for reasons that have been discussed already. Fourth, and finally, the contemporary revivification of memory often conceals a hostile intent that is completely absent in Durkheim's discussion. Thus, the Serbs' revival of the memory of the Battle of Kosovo, which they lost to the Muslims in 1389, is used to rationalize an aggressive, genocidal nationalism against contemporary Muslims, not the cosmopolitanism that Durkheim described. How innocent Durkheim seems in contrast to the uses and misuses of historical memory nowadays!

In summary, postemotional, post-other-directed society is too sophisticated cognitively to commemorate or remember any historical event without arguing about its meaning, cynically debunking someone else's interpretation in order to promote one's own, and, ultimately, without Balkanizing. Traditional and inner-directed societies apparently had a much easier time agreeing on the meaning of historical events that were revivified. Consider one final illustration of all these postemotional elements in contemporary commemorations, the rescue of Captain O'Grady from Bosnian Serb territory after his NATO warplane was shot down by the Serbs in June 1995. O'Grady was flown to Washington, DC, to receive a hero's welcome commensurate with what Bellah called American Civil Religion. Yet several aspects of this commemoration of his American heroism seemed anomalous. First, Captain O'Grady was hailed as a hero even though he saved only himself, whereas, traditionally, heroes are those who save others. Second, he wept during a televised news conference in response to a question about how he felt before being rescued. Traditionally, professional soldiers did not weep in public, in line with the hazing and suffering aspects of becoming a soldier that Durkheim described. Third, President Clinton turned O'Grady's rescue into a postemotional spectacle, as explained eloquently by Michael Dorris:

> President Clinton spontaneously remarked that Captain O'Grady's story would someday make 'a very great movie.' It was a curious but telling response, as if the happy event could not be complete until it was turned into a popular fiction. The appeal of the idea is obvious. When experience is transformed into uplifting entertainment, it can be broken down into separate acts that lead to tidy conclusions about good guys who beat odds. . . . Presto, the mind-numbing tragedy of the Bosnian War becomes background noise for relief at one tough, resourceful American's narrow escape. The message: 'This time, we won. We're outta there in one piece.' But this apparent reaction reflects a kind of myopia that all but obscures more difficult matters. We are invited to glean hope from a single success of one good officer removed from a setting of overwhelming defeat. . . . There's something essentially wrong with this response; our collective mood of congratulations over his escape seems self-aggrandizing. By distilling the parochial 'we' out of a global 'us,' we absolve ourselves from sustained empathy and responsibility for the lives of Sarajevo's residents and the other places of Bosnia. In fact, as part of a NATO patrol over Bosnia, Captain O'Grady was assigned to observe rather than fight a war.[90]

Dorris is right: When viewed in a larger context, O'Grady's rescue was not really a cause for collective commemoration of Americanism because US policy failed miserably (along with the Europeans) to stop Serbian genocidal aggression in Bosnia. Of course, one is happy that he was rescued, but the plight of Bosnians who were *not* rescued makes this particular commemorative rite seem hollow. Furthermore, it is a telling observation that the postemotional President, Bill Clinton, wanted to turn Captain O'Grady's rescue into a movie. The movie would automatically render his experience into a postemotional event because it would entail a script, complete control settings, the bias of the producer and director, commercial concerns, guidelines for public relations, and so on.

Durkheim refers to piacular rites as those that are inspired by sentiments of sorrow and fear.[91] These rites are celebrated in a state of sadness or uneasiness. Mourning related to funerals is the most obvious example of such rites. According to Durkheim, in piacular rites, anger may be mingled with sadness (for example, the vendetta), and, in general, dejection, cries, and tears are the rule.[92] Mourning is a duty and obligation: Piacular rites in general come out of collective ceremonies that produce a state of collective effervescence. In line with the overall focus of Durkheim's work on collective integration, he asserts that society cannot allow members to be indifferent to the loss of one of its members through death.[93] Death requires an affirmation of moral unity and cohesion by society. While contemporary societies still hold funerals, it is an open question whether they still serve an integrative function. One could argue that postemotional types are increasingly 'indifferent' to the death of loved ones as well as televised deaths of strangers from Cambodia to Bosnia, even when they go through the motions of expressing the appropriate emotions. Funerals grow ever shorter and death becomes an issue that involves expense, the consumption of precious time, and legal obligations. It is not even obvious that sorrow is the conventional response to death. Thus, the Day of the Dead, celebrated in traditional societies from Poland to Mexico in a great collective effervescence of sorrow, has been transformed into the fun of Halloween in the USA.

Regarding piacular as well as all other rites, Durkheim asserts that human sentiments are intensified when affirmed collectively.[94] But is the mechanical reproduction of 'collectivity' through television sufficient for such intensification? I agree with Keith Tester that it is not.[95]

Conclusions

According to Durkheim, 'It is life itself, not a dead past, that can produce a living cult.'[96] But we have seen in this chapter and throughout this book that postemotional types focus their attention increasingly on the dead past through recycling and simulation. Durkheim also claimed that faith is before all else an impetus to action.[97] But again, we have seen that postemotional types seem unable to match an appropriate action to a particular insight. Postemotional types are cynical: They have lost the capacity for faith. Referring back to Riesman's metaphor of the Milky Way of choices that confronts the other-directed type, one can rephrase this as follows: There are too many alternatives, choices, and interpretations in the postemotional sky – all of which can be debunked, deconstructed, and de-differentiated – to allow the postemotional type to feel faith in his or her decisions to act. One senses this loss of faith in phenomena that range from the inability of many persons to choose a person to marry to the inability of the West to choose a course of action to stop the slaughter in Bosnia.

Although he sometimes seems naive, Durkheim was aware that collective concepts as well as sentiments are retouched, modified, and consequently falsified as they become individualized.[98] There is slippage in the transference of collective phenomena to the individual comparable to mutation in biology. No one individual in any of the rituals that Durkheim describes experiences the collective effervescence in exactly the same way. Nevertheless, Durkheim felt that a genuinely collective experience was possible despite this slippage. I am suggesting that in postemotional society the slippage has become an avalanche and the mutation of meaning has developed into a leukemia. The individual's cognitive modification of collective phenomena has become so extreme that a genuinely collective experience has become almost impossible.

Durkheim concluded that despite individual differences in interpreting events, collective representations present guarantees of objectivity precisely because they are collective, hence generalized and persistent.[99] This faith in the objectivity of the collectivity was the basis of his infamous concept of 'social facts.' Interestingly, this is one of the most vilified concepts in sociology. American sociologists, especially, object to the apparent anti-individualism that accompanies this concept. Yet without this guarantee of some sort of objectivity, individuals are left in a Tower of Babel of private meanings, and are unable to produce states of collective effervescence. Ironically, I believe that quite apart from the criticisms levelled at him on the ideological grounds of individualism, Durkheim's faith in collective meanings no longer applies to postemotional societies. This is because, as stated above, postemotional individuals are too cynical and too skilled at deconstruction to 'let go' emotionally and experience collective effervescence.

Durkheim also felt that concepts derive their authority not uniquely from their objective value but from their harmony with other beliefs and opinions and collective representations, hence, from a collective faith.[100] Alas, Durkheim's idealized social harmony has degenerated into a smorgasbord of widely divergent beliefs, opinions and collective representations that can never harmonize. The postemotional social world is one of competing viewpoints, interpretations, ideologies, and representations. Publicly expressed faith in any one of them exposes one to the indignation of individuals and groups who hold differing views.

Durkheim believed that concepts were linked to emotions and to sociability itself in the following way: Conceptual thought is coeval with humanity itself. A human who did not think with concepts would not be a social being because concepts bind one emotionally to the group.[101] In postemotional society, it seems that concepts antagonize other individuals and groups. Durkheim felt that collective consciousness is the highest form of psychic life.[102] I have suggested, contrary to Durkheim, that collective consciousness no longer exists.

In many ways, Durkheim, like Riesman, expresses an innocence concerning social relations that is appealing, but ultimately out of sync with the realities of postemotional societies. Durkheim's *Elementary Forms* presents us with a 'Paradise Lost' portrait of genuine, collective emotions. Postemotional types go through the emotions of all the rituals that Durkheim describes, but they can no longer achieve the spontaneous collective communion in his vision of the past.

Notes

1. In the *Westiminster Gazette*, 16 August 1916.
2. Fustel de Coulanges, *The Ancient City: A Study on the Religion, Laws, and Institutions of Greece and Rome* (Boston: Lee and Shepard, 1889).
3. Jean-Marie Guyau, *The Non-religion of the Future* (New York: Shocken Books, [1887] 1962).
4. Wilhelm Wundt, *Elements of Folk Psychology* (London: Allen and Unwin, [1887] 1916).
5. Émile Durkheim, *The Elementary Forms of the Religious Life* (New York: Free Press, [1912] 1965).

6. Émile Durkheim, *Professional Ethics and Civic Morals* (Westport, CT: Greenwood Press, [1950] 1983).

7. Émile Durkheim, *The Division of Labor in Society* (New York: Free Press, [1893] 1933).

8. Émile Durkheim, *Suicide* (New York: Free Press, [1897] 1951).

9. W. Robertson Smith, *Lectures on the Religion of the Semites* (London: Adam and Charles Black, 1894).

10. Reprinted in Émile Durkheim, *Incest: The Nature and Origin of the Taboo* (New York: Lyle Stuart, [1898] 1963).

11. Stjepan G. Meštrović, *Émile Durkheim and the Reformation of Sociology* (Totowa, NJ: Rowman and Littlefield, 1988).

12. Émile Durkheim, *Sociology and Philosophy* (New York: Free Press, 1974), pp. 1–34.

13. Durkheim, *Elementary Forms*, p. 13.

14. Ibid., p. 16.

15. Ibid., p. 21.

16. Ibid., p. 22.

17. See, for example, Stjepan G. Meštrović, The Coming *Fin de Siècle* (London: Routledge, 1991).

18. Durkheim, *Elementary Forms*, p. 53.

19. Ibid., p. 301.

20. See, for example, William Pickering, *Durkheim's Sociology of Religion* (London: Routledge and Kegan Paul, 1984).

21. Durkheim, *Elementary Forms*, pp. 57–8.

22. Ibid., pp. 59–60.

23. Ibid., p. 60.

24. Ibid., p. 405.

25. Ibid.

26. See especially Steven Lukes, *Émile Durkheim: His Life and Work* (New York: Harper and Row, 1972).

27. Daniel O'Keefe, *Stolen Lightning: The Social Theory of Magic* (New York: Random House, 1982).

28. Durkheim, *Elementary Forms*, p. 107.

29. Ibid., p. 86.

30. Ibid., p. 258.

31. Ibid., p. 259.

32. Ibid., pp. 220–52 passim.

33. Ibid., p. 246.

34. Stjepan G. Meštrović, *The Barbarian Temperament* (London: Routledge, 1993).

35. Durkheim, *Elementary Forms*, p. 140.

36. Ibid., p. 143.

37. Ibid., p. 157.

38. Ibid.

39. Ibid., p. 174.

40. Ibid., p. 179.

41. Ibid., p. 180.

42. Ibid., p. 189.

43. Ibid., pp. 190–2.

44. Ibid., p. 195.

45. Ibid., p. 199.

46. Ibid., p. 200.

47. Ibid., p. 207.

48. Ibid., p. 208.

49. Ibid., p. 210.

50. Ibid., p. 217.

51. Ibid., p. 245.

52. Ibid., p. 475.

53. Robert N. Bellah, 'Civil Religion in America,' *Daedalus*, 96 (1967), pp. 1–21.

54. Bellah did make such an attempt, however. See Robert N. Bellah and Peter E. Hammond, *Varieties of Civil Religion* (New York: Harper and Row, 1980).

55. See Robert N. Bellah, 'Reply to "Twenty Years After Bellah,"' *Sociological Analysis*, 50, 2 (1989), p. 149. Discussed in Stjepan G. Meštrović, *Durkheim and Postmodern Culture* (Hawthorne, NY: Aldine de Gruyter, 1992). Let me make it clear that some efforts were made to extend the concept of 'American Civil Religion' by studying the civil religions of other nations, but there were not many such efforts, and their impact on sociology was negligible.

56. Durkheim, *Elementary Forms*, p. 241.

57. Ibid., p. 250.

58. Pam Belluck, 'Pilgrims Wear Different Hats in Recast Thanksgiving Tales,' *New York Times*, 23 November 1995, p. A1.

59. Durkheim, *Elementary Forms*, p. 256.

60. Ibid., p. 262.

61. Ibid., p. 263.

62. Ibid.

63. Ibid., p. 264.

64. Ibid., pp. 324–5.

65. Ibid., p. 474.

66. Émile Durkheim, *Moral Education* (Glencoe, IL: Free Press, [1925] 1961), p. 74. For an extensive discussion of Durkheim's theory of nationalism as it relates to cosmopolitanism, see Stjepan G. Meštrović, Miroslav Goreta, and Slaven Letica, *The Road From Paradise* (Lexington, KY: University Press of Kentucky, 1993).

67. For an extended discussion, see my *The Balkanization of the West* (London: Routledge, 1994).

68. Hubert J.M. Hermans, Harry J.G. Kempen, and Rens J.P. van Loon, 'The Dialogical Self: Beyond Individualism and Rationalism,' *American Psychologist*, 47 (1992), pp. 23–33; Hubert J.M. Hermans and Harry J.G. Kempen, 'Body, Mind and Culture: The Dialogical Nature of Mediated Action,' *Culture & Psychology*, 1 (1995), pp. 103–14.

69. Durkheim, *Elementary Forms*, p. 338.

70. Ibid., p. 339.

71. Ibid., p. 347.

72. Ibid., pp. 350–5.

73. Ibid., p. 356.

74. Ibid., p. 358.

75. Ibid., p. 362.

76. Ibid., p. 387.

77. Ibid.

78. Ibid., p. 475.

79. Ibid., p. 393.

80. Ibid., p. 401.

81. Ibid., p. 403.

82. Ibid., p. 473.

83. Ibid., p. 420.

84. Ibid., p. 423.

85. Ibid., pp. 424–7.

86. 'David Crockett Died a Hero,' *Bryan-College Station Eagle*, 30 January 1995, p. A6.

87. Karen de Witt, 'US Exhibit on Enola Gay in Jeopardy,' *New York Times*, 28 January 1995, p. A8.

88. Karen de Witt, 'Smithsonian Scales Back Exhibit of Plane in Atomic Bomb Attack,' *New York Times*, 31 January 1995, p. A1.

89. Robert Frank and Elena de Lisser, 'Dr. King's Heirs Fight Accusations of Greed Over Theme Park Plan,' *Wall Street Journal*, 9 January 1995, p. A1.

90. Michael Dorris, 'O'Grady's Pluck Lets Us Forget,' *New York Times*, 13 June 1995, p. A11.

91. Durkheim, *Elementary Forms*, p. 435.

92. Ibid., p. 442.

93. Ibid., p. 445.

94. Ibid., p. 446.

95. Keith Tester, 'Moral Solidarity and the Technological Reproduction of Images,' *Media, Culture and Society*, 17 (1995), pp. 469–82.

96. Durkheim, *Elementary Forms*, p. 475.

97. Ibid., p. 479.

98. Ibid., p. 484.

99. Ibid., p. 486.

100. Ibid.

101. Ibid., p. 487.

102. Ibid., p. 492.

6

Death and the End of Innocence

When did postemotionalism begin? Similar questions have been and continue to be asked regarding modernity, modernism, and postmodernity, with diverse answers supplied by different authors. With regard to the beginnings of postmodernity, some of the answers, such as Chris Rojek's in *Ways of Escape*, go as far back as the Renaissance and the Reformation, while others, such as David Harvey's, pinpoint them to the destruction of an urban housing project in the USA in the 1970s.[1] If one were to begin to try to answer this question with regard to postemotionalism, one might look for an era in which collective innocence began to mutate into cynicism, in which television first became the social force that it is today, and in which the moral authority of the collective consciousness began to wither. The diminution of the collective consciousness, especially, would signal the drying up of the category of the sacred and of less availability for people to engage in collective effervescence. I might point to the early 1960s as such an era, and therefore locate the origins of postemotionalism in the most other-directed geographical locations of the United States, namely, the large cosmopolitan cities such as New York and Los Angeles, and to university campuses. I see no reason to abandon one of the guiding premises of the present argument, refracted from Baudrillard, Riesman, and others going back to Alexis de Tocqueville, that the USA serves as a cultural beacon for the rest of the world. Postemotionalism began in the USA, and could not have taken root in more traditional or inner-directed societies, not even Western Europe, in which many traditions persisted alongside modernity, at least until recently. In 1960, television began to dominate cultural life following the Nixon–Kennedy debates, which were the first televised Presidential debates in US history. In 1962, the Vietnam War protests began in earnest, which signalled the beginning of the erosion of adult authority for an entire generation of young people, and also marked widespread cynicism and suspicion concerning the US government. In 1963, President John F. Kennedy was assassinated in Dallas, Texas, and the assassination was followed on television. The vast majority of the US population today has concluded that Lee Harvey Oswald was *not* the lone assassin, and many believe that the US government played a role in his assassination. These beliefs run against the grain of the official Warren Commission report, and indicate a widespread cynicism that older generations could not imagine. Older Americans cannot even entertain the notion that the death of Kennedy might have been a coup orchestrated by the US government.

What is collective innocence, sociologically speaking? As suggested by

David Riesman,[2] post-World War II American innocence included a general mood of optimism, a sort of temporal hubris in which the USA was perceived to be an invincible power, a provincial self-righteousness, and an over-confident faith in the American dream. At least in the 1950s, the American dream was not yet mean-spirited, nor was it stingy (recall the Marshall Plan). Innocence is not exactly the same as naivety. Rather, innocence involves a collective and easy confidence in tackling large problems on the basis of limited evidence, an American 'can-do' attitude. Americans in the 1950s thought that social problems were accessible to understanding and even, in some measure, to resolution. Even sociologists in the 1950s were innocent: Many had not learned the rules of sociological method in a formal way, nor studied the history of the discipline. A knowledge of Parsons sufficed, and sociologists thought they could cure America's ills. In many ways, these American traits from a by-gone era resemble Durkheim's description of the boldness, courage, and 'happy confidence' that are the hallmarks of an integrated society. It would be an interesting study to compare and contrast American innocence with the forms that innocence takes in other cultures.

But things are much different in the USA in the post-innocent 1990s. If Americans learned to hate and fear the Soviet Union during the Cold War, many of them now hate and fear their own government (consider the Oklahoma City bombing and many related incidents in America's Far West). Optimism has given way to widespread pessimism concerning the future. The reduction of voter turnout in elections, a palpable decrease in general trust, and an increase in cynicism all serve to mark the end of American innocence. Americans are much more cosmopolitan and knowledgeable about the world today than they were in the 1950s, yet all this knowledge only makes them feel helpless in tackling what seem to be insurmountable social problems domestically as well as internationally. In contradistinction to Anthony Giddens's writings on empowerment, Americans feel powerless as they become more knowledgeable. The American dream in the 1990s is mean-spirited toward immigrants, have-nots, and the disadvantaged. It has also become stingy: Americans questioned why the USA should spend any money to reconstruct war-shattered Bosnia when that money could be used to reconstruct tattered American cities. There is little confidence in tackling large problems. The more common reactions include exasperation and 'compassion fatigue,' captured by the refrain 'America is not the world's policeman.' Social problems are no longer seen as accessible to understanding or resolution. Rather, as I have suggested throughout this book, Americans seem unable to comprehend the US budget deficit, O.J. Simpson verdict, Bosnia, and other events. Even in academe, highly socialized sociologists tend to promote some aspects of postmodern doctrine which promulgate ambivalence, ambiguity, and a sense of helplessness concerning world events. The era of innocence is over.

Yet collective innocence does not suffer an easy death. Postemotional society tries desperately to synthetically re-create the innocence of the 1950s.

President Clinton, who began his Presidency on the cynical note that the USA is just one nation among many, tried to re-create the sense that America is special in his address to the nation concerning US involvement in Bosnia. He did not convince most Americans or Congress. The 1950s serve as a focal point for recycling in popular culture from the Nostalgia Channel on cable television to remakes of old movies, songs, themes, and icons. Witness Coca-Cola's recycling of 1950s' Coke advertisements. Pundits talk of America as the lone super-power in the world, but most Americans feel that they are falling behind Japan and Germany in quality of life. Many in the current generation of young Americans mouth the tenets of the American dream, but are not sure if they will ever be able to afford the purchase of a home. Democracy and capitalism are still touted as American gifts to the world – and especially to the former Soviet Union – but there is a sense that these have become empty slogans. If America tried to democratize and capitalize the former Soviet Union, it was a half-hearted and stingy effort at best, and it failed in any case.

If postemotionalism appeared in its incipient stages in the 1960s, it took a long time to mature and ripen. It is my contention that it has reached its apex in the 1990s *vis-à-vis* the television coverage of genocide in Bosnia and the television coverage of the O.J. Simpson trial. Bosnia is not just one instance of genocide among many: Its uniqueness stems from the fact that it was followed closely, often day-by-day, by Americans (and others) on television. This time, nearly everyone in the USA knew about this most evil of crimes, in 'real' time, often on live television, yet felt impotent to stop it, despite feeling horrified. This collective reaction shattered the innocent American can-do attitude of by-gone days. Europeans took the typically European attitude toward Bosnia (namely, it is an instance of tribalism characteristic of the Balkans), and various European countries took positions along the cleavages of traditional alliances and the widespread, racist feeling that this is what the sub-civilized, not-yet-European people in the Balkans do. France, Britain, and Russia essentially became silent collaborators with Serbia. Meanwhile, Americans agonized over Bosnia, yet could not act for various reasons: The ghost of Vietnam haunted them; they were suspicious of their postemotional President, Bill Clinton, whose foreign policy is driven by domestic politics; and they were bombarded with so much emotionally laden information that they felt confused and complained of compassion fatigue. The most important point is that the television coverage of Bosnia forced Americans to take on the role of voyeurs. The rationalization left over from the Holocaust, 'We didn't know,' was shattered for ever. This time, we knew, and realized that knowledge is not enough.

Similarly, the television coverage of the O.J. Simpson trial brought to a head a number of festering lesions in the American social body. Americans began to realize that the state of race relations in the USA had deteriorated incredibly since the racist but still innocent times of Martin Luther King Jr. American cynicism regarding both lawyers and litigation itself reached its culmination point: Most people concluded that wealth can buy an acquittal, thereby shattering one of the cornerstones of American Civil Religion, equal justice under the law.

I have picked these two events in the 1990s against the backdrop of many others for the primary reason that they received the most television coverage, and therefore engaged the post-emotions of Americans. Other events, such as the collapse of Communism, may have been more important historically, but they were not as televised, and did not engage Americans to the same degree. Similarly, there were many other deaths, assassinations, wars, and events between 1960 and the present that might qualify as pivotal events in the eyes of other analysts. I do not intend to be dogmatic about my choice of the events I have chosen for analysis, and leave open the possibility that other events might be just as important. Nevertheless, I maintain the position that the confluence of television with post-other-directed social forces culminated in the cynicism, collapse of the collective consciousness, and atomization of the social fabric that constitute postemotionalism and the end of collective innocence.

Nor do I intend to be dogmatic about choosing the USA or the 1960s as the beginnings of postemotionalism. Such choices are necessarily somewhat arbitrary. One could argue that Nazi Germany was the true birthplace of postemotionalism. (I would reply that Hitler and the Nazis were too inner-directed and obnoxious to be postemotional, though they certainly manipulated real emotions.) One might point to Edward Teller's dreadful victory, the invention of the hydrogen bomb, as the beginning of the end of innocence. And so on. I recognize that the question of where and how postemotionalism began is debatable, and do not intend to close the debate with my choices. Nevertheless, I have given some justifications for making the choices that were made for the purposes of the present discussion.

No one can foretell the future, of course, but if these assumptions are correct, it is reasonable to conclude that there will be many more televised Bosnias and Simpson trials in the future. America may drift along the postemotional cultural trajectory for a long time to come, thereby influencing the postemotionalism of the rest of the world, or it may suddenly revivify its collective consciousness and American Civil Religion. Boldness, courage, happy confidence, faith, and trust may still emerge from the ruins of Americanism. Nonetheless, a theme seems to bind together the events chosen for analysis above with themes touched on in the course of the present discussion: the death of Kennedy, televised death in Bosnia, dead emotions, the dead past, a dead cult, the death of innocence – death. Ironically, so-called postmodernism is obsessed with death without conscious awareness of this fact in its focus on the animation and the simulation of the dead past in cartoons, museums, theme parks, and television. Animation is the simulation of life, but is not life itself. To simulate is to fabricate, ape, imitate, copy, and mimic what is or was alive. Thus, the concept of death demands postemotional analysis.

Reconceptualizing Death

In October 1995, scientists announced that they had found the 500-year-old frozen remains of a woman's body in the Peruvian Andes. She had been sacrificed to Inca gods. 'But beyond the scientific intrigue,' the story ran, 'was an object of morbid curiosity: What did the dead woman look like?':[3]

> What makes her attractive is the same thing that draws people to ancient Egyptian mummies, to the relics of the saints, to bodies that have been dug up from bogs, to the bones of Holocaust victims and to the embalmed corpse of Lenin, which has outlasted Soviet communism. Dead bodies are magnetic not as examples of extinct cultures, proofs of ritual sacrifice, evidence of human atrocities or emblems of political movements but as fleshy humans who chewed with these very teeth, walked on these very legs and furrowed these very brows.[4]

We have seen in the previous chapter on Durkheim that traditional interest in the dead and their relics was tightly controlled by ritual. Today's morbid curiosity is less a matter of even secular relics than a profane interest in death devoid of ritual. Why would people want to 'know' that their predecessors were as human as they are when they already know that?

One outcome of recycling dead emotions and of transforming living emotional cults into unemotional individualism is that death itself becomes an important site of interest for postemotional types. This is not a new observation in and of itself. In *The Transparency of Evil* and other writings, Jean Baudrillard has already suggested that Western culture is dead and therefore fascinated by death. Pope John Paul II recently called Western culture a 'culture of death' because of its proclivity toward abortion, euthanasia, murder, and suicide.[5] Hitler's death still continues to fascinate people.[6] One should also take into account the existence and widespread viewing of films that show real executions and death for teenage entertainment. Even the widely popular animated film industry and the budding virtual reality industry may be reconceptualized as pathological concerns with the illusion of life in contrast to life itself. And of course, death, real or 'animated,' is splattered across television and cinema screens, in graphic detail and in 'living' color. The fear of death is diffused throughout postemotional society in various forms. Concerns with air pollution, the disposal of hazardous substances, and the fear of AIDS are among the various forms that it takes.[7]

Chris Rojek has made the important observations that sites of death and suffering have become tourist attractions in recent years.[8] Tourists flock to Jim Morrison's tomb in Paris, to the site of John F. Kennedy's assassination, to the site of Marilyn Monroe's death, to the site of the burned Branch Davidian compound in Waco, Texas, and so on. Or they take tours of barrios in San Antonio, Texas, or Harlem or other sites of widespread social suffering. One must keep in mind that the tourist industry is just that, an industry that has codified, rationalized, routinized and otherwise converted these experiences of death and suffering along the tenets of Modernity 2.

Nevertheless, it is important to relate the theme of innocence to this morbid fascination on the part of Americans. JFK, Elvis Presley, Marilyn

Monroe, Jimmy Dean, Jim Morrison, and most recently, Selena, all became objects of a sort of cult worship following their deaths. All of them also exhibited characteristics of the innocent American dream alluded to previously. In the unending mourning of their deaths, illustrated by the almost fanatical devotion by Americans to these death figures, Americans may really be mourning the death of the collective ideal of innocence represented by these and other cultural icons.

Another new point I wish to make is that death has been profaned. By profaned, I mean what Durkheim meant by the concept of the profane: Death has been made ordinary, pedestrian, the stuff of everyday experience devoid of the rituals and collective effervescence that used to keep it sacred. In the 1990s, a family is likely to sit down to dinner while watching the evening news on television, wherein they will see the brains of a child splattered on a Sarajevo pavement as a UN peacekeeper looks on, or mutilated corpses as they are being taken away from a train wreck, or the blood-splattered scene of yet another murder, and so on. The family keeps on eating. More poignant is the fact that children no longer regard death as a mystery. Those persons who would never dream of taking a child to a morgue do not seem to notice that Western children are exposed to images of death on television as if they were at a morgue. To some extent, television has become the simulation of a mortuary.

To be sure, death still makes people feel squeamish, uncomfortable, and at times even horrified. Nevertheless, without the collective effervescence and collective rituals in place to create as well as channel genuine emotions of rage and grief following death, especially the death of small children, the contemporary person experiences a mostly private, postemotional grief, rage, and horror. These post-emotions are quickly absorbed into the postemotional pattern of the rest of everyday life. The banality of death in the current *fin de siècle* is what makes it extraordinary, sociologically speaking.

The Break with Traditional Approaches to Death

In this section, I will offer a brief analysis of Robert Hertz's neglected book *Death and the Right Hand*,[9] concentrating on his Durkheimian discussion of the sociological significance of death. Hertz, who was one of Durkheim's most brilliant disciples, had his career cut short by his own death in World War I. I will then move in the following section to discussions of how John F. Kennedy's death and the many deaths in the current Balkan War illustrate the postemotional theme that is the subject of this book.

Hertz completes a thought found in Durkheim's *Elementary Forms* that was merely touched on in the previous chapter, namely, that society cannot allow the death of one of its members to occur without revivifying itself. The concept of 'society' for Durkheim scans the spectrum from the cosmopolitan society of humankind to the smallest society, the family. Hertz elaborates on Durkheim as follows:

Death does not confine itself to ending the visible bodily life of an individual; it also destroys the social being grafted upon the physical individual and to whom the collective consciousness attributed great dignity and importance. The society of which that individual was a member formed him by means of true rites of consecration, and has put to work energies proportionate to the social status of the deceased: his destruction is tantamount to a sacrilege, implying the intervention of powers of the same order but of a negative nature. God's handiwork can be undone only by himself or by Satan. This is why primitive peoples do not see death as a natural phenomenon: it is always due to the action of spiritual powers, either because the deceased has brought disaster upon himself by violating some taboo, or because an enemy has 'killed' him by means of spells or magical practices.[10]

Animals do not have this uniquely human response to death. Typically, animals will sniff the dead carcass and either devour it or walk away if it is one of its kind. But traditional humans represent death cognitively and *emotionally* as an affront to the collective consciousness and as sacrilege that must be undone through funeral rites:

Indeed society imparts its own character of permanence to the individuals who compose it: because it feels itself immortal and wants to be so, it cannot normally believe that its members, above all those in whom it incarnates itself and with whom it identifies itself, should be fated to die. . . . Thus, when a man dies, *society loses in him much more than a unit; it is stricken in the very principle of its life, in the faith it has in itself.*[11] (emphasis added)

For this reason, traditional societies have subscribed to myths that refuse to consider that death is irrevocable: 'The last word must remain with life: the deceased will rise from the grip of death and will return, in one form or another, to the peace of human association.'[12] Christianity guarantees resurrection and life everlasting. Other religions make similar guarantees concerning the indestructibility of the soul. The soul is reincarnated in Hinduism and Buddhism, for example. This general principle seems to hold across diverse societies in the world: Exclusion through death is always followed by a new integration. The fact that postemotional types no longer subscribe to these myths of regeneration to the extent that their ancestors did, because religious affiliation is declining, raises the important question of how postemotional types can participate in the emotional revivification that Hertz describes. The answer seems to be that, increasingly, they cannot. Death is fast becoming a brute fact. Human death all too often is treated as if it were the death of an animal.

In traditional societies, funeral rites were long and elaborate, sometimes lasting for months, because human consciousness could not accept the finality of death:

The brute fact of physical death is not enough to consummate death in people's minds: the image of the recently deceased is still part of the system of things of this world, and looses itself from them only gradually by a series of internal partings.[13]

But contemporary funeral rites grow increasingly faster in pace and shorter in duration. Increasingly, death provokes weak social reactions and funerals become practically instantaneous. (One might characterize this process as a

cultural extension from instant coffee to instant funerals.) Dead members of
society are excluded today quickly and with minimal psychic pain to the
grievers. Marcuse's 'happy consciousness' is extended to death. For example,
in traditional societies the widow was allowed to wear the black clothing of
mourning for many years to mark her sorrow, but such behavior in postemotional society would be regarded as an aberration and might very well result
in psychiatric commitment. Postemotional types are expected to grieve
quickly, return to work, and 'bounce back' in a matter of days.

Using the terminology of previously analyzed theorists, one might paraphrase this insight into the postemotional attitude toward death as follows:
Postemotional society has McDonaldized death. Funerals are quick, efficient, and rational. The contemporary disposal of the dead body has become
part of machine culture as a whole. Nor is this surprising in the context of
previous discussions of the McDonaldization of society. McDonaldization,
as the American embodiment of efficiency and standardization, has extended
to all social realms, including the realm of death.

Another telling cultural indicator of a fundamental change in collective
consciousness toward death is the stark contrast between cemeteries a century
ago and cemeteries today. Older cemeteries, especially in Europe, resemble
arboretums with their flowers and landscaping. They are often so aestheti-
cally pleasing that they still serve as tourist attractions. The living would
often bring fresh flowers, even food, to the graves. Apparently, our ancestors
had a very hard time letting go of their loved ones. This is especially evident
with regard to small children, who used to be killed in large numbers due to
influenza and pneumonia: The heartfelt inscriptions on their tiny graves in
older Texas cemeteries, for example, are enough to bring tears to one's eyes.
In Durkheimian terms, the child is society's investment in its own future,
which makes the death of a child especially devastating.[14]

By contrast, contemporary cemeteries resemble lawns or golf courses for
the most part. A small slab in the grass marks the spot where the ashes of the
dead are buried. There may or may not be plastic flowers at the gravesite –
plastic flowers as the postemotional throwback to the intricate thought and
action that resulted in fresh flowers in the past – but, either way, the living are
not likely to visit the gravesite ever again. The dead are dead and gone, and
life is for the living. This modernist motto runs against the Durkheimian
grain in Hertz's analysis of death, that life can be lived fully only when death
is commemorated and exorcized passionately.

The concluding paragraph of Hertz's analysis bespeaks the naivety and
innocence that I have already noted with regard to all of the social theorists
from the past whose thought has been analyzed in this book:

> For the collective consciousness death is in normal circumstances a temporary
> exclusion of the individual from human society. This exclusion effects his passage
> from the visible society of the living into the invisible society of the dead.
> Mourning, at its origin, is the necessary participation of the living in the mortu-
> ary state of their relative, and lasts as long as this state itself. In the final analysis,
> death as a social phenomenon consists in a dual and painful process of mental

disintegration and synthesis. It is only when this process is completed that society, its peace recovered, can triumph over death.[15]

But postemotional society is unable to triumph over death. For the most part, it no longer subscribes to the mythical beliefs or rituals regarding death that are found in traditional religions. The collective consciousness is weak and treats the death of its members with considerable indifference. The mourning process is never really completed – a final catharsis is not reached, in Freudian terms – because contemporary societies allow less emotional space for passionate grieving in contrast to traditional societies. Ironically, in postemotional societies, death has triumphed over life. This may be one reason among many why postemotional types are obsessed with the simulation of life as well as death: It is a sort of collective 'compulsion to repeat,' the most ineffective and desperate form in Freud's arsenal of forms of catharsis.

The Death of JFK: Catharsis Denied

Many aspects of the assassination of President John F. Kennedy stand out as peculiar when viewed through the traditional eyes of Durkheim and Hertz. First, his assassination was seen and continues to be seen repeatedly either on the original film or in countless simulations. This fact alone profanes his death by making it public. The emotional barrier to death as a sacred event has been severed by the television camera: 'You are there' as portions of his brain are splattered over the back of his limousine. Second, the elaborate funeral that JFK received – which was again televised – was apparently not enough to achieve catharsis and psychic peace among Americans. JFK's death is referred to as an event that changed America,[16] and it continues to be the subject of films, documentaries, and treatises. His image has been co-opted postemotionally by President Bill Clinton, who tries to come across as the new Prince Charming in search of another Camelot.[17] The site of JFK's assassination in Dallas has become a popular tourist attraction. When tourists ask what one can see and do in Dallas, the immediate answer is that one should go to the museum on the sixth floor of the infamous Texas School Book Depository building, where Lee Harvey Oswald allegedly performed this vicious deed. Jim Schutze depicts the site of JFK's death in an interesting and relevant way (from the perspective of the present discussion): 'Like a theme park of grief, Dealey Plaza is now a full-range experience, extending from the sacred to the profane,'[18] from the official JFK museum run by the government to the unofficial conspiracy museums and tours. This observation is commensurate with the general trend we have uncovered in the course of this discussion, that all events in postemotional society, from Thanksgiving and Christmas to birthdays, are celebrated along factionalized lines. Thus, there is a JFK museum aimed at those who believe the Warren Commission and a JFK museum for 'conspiracy nuts.' Third, Oswald was never put on trial, and this factor has denied the American public the emotional catharsis and final sense of closure that traditional trials provided. Fourth, the Warren

Commission report, and its conclusion that Lee Harvey Oswald acted alone, marks the beginning of postemotional reactions to highly publicized deaths. The public had to wait for many years for the Commission to go through a rational, bureaucratized, and highly intellectual exercise to arrive at a conclusion that most people in the USA emotionally reject.

This has become the new norm in dealing with highly visible death: set up a commission to investigate, observe, and coldly analyze an emotionally charged death or deaths, and let the collective conscience hold back its emotional reaction. This is especially true regarding genocide in Bosnia, which has been investigated by seemingly countless commissions over the course of four years. It is worth speculating how this process is different from Max Weber's rationalization thesis and his general claim that the modern world suffers from disenchantment. The difference that Weber did not anticipate is that enchantment rises up, phoenix-like, from the ashes created by excessive rationality: Reality is *re-enchanted* on a rational, systematic basis, hence made postemotional. In the case of JFK, the Warren Commission verdict is made sacrosanct and is tied to the emotional aura of American Civil Religion – it is considered unthinkable that the US government would play a role in killing its head of state. In the Bosnian case, the humanitarian aid is depicted in hallowed tones of Western compassion and goodness, *not* in the coldly cynical language that the West might have sent food and bandages so that it would not have to take a military stand against Serb-sponsored genocide.

This rational-legal brake to emotional catharsis stands in sharp contrast to the relatively swift justice exacted on Nazi leaders and Nazi collaborators following World War II. Even if the Nuremberg War Trials are regarded cynically as a trial of the victors, the more important point is that the collective consciousness accepted the fairly quick verdicts because it needed catharsis. One should recall that anger and the desire for revenge are part of piacular rites for Durkheim. Mussolini was quickly executed by an Italian mob. If one asks any Norwegian what happened to Quisling, the typical reply is, 'He was shot, of course.' The 'of course' would be problematic nowadays. If we perform a thought experiment to ask what would have happened to Quisling in the 1990s, a likely response is that he would have been put on trial, which would have lasted for many years, and he would have purchased the services of the best defense lawyers to ensure that he received a 'fair trial.' In the end, he might even have been acquitted.

I put less stock than most analysts into the other reasons cited as to why JFK's death continues to haunt Americans. The typical reasons that are given include that he was young and charismatic, even handsome; that his death represents a martyrdom akin to the death of Jesus; and that he represented a Camelot dream for most Americans that made his assassination particularly traumatic.[19] But one has to keep in mind that JFK won the Presidential election by the narrowest margin in US history; that he was openly despised by many, especially in the American South; and that he was not a popular President prior to his death. In his Presidency, JFK clearly did not represent the American collective consciousness. What really galvanized the American collective consciousness was the unbelievable (literally) conclusion reached by the Warren Commission that a single bullet fired by Oswald killed Kennedy. Despite the best scientific evidence for the single bullet theory mustered by the Warren Commission, subsequent commissions, and other investigators, the American public remains unconvinced. The widespread suspicion that the US government was involved in JFK's assassination and then covered up this involvement lingers, and is still festering. It leads to the unwelcome and sociologically devastating suspicion that the US government, as the highest representation of the American collective consciousness, participated in the liquidation of its official incarnation. In other words, the American people suspect that the collective consciousness turned against itself, like a cancer. This is a possibility that Durkheim and Hertz never entertained.

There are peoples and nations that would not regard as problematic or traumatic the suspicion that the government assassinated its own President. Such behavior is the rule, not the exception, in some countries. But Americans cannot simply accept such a suspicion, for it tears at the heart of American Civil Religion, which conceives of America as a special place, blessed by God, and as fundamentally democratic. The outcome of the Warren Commission report sowed the seeds of anti-government sentiment, even hatred of the government, that persists in the USA even today. Thus, US government misconduct in Waco and Ruby Ridge touches on the JFK trauma, and is related to the Oklahoma City bombing. The Republican Party in the 1990s rode to power on the widespread wave of anti-government sentiment in the USA. Even the O.J. Simpson trial invoked the ghost of Kennedy: Many commentators observed that if the government might have been implicated in JFK's death, it stood to reason that the government might have framed O.J. Simpson. Such thoughts would have been unthinkable a generation ago. American innocence has been shattered, at least for the present generation.

Incidentally, Israel is experiencing a somewhat similar sociological phenomenon following the assassination of its Prime Minister at the hands of a Jew in November 1995. Most Israelis were shocked that a Jew could kill a fellow Jew. Again, objectively speaking, this is no more shocking than the possibility that a government might assassinate its own head of state. But in the context of the Holocaust, and of the cultural belief that Israel, like the USA, is a special place, albeit for different reasons, this Israeli reaction is understandable. It is a lighter shade of the phenomenon uncovered regarding JFK's death: the collective consciousness turning on itself. Of course, I am not claiming or implying that there are any other similarities between the assassinations of JFK and Rabin.

Returning to JFK, one observes that widespread anti-government sentiment in the USA has not been transformed into riots or outright rebellion or violence (with the possible exception of the Oklahoma City bombing). It has been transformed, instead, into widespread cynicism concerning the government, as indicated by opinion polls. This means that catharsis has not been achieved, and that JFK's death remains a major trauma in the American psyche, alongside the Vietnam War.

A field trip to the site of JFK's assassination in Dallas reveals other clues about the significance of his death. The first thing that strikes the visitor is that there is no marker, plaque, or monument on or near Dealey Plaza to commemorate his death. Of course, everyone knows the general area where the event occurred, and 'conspiracy tour' guides can be seen directing individuals to specific places in the area where specific events occurred. But that is beside the sociological point. A monument or a commemorative marker or even a statue would have served to fulfill some of the revivifying functions that Durkheim clearly felt were necessary. One of the tour guides even remarked that it is a disgrace that the city of Dallas does not maintain the grass in the grassy knoll in good condition. One detects the Durkheimian echo in his comment that this is sacred ground because of its association with JFK's death, and should be treated with some sort of visible awe or reverence. But clearly, it is treated as if it were any other portion of Dallas.

There are two museums in the vicinity of the assassination site. One is run by the government and is located on the sixth floor of the Texas School Book Depository building. The other is referred to as the 'conspiracy museum'[20] and is located a few blocks from the assassination site. It is fascinating, from a Durkheimian perspective, that the visitor cannot experience an unequivocal revivification of American Civil Religion *vis-à-vis* JFK's death. Rather, his death has Balkanized Americans into two groups, the conspiracy believers versus the believers in the government version of what happened. One must pass through metal detectors to enter the government museum, which is an eerie reminder of the fear of violence in American society. The visitor is handed a taperecorder and set of headphones with which to listen to a pre-recorded lecture as he or she walks, in virtual solitude, despite the physical presence of others, through the exhibits. The exhibits basically give the visitor the government 'line': The Warren Commission's conclusions are held to be the right ones; conspiracy theories are mentioned and dismissed. There is no opportunity to engage in any sort of collective effervescence because the visitor is alone with his or her taperecorded message. It is a pre-packaged experience, the McDonaldization of the death of JFK. JFK's death is experienced through the inner-directed coldly rational techniques characteristic of *Gesellschaft*. The government museum tries to preserve the 'happy consciousness' in America: Oswald was a 'lone nut' who killed JFK, but America is a good, happy place.

Nevertheless, it is surprising to go through the pages of comments written by some visitors in the guest book that is to be found at the end of the tour. A sort of collective effervescence tries to break through the inner-directed cultural restraints in the museum. Page after page is filled with cynical statements such as: 'The CIA did it'; 'Lee Harvey Oswald didn't act alone'; 'My own government did this;' and so on. It is true that such comments cannot be relied upon for drawing conclusions because self-selection may be operating: Cynical visitors may be the ones who write in the guest book while those visitors who agree with the government version of what happened are reluctant to express their feelings. It would be an interesting study, nevertheless, to do a content analysis or other empirical study of the comments in the guest books spanning several years. And it should be kept in mind that the overall cynicism found in the guest book is commensurate with the cynicism concerning the government version of what happened that is found repeatedly in opinion polls.

The conspiracy museum is another matter entirely, sociologically speaking. Visitors can be found engaged in passionate discussion with each other and with the tour guides. Unlike the government museum, the conspiracy museum offers bus tours that purport to re-create the entire story behind the assassination: One retraces JFK's entire visit to Dallas, starting with the airport. The guides stop the bus at various points and take the visitors outside to offer their theories of what 'really' happened, and where. The tour includes: a visit to the picket fence where conspiracy theorists believe a second gunman waited for JFK; Lee Harvey Oswald's residence; Jack Ruby's residence; the street on which officer Tippitt was shot; the theater in which Oswald was arrested; even the police station where Oswald was killed by Ruby – among other sites. There is plenty of collective effervescence: On the tours that I took, the visitors engaged each other and the guides in what seemed to be spontaneous and passionate discussions.

Several sociological factors distinguished the conspiracy tour from a visit to the government museum. First, in a Durkheimian sense, the visitor engages in a ritual somewhat akin to the Stations of the Cross (if one really likens JFK's death to the death of Jesus) by visiting and stopping at specific 'sacred' sites (albeit, all unmarked *vis-à-vis* JFK's death). Second, the visitor experiences what Walter Benjamin called 'aura' rather than experiencing photographs of a reality that lies outside the sixth floor of the School Book Depository. (It really is strange that a museum would try to re-create reality second-hand when some of it is so close at hand.) Third, the conspiracy museum staff did not seem to have to prod visitors very hard to try to convince them that the government was capable of conspiring in and covering up the JFK assassination. Visitors seemed primed for this message. Again, self-selection is at work, without a doubt. Nevertheless, one wonders whether the conspiracy museum would draw any visitors had the government commemorated JFK's death along Durkheimian lines by erecting monuments and sites that would promote collective effervescence. It seems to this observer that in the absence of sites and rituals for a collective effervescence that would bind people into American Civil Religion at the sites related to JFK's death, an anti-government 'religion' has sprung up in its place.

From Dallas to Sarajevo

If JFK's death is a trauma that still needs collective catharsis, ritual, and effervescence, and the absence of outlets for channelling these needs fosters the JFK mystique such that his unexpiated death symbolizes in some ways the death of emotional life in America, something similar seems to be happening in relation to the horrifying deaths in Bosnia. The American television-viewing public has been exposed to a steady stream of images from Bosnia that include blood-drenched streets in which innocent men, women, and children have been slaughtered. Objectively speaking, such slaughter is no more unusual than the assassinations of national leaders. But, to repeat, both sets of events involve televised imagery, thereby involving millions of people emotionally. The US government's insistence that a single bullet fired by a single madman killed JFK has an effect on the masses similar to the insistence by the UN and other international bodies that it does not know who is responsible for the slaughter in Bosnia, and if it did, it would be powerless to do anything about it. Such bureaucratized newspeak is almost instinctively resisted by the masses, who, to the extent that some fragments of collective consciousness are left intact, demand emotional catharsis and effervescence in response to death. As Hertz noted, any other response would make humans less than human.

The UN indicted Serb leaders Radovan Karadžić and Ratko Mladić for crimes against humanity and genocide, but, as of this writing, the USA and other Western nations refused to make the Belgrade regime hand them over for trial as a condition for the peace agreement in Dayton, Ohio.[21] The rationalization offered by the USA is that handing over Karadžić and Mladić to the International War Crimes Tribunal would jeopardize the peace process.[22] From a Durkheimian perspective, their proposed trial would be more than a legal exercise. It would have been an emotional catharsis that would have produced collective effervescence, and eventually, emotional healing.[23] But as in the case of the televised murder of JFK, catharsis has been denied with regard to televised genocide in Bosnia.

To be sure, the death of innocents in Bosnia seems far away for Americans. But given that Durkheim conceived of the collective consciousness as a spectrum that ranges from cosmopolitan humanity to one's immediate family, even geographically distant death demands the revivification of life that is essential for healthy social functioning. This is especially true regarding Bosnia because, as I have noted already several times, television brought the slaughter into the living rooms of ordinary Americans. (Nor should one overlook the fact that JFK's death was traumatic for many persons around the globe, and for the same reason: television.)

Let me begin this segment of the discussion with a thought experiment by imagining what should have been the idealistic Western response to the Serbian war of genocidal aggression against some of its neighboring countries that used to be part of the former Yugoslavia. This response should have been based on the real Enlightenment tradition of the West, the principles enshrined in the UN Charter, and the findings of the world's respected fact-gathering organizations concerning the culpability of the various actors in this war. Croatia and Bosnia-Herzegovina are real, duly recognized nation-states and members of the United Nations. Article 51 of the UN Charter specifies that all nations have an inherent right to self-defense, which means that this right existed prior to the creation of the United Nations and that it cannot be abridged for any reason. Fact-gathering organizations such as the UN, the US State Department, the CIA, Helsinki Watch, and others have concluded unanimously that the Serbs have committed 90 percent of the atrocities in this Balkan War and have committed 100 percent of the genocide[24] according to the UN definition of genocide, that is, the organized, planned, and systematic destruction of a people in whole *or in part* based on ethnicity, religion, or other group identity. Thus, if the West had taken all these factors seriously, it would have been obligated to respect the territorial integrities of Croatia and Bosnia-Herzegovina, lift the illegal weapons embargo imposed on these nation-states at Serbia's request, and do all that it could to put a stop to the genocide as soon as it had been ascertained.

While all this sounds coldly logical and rational, it actually bespeaks a significant role for the emotions. This is because the UN Charter's obligation for member states to take all steps necessary to stop genocide may involve, in this case, punishing military action against Serbia. In a Durkheimian sense, punishment always involves the emotional complex related to revenge.[25] When the state punishes domestic or international criminals, it reaffirms society's collective norms and revivifies the collective consciousness. This is one of Durkheim's most important insights regarding the sociology of law. But Durkheim also claimed that if the state fails to punish crime, society is diminished and the collective consciousness is weakened. Thus, the international community's failure to stop widely known genocide over the course of four years in Bosnia is having the same effect on the cosmopolitan collective consciousness as a domestic government's failure to punish murder might have on the national collective consciousness. The state must punish crime, not out of cruelty, but because this organized form of vengeance is part of society's need to revivify itself in the face of all crime, and especially crime that leads to murder.

The West did not take these steps, which are rooted in its ideals, Enlightenment tradition, and respect for the rule of law. Instead, Western media, diplomats and politicians invented a host of postemotional rationalizations and excuses for letting the slaughter continue up to the signing of the Dayton Accords in 1995. The standard responses to the Balkan War were as follows: All sides are equally guilty; the fighting is horrible, but we can't do anything to stop it; the bloodshed is contained in the territory of the former Yugoslavia so it has no larger meaning for those who do not live there; Croatia and Bosnia-Herzegovina are not 'real countries' so that this is a 'civil war'; lifting the arms embargo would only prolong the fighting. These rationalizations have eased Western consciences in the short run, but will not stand up to honest scrutiny in the long run. More importantly, they have damaged the international collective consciousness.

In the first place, as we have just noted, respected Western fact-gathering organizations have concluded that the overwhelming majority of the atrocities and 100 percent of the *genocide* in the Balkan War were committed by Serbs. Genocide is the most serious of international war crimes, and the West failed to put a stop to it. The Dayton Accords were merely one step in a long series of appeasement. The reality of genocide was obscured by using the Serbs' clever and neo-Orwellian use of the term 'ethnic cleansing,' and then charging that all sides have engaged in it. It is true that all sides in this Balkan War have committed atrocities, but this does not mean that all sides have committed genocide, nor that all sides are morally equivalent. One should recall that during and immediately following World War II, the Allies also committed considerable atrocities, ranging from revenge killings of Germans and their collaborators to the merciless bombing of civilians in Dresden, Tokyo, Hiroshima, and Nagasaki, among other sites. On a recent visit to the Netherlands, I learned that Nijmigen was bombed 'accidentally' by the British, who meant to bomb German civilians across the nearby border. But no respectable historian would conclude that the Allies and Nazis are morally equivalent. Thus, the revenge killings committed by some Croats of Serbs in the liberated Krajina region, while deplorable, are neither the same as Serb-sponsored genocide nor the moral equivalent of Serbian atrocities. Serbs in the Krajina fled at the urging of Serbian leaders in the Krajina. By contrast, Croats and Muslims were expelled by Serbs with carefully organized terror that included mass rape, torture, the slashing of throats, and other ghastly deeds. All this is documented rigorously in Norman Cigar's recent book, *Genocide in Bosnia-Herzegovina*.[26] But it is also well known to anyone who reads the *New York Times* faithfully.

Second, Croatia and Bosnia-Herzegovina are 'real' countries. The West supervised the elections that led to their secession, the drafting of their constitutions, and their implementation of human rights standards. If one persists in claiming that their situation is not the same as Hitler's taking over of *bona fide* nation-states, a moment's reflection will reveal that the situation is actually chillingly similar. Hitler claimed that Austria and portions of Czechoslovakia and Poland were not real countries, and that he was actually liberating the Germans living there. Similarly, the propaganda emanating from Belgrade insists that Bosnian Muslims are not real Muslims, but are Serbs, and that Croats are really Serbs, and that the Serbs' genocidal campaign is really a campaign to 'liberate' these counterfeit Serbs.

Third, the argument that lifting the arms embargo would have only prolonged the fighting would sound different to Western ears today if the United States had said to Churchill, when he begged Roosevelt for assistance to fight the Nazis, 'No, our help would only prolong your agony. Join the rest of Europe and succumb to the Nazis.' The euphoria, atmosphere of boldness, and *innocent joy* that followed American ascension to a world power following World War II stems in part from the widespread collective belief that the USA stood up to and defeated fascism. The consequences of this revivification of American Civil Religion lasted through the first decades of the Cold War and did not begin to diminish until the Vietnam War. But by the same Durkheimian logic, it seems to be the case that America's capitulation to Europe regarding the appeasement of Serbian genocidal aggression is deepening the wounds to American Civil Religion that the Vietnam War inflicted.

Fourth, it is not true that the West was powerless to stop Serbian genocidal aggression. The swift victory by the Croats over their Serbian occupiers in the Krajina demonstrated clearly that the Serbs are not invincible, even though they enjoy a decisive military advantage because they took over most of the armament of the Yugoslav Federal Army. The logical conclusion drawn by the West should have been that with the lifting of the arms embargo, the Croat–Muslim federation could have driven out the Serb occupiers from Bosnia-Herzegovina as well, with no loss to Western lives. The Bosnian government has maintained consistently the position that it was asking not for Western soldiers to fight on their behalf, but to be given the tools, in Churchill's words, to finish the job of liberation.

Fifth, this Balkan War was not really confined to the former Yugoslavia. Thanks to the miracle of television, and the massive coverage given this war – second only to the media coverage of the O.J. Simpson trial – this war entered the living rooms of nearly everyone in Western, industrialized nations. Thus, and in contrast to other instances of genocide, ranging from the Holocaust to more recent instances in Rwanda and Cambodia, this one in the Balkans was televised. Let me repeat that the comparison to the Holocaust does *not* mean that genocide in Bosnia is comparable to the number of Jews killed in the Holocaust, nor the effort to exterminate all Jews, nor even to the Holocaust as a sacred site of Jewish memory. But in addition to being all these things, the Holocaust was *also* a site of genocide, and is comparable to other sites of genocide strictly on the basis of genocide.

Thus, the rationalization given for genocide in World War II, that 'We didn't know,' does not hold for the genocide in the Balkans. Thanks to the information revolution, nearly everyone in Western countries knew about this genocide. But this fact raises serious moral issues, ranging from the question, 'Would genocide in World War II have been stopped had people known about it?,' to why knowledge of genocide in the 1990s did not lead to the appropriate moral and military action to put a stop to it. A possible sobering answer to the first question is that no, the Holocaust would not have been stopped. A possible affirmative answer would assume that inner-directed types would have been more likely to stop genocide had they possessed mass-knowledge of it, but the caveat to that conjecture is that the mass dissemination of information via television is commensurate with other-directedness. Sociologically speaking, television is more than a technological invention. Its widespread use must go hand in hand with a particular type of social character, and what Riesman called other-directedness seems to be the type most suited to it. In any event, in the postemotional 1990s, 'We didn't know' was finally exposed as a rationalization, and can no longer be accepted as a truism. It has become problematic. The answer to the second question posed above is that mere information is not enough to translate knowledge into appropriate moral action. This is something that supporters of the information revolution do not consider, for they seem to assume that knowledge alone is sufficient to create a global community. What they overlook is action based on information assumes an emotional base, and this emotional base is ideally provided by a healthy collective consciousness.

Sixth, the Balkan War became internationalized early because of the involvement of NATO, the United Nations, Russia, much of the Islamic world, and many European nations. It was a 'world war,' not in the sense of many countries going to war with each other but in terms of the focus, money, alliances formed (for example, Russia, Serbia, and Greece against the West) and alliances discredited (such as NATO, the CSCE, the European Union, and the UN). The Poles, for example, regard as hollow NATO's promises that it will protect them from a feared Russian invasion. Analysts such as Francis Fukuyama who dismiss the genocide in the former Yugoslavia as irrelevant to the West because it was 'contained' geographically fail to take into account that it was not contained in any other way. On the contrary, it was a highly international event.

The evil of mostly secret genocide in World War II led to numerous scholarly efforts to understand the minds of the Nazi criminals who were responsible for it. The healthy attempt at international revivification of collective morality focused on the question, 'How was Auschwitz possible?' The evil of the highly visible genocide in the Balkans in the 1990s must eventually lead to scholarly efforts to understand not only the minds of the criminals who perpetrated it, but also the minds of those who stood by, watched it, and failed to stop it decisively and militarily. As mentioned previously, critical theory took on the task of attempting to understand fascism sociologically. But it seems that postmodernism is inadequate for the task of understanding the collective voyeurism of the 1990s, and that postemotionalism might be better suited for this task.

One such effort at understanding the minds of the voyeurs – namely, the television-viewing public – is made by the postmodernist writer Jean Baudrillard. I have already analyzed his three articles published in 1995 in *La Libération* on the international significance of the Balkan War. I have noted that I take issue with his conclusion that the West is imposing its disorder onto the world *vis-à-vis* Bosnia. Baudrillard's version of postmodernism tries to depict a social world of randomly circulating, rootless fictions that have no referent or origin. Using postemotionalism, I argue that the fictions are ordered and rooted in dead emotions from the various histories of countries that are usually referred to as Western.

Thus, the West did not wish to confront Greece's seemingly silly quibbling with neighboring Macedonia over its name because it did not wish to confront a NATO ally. The memory of Alexander the Great was actually revived in the 1990s by the Greeks in this dispute. The British were still acting on their perceived 'lesson of history' that in dealing with regional conflicts one should isolate the combatants and support the strongest party. Thus, in the Balkan Crisis of the 1860s, in which the Turks persecuted Christians in Bosnia and Bulgaria, London supported the stronger Turks. It followed a similar strategy in Ethiopia, the Spanish Civil War, and in response to Hitler's annexation of Czechoslovakia. What some historians call British appeasement is still seen by London as the right lesson to be drawn from history, and was applied in the Balkans. But this is a postemotional lesson, as if the British government were stuck in a time warp from a century ago. The British were also anxious to contain so-called 'German expansionism' in the Balkans and to send a message to secessionist-minded folks in Scotland, Wales, and Northern Ireland that secessionism does not pay.

The French referred to the Serbs as their allies, but in fact both France and Serbia suffer from a similar postemotional complex of failing to admit the full extent of their collaboration with the Nazis. The former President of France, François Mitterrand refused to acknowledge the reality of Vichy by dismissing it as a non-French phenomenon. The Serbs similarly simply deny their own Nazi collaboration during World War II.[27] Thus, both the French and the Serbs are suffering from a postemotional revisionism in their ostentatious claims that they were America's unequivocal allies against fascism.

The United States is still suffering from its Vietnam Syndrome, its humiliating loss in that war and the divisiveness it caused. As a result of this wound to its Civil Religion, the USA is willing to enter wars only if they are short, winnable, and, above all, if they do not result in a sizeable number of body bags of its soldiers sent home. Thus, the USA saw in the Balkans a 'Vietnam quagmire.'

The Russians saw in this Balkan War a chance to compensate for their own humiliating loss of status in the former Soviet Empire, to 'pay back' the West for the hardships caused by the imposition of pure capitalism following the collapse of Communism, and for pursuing their own sort of Monroe Doctrine. Thus, the Russians upheld the Serbs as their 'little Slavic brothers,' called the NATO air strikes 'genocide' against the Serbs, and continue to persecute the Muslims in Chechnya with impunity as they threaten neighboring countries that used to constitute the Soviet Empire. The West is all too willing to oblige them rather than risk a confrontation with Russia.

As of this writing, the latest excuse offered by the West is that 'this time' the 'new peace plan' signed in Dayton, Ohio, on 21 November 1995 will work so there is no need to engage in a sobering analysis of its motives. But consider that President Clinton's 'new' peace plan is actually the 'old' plan for the ethnic partition of Bosnia-Herzegovina that was offered by the Europeans early in the conflict; that ethnic partition is a repulsive idea that runs contrary to Western ideals of multiculturalism; and that this plan actually rewards Serbian genocidal aggression. President Clinton's mastery of Newspeak in masking these realities so that he can be hailed as a peacemaker rivals any of George Orwell's illustrations. I could go on analyzing the West's excuses and rationalizations for not taking a decisive stand against televised Serbian genocidal aggression, but in the end, all these excuses amount to the same thing: The West refused to abide by its most hallowed principles, and it chose to ignore the findings of its allegedly respected fact-gathering organizations. It expressed other-directed curdled indignation at the Serbs, but was unwilling to take punitive military action that would have revivified collective morality. Even the 'massive NATO air strikes' against the Serbs were nothing more than massive NATO pinpricks, because NATO refused to bomb the 300 tanks and artillery pieces that surrounded Sarajevo. Such action would have made NATO seem less than 'neutral.' The West preached a phony, provincial multiculturalism for 'us,' but tolerated genocide for 'them' in the Balkans. 'They' were deemed unworthy of 'our' multiculturalism. They had to settle for ethnic partition.

In *The Anatomy of Human Destructiveness*,[28] Erich Fromm examined the criminal minds of Hitler, Himmler, and Stalin. But for reasons stated above, the circumstances surrounding genocide in the Balkans have changed from World War II genocide because of massive media coverage. In line with Hannah Arendt, Erich Fromm, and others who analyzed the 'minds of the criminals' from the Nazi era, one could examine outpourings from the mind of the indicted Serb war criminal Radovan Karadžić, as well as the rationalizations of his henchmen. (They are all too willing to give their points of view on Western television.) We would not learn much more about them than we already know about such criminals based on studies of Hitler, Himmler, and Stalin. What we really need is to probe into the reasons why Westerners were generally taken in by the rationalizations for genocide offered by indicted Serbian war criminals.

The postemotional rationalizations I am referring to include the following by Radovan Karadžić: The Serbs were forced to commit pre-emptive geno-cide against Croats and Muslims due to fears of them that stem from atrocities committed by the World War II Croatian Nazi collaborationist regime, the Ustasha, and fears of Bosnian Muslims harking back to the Turkish victory over the Serbs in 1389. Karadžić's right-hand man, General Ratko Mladić, adds that the Serbs have been the West's consistent allies. For example, Roger Cohen writes in the *New York Times*:

> General Ratko Mladić, the commander of the Bosnian Serbs, accused NATO of attacking the Serbs in a more brutal way than Hitler. . . . The reference to Hitler by General Mladić underscores the way in which the Serbs' war-ravaged history, marked at times by stoical heroism, and their contribution to allied victories in two world wars, has been repeatedly invoked by political and military leaders. . . . They ask why the Serbs are thus persecuted and conclude that it is all an American-led plot against them. . . . They have suffered unduly.[29]

Through postemotional Newspeak, Mladić became the object of sympathy. Thus, David Binder

> called it 'debatable' whether General Mladić, whom he has met several times, is a war criminal. 'I think he [Mladić] has been trying to create a situation that would lead to peace in Bosnia for some time. I think he can live quite comfortably with a genuine peace settlement.'[30]

The actual history of the former Yugoslavia is much more complex: The crimes of the Croatian Ustashe were terrible, but the Serbian Chetniks also collabo-rated with the Nazis in addition to opposing them at times during World War II. Serbia was not just *occupied* by the Nazis, but actively *collaborated* with them under the quisling rule of Milan Nedić.

But any respectable historian and journalist should have known that pup-pet regimes in World War II Yugoslavia, including that of Serbia, collaborated with the fascists. This should not be surprising given the larger context of fascist collaboration even by America's allies France and Italy. The rationalizations and distortions offered by Serbian war criminals in the 1990s should have been challenged and debunked on the basis of facts, but clearly were not. Most commentators who denounced Serbian atrocities in the 1990s nevertheless reserved sympathy for Serbian fears of Croats and Muslims that supposedly led them to commit evil – as if Serbia's contemporary victims would not have had good grounds to fear the Serbs based upon their history. This widespread acquiescence by Westerners to postemotional arguments really raises the haunting question of how post-World War II genocide is possible.

The reply based on the postemotionalism concept includes the following: Other-directed types are prone to ambivalence because they are sensitive to all sides of every issue, including the point of view of the victimizer. This is especially true if the victimizers come across on the television screen as charming and sincere. The result of this sensitivity is that other-directed postemotional types are left feeling confused and unable to translate indignation into action. The result of this inability to act decisively is that the senseless death of innocents, even when it is widely known, goes unpunished. Society is unable to reaffirm life and to revivify itself. The collective consciousness is weakened and Balkanized. A moral climate is established internationally in which the death of innocents, including genocide, is tolerated. This toleration further weakens the collective consciousness thus further promoting similar evil. A vicious spiral has been established that will not be broken until collective morality is revivified.

Conclusions

Innocence is not the same as authenticity, though the two phenomena overlap to some extent. Innocence is a child-like quality that is integral to the healthy functioning of individuals as well as societies. The innocent possess 'happy confidence,' are willing to take risks because they don't fully realize the dangers of the world, and they look forward boldly to the future. No child, or society for that matter, could possibly develop in a normal fashion without some degree of innocence. On the other extreme of innocence, the corrupted, knowledgeable human agent of the modernist era simply knows too much to feel happy confidence, boldness, or genuine optimism concerning the future. The postemotional type has been the victim of guile and circumstance too many times to maintain an innocent attitude.

Yet innocence is such an integral aspect of healthy living that it is hard to let go of it. Thus, and not surprisingly, an innocence industry springs up. Postemotional types try to reinvent innocence synthetically. President Clinton reinvents himself *vis-à-vis* the innocent image of JFK.[31] Postemotional society is obsessed with its children; it spoils them even as it corrupts them with knowledge of AIDS, cocaine use, and other evils before they are ready to apprehend such things. One cannot escape the conclusion that postemotional adults are desperately trying to retrieve their lost innocence through their children. Perhaps parents have done this to some extent in all eras, but in the postemotional era the window of opportunity has shrunk to only a few years: Children grow up faster than ever in postemotional society. Disneyworld stands as a shrine to synthetic innocence.

The loss of innocence helps to explain Western obsession with specific cult figures – especially following their deaths. Elvis, Marilyn, Selena, and others captured this sense of innocence as defined above. Many of them have become cult heroes in Western countries other than the USA, yet they incarnate primarily the American dream of innocence, which, incidentally, used to inspire many other peoples in the world. America was the land of happy confidence, of boldness and optimism. In recent years, America has come to resemble France, Britain, and Germany in its lack of self-confidence, anxiety, and uneasiness about the future. Thus, people cling to the past, to idealized nostalgias of innocent times.

Death has always been an affront to human consciousness, on the individual as well as collective levels. If one takes the Durkheimians seriously, it seems to be the case that traditional societies responded to death on an emotional level of *innocence*. Simply put, the innocent soul cannot let death have the last word. Life must have the last word for the innocent. Society had to revivify life, and its own existence, in the face of death. It did this simply, spontaneously, and naturally – without rationalization – through the many rituals that traditional societies developed in response to death.

By contrast, postemotional society rationalizes death. We have noted this with regard to the death of JFK as well as the deaths in Bosnia. Governments as well as the information media offer rationalizations, facts, and figures instead of emotional outlets for catharsis, from the single-bullet theory to the incredible array of excuses offered for why genocide in Bosnia could not be stopped. More often than not, these rationalizations seek to justify *lack of confidence*, not happy confidence. Postemotional societies rationalize a sense of impotence and a pervasive sense of innocence lost. JFK's death could not have been prevented. Genocide in Bosnia could not be stopped by NATO, the world's mightiest military alliance! Postemotional types are clever, and don't really believe the rationalizations. This may be one significant reason why JFK's death continues to haunt America. And for the same reason, Bosnia may haunt the Western world for many years to come.

Notes

1. David Harvey, *The Condition of Postmodernity* (Oxford: Basil Blackwell, 1989).

2. David Riesman, 'Innocence of the *Lonely Crowd*,' *Society*, 27, 2 (1990), pp. 76–9.

3. Sarah Boxer, 'Body Language: The Lure of the Dead,' *New York Times*, 29 October 1995, p. E1.

4. Ibid.

5. 'Culture of Death?' *Commonweal*, 21 April 1995, p. 3.

6. Stephen Kinzer, 'The Day of Hitler's Death: Even Now, New Glimpses,' *New York Times*, 4 May 1995, p. A5.

7. Ed Vulliamy, 'Death in Dreamland,' *World Press Review*, 42 (1995), pp. 38–9.

8. Chris Rojek, 'Indexing, Dragging and the Social Construction of Tourist Sights,' in Chris Rojek and John Urry, *Touring Cultures: Transformations in Travel and Theory* (London: Routledge, 1996).

9. Robert Hertz, *Death and the Right Hand* (Aberdeen: Cohen & West, [1907] 1960). I shall concentrate on the essay in the book entitled 'A Contribution to the Study of the Collective Representation of Death.'

10. Ibid., p. 77.

11. Ibid.

12. Ibid., p. 78.

13. Ibid., p. 81.

14. Hertz and Durkheim take diametrically opposing positions on the death of children. It would derail the present discussion to dwell on this internal debate. I have taken Durkheim's position.

15. Hertz, *Death and the Right Hand*, p. 86.

16. Michael R. Beschloss, 'The Day That Changed America,' *Newsweek*, 22 November 1993, pp. 60–2.

17. Gwen Ifill, 'Clinton and Kennedy: In 30 Years, a Full Circle,' *New York Times*, 25 August 1993, p. A10; Richard Reeves, 'Why Clinton Wishes He Were JFK,' *Washington Monthly*, September 1995, pp. 16–20.

18. Jim Schutze, 'Selling JFK,' *Houston Chronicle*, 22 November 1995, p. A1.

19. See Arthur M. Schlesinger, 'Camelot Revisited,' *The New Yorker*, 5 June 1995, p. 33; Max Holland, 'After Thirty Years: Making Sense of the Assassination,' *Reviews in American History*, 22 (1994), pp. 191–209; Steven D. Stark, 'The Cultural Meaning of the Kennedys,' *Atlantic Monthly*, January 1994, pp. 18–36; Kenneth W. Thompson, 'John F. Kennedy and Revisionism,' *Virginia Quarterly Review*, 70 (1994), pp. 430–43; Robert Niemi, 'JFK as Jesus,' *Journal of American Culture*, 16 (1993), pp. 35–40; Wendy Leigh, 'Prince Charming,' *Ladies' Home Journal*, November 1993, pp. 202–3; Richard Reeves, 'Why Camelot and Kennedy Endure on TV,' *TV Guide*, 20 November 1993, pp. 22–5.

20. David Barboza, 'Conspiracy Museum Draws Visitors Who Consider the Plot the Thing,' *New York Times*, 28 May 1995, p. A22.

21. Alan Cowell, 'War's Crimes and Punishments, Then and Now,' *New York Times*, 20 November 1995, p. A4.

22. Elaine Sciolino, 'US Tells Leaders of Balkan States to Wind Up Talks,' *New York Times*, 20 November 1995, p. A1.

23. Though they do not use Durkheimian terminology, Anthony Lewis and Judge Richard Goldstone make a similar case for the need to put Mladić and Karadžić on trial. See Anthony Lewis, 'No Peace Without Justice,' *New York Times*, 20 November 1995, p. A11.

24. For extensive documentation of these and related figures, see Stjepan G. Meštrović, *Genocide After Emotion: The Postemotional Balkan War* (London: Routledge, 1996).

25. Émile Durkheim, *The Division of Labor in Society* (New York: Free Press, [1893] 1933).

26. Norman Cigar, *Genocide in Bosnia-Herzegovina* (College Station, TX: Texas A&M University Press, 1995).

27. See Philip J. Cohen, *Serbia at War With History* (College Station, TX: Texas A&M University Press, 1996).

28. Erich Fromm, *The Anatomy of Human Destructiveness* (New York: Holt, Rinehart and Winston, 1973).

29. Roger Cohen, 'Calling History to Arms: Serbs Invoke Their Past,' *New York Times*, 8 September 1995, p. A1.

30. Pamela Taylor, 'Closeup,' Voice of America broadcast, 28 September 1995.

31. Alison Mitchell and Todd S. Purdum, 'Clinton the Conciliator Finds His Line in Sand,' *New York Times*, 2 January 1996, p. A1.

7
Conclusions: The Final Triumph of Mechanization

Nearing the end of this discussion, the distinctive aspects of the contemporary social world conceived as postemotional as opposed to modern – based on the Enlightenment project – or postmodern – based on rebelling against the Enlightenment project – should be apparent. The Enlightenment project itself is spurious in the society of simulation. The need to make it a mechanized project demonstrates that its authentic power has been lost. Postemotional society is made possible by a social character that succeeded Riesman's other-directedness in which the bulk of people's emotional reactions have been reduced to being 'nice' versus indignant. The collective consciousness has all but disappeared, and has been succeeded by widespread Balkanization and social fission – in Western, industrial countries, and not just the Balkans. The cleavages in postemotional society are not exclusively ethnic, but also include gender, sexual preference, life-style, and a myriad of other group identifications. Yet despite this underlying lack of social unity, postemotional society is an extension of the cult of the machine such that emotions have been McDonaldized, petrified, routinized, and otherwise made artificial. Mechanization has extended its imperialistic realm from technology and industry to colonize the last bastion of nature: the emotions. Many writers from the previous turn of the century foreshadowed but could not quite discern the full ramifications of this momentous social transformation, including Henry Adams in his writings on the dynamo; Fyodor Dostoevsky in his portrait of the underground man who lives in the unnatural, artificially constructed city of St Petersburg; and Émile Durkheim in his dark vision of the social disintegration caused by modernity – among many other writers from the previous *fin de siècle*. Most everyone today knows what post-emotions must be presented in social interaction in order to make it run smoothly and efficiently. George Orwell worried about fascism and totalitarianism based on the fledgling Newspeak that he uncovered. His fears were proved correct, and he did foresee World War II in the crystal ball that was the Spanish Civil War.[1] But postemotionalism holds the potential for degenerating further into an entirely new form of totalitarianism, one that is so 'nice' and charming that it cannot lead to indignation or rebellion. The postemotional packaging of the Balkan War[2] is the contemporary crystal ball into a disturbing social future for reasons that have already been analyzed at length.

Of course, books should not end on such discordant notes. A postemotional writing style already exists and requires that one should expose the good as well as bad aspects of any phenomenon under discussion, the hopeful in addition to the distressing, the optimistic scenarios to offset the pessimistic. If I were to follow this style, I should end this book with an analysis of the positive aspects of postemotionalism. At the very least, I am expected to list the ways that an individual who might be outraged by postemotionalism should fight it. 'What can we do about it?' is a fairly typical American response to this or any other problem. I am sympathetic to such a reaction, which is rooted in a long-standing American tradition of populism and resistance to centralized authority of any sort going back to the rebellion against British colonial rule. But the heritage of Durkheim's version of sociology should make one aware that the individual is powerless to change the course of social events without the help of his or her fellows through collective effervescence. And it must be a spontaneous, genuine collective effervescence, not the deliberately rehearsed and planned public spectacles that have been the subject of postmodern analyses.

In his book *The McDonaldization of Society*,[3] George Ritzer foreshadows the concept of postemotionalism. Phrased differently, his argument can be extended to the realm of the emotions. Ritzer is correct that McDonald's stands for the values for efficiency, quantification, calculation, predictability, and control. I also agree with him that 'the fast-food restaurant has become the model of rationality'[4] in other spheres of social life. In attempting to delineate ways of escaping this excessive rationality, he notes that 'the escape routes from rationality have been rationalized. There is no way out.'[5] As noted previously, Chris Rojek arrives at a similar conclusion in his book *Ways of Escape*:[6] All forms of escape are eventually co-opted (commodified). If one seeks escape through leisure, one will find that leisure has been McDonaldized. If one tries to resist by using inner-directed fantasy, one encounters the routinization and automatization of fantasy, as in current romance novels that follow predictable formulas. And so on. Nevertheless, Ritzer tries very hard to find ways to resist McDonaldization, and makes specific suggestions in this regard, including but not limited to the following:[7]

- Avoid daily routine as much as possible. Try to do as many things as possible in a different way from one day to the next.
- The next time you need a pair of glasses, use the local store-front optometrist rather than the Pearle Vision Center.
- At least once a week, pass up lunch at McDonald's and frequent a local greasy spoon. For dinner, again at least once a week, park the car, unplug the microwave, avoid the freezer, and cook a meal from scratch.
- Send back to the post office all junk mail, especially that which is addressed to 'occupant' or 'resident.'
- Seek out small classes; get to know your professors.

But in all honesty, I do not think that Ritzer's suggestions for resisting McDonaldization are practical. If one were to follow his suggestions, one would soon find oneself falling behind in work and family obligations – resistance to McDonaldization is time-consuming. One needs the cooperation of others in this proposed war of solitary resistance. Suppose, for example, that a student tries to get to know his or her professor, but the professor is comfortable with the McDonaldization of teaching because it is the most efficient way for structuring his or her work and family life. Even the arenas of social life that Ritzer assumes have not yet been McDonaldized actually have been. The store-front optometrist and the proprietor of the greasy spoon are no doubt emulating McDonald's in their quests for efficiency, and if they are not, they are probably on the verge of going out of business. Finally, note the irony in Ritzer's deliberate rehearsing and scheduling of anti-McDonald's behavior: He is unwittingly McDonaldizing the proposed rebellion against McDonaldization.

Suppose, for example, that a concerned citizen has a genuine emotional response to some social problem, and writes a sincere letter to his or her Senator or even to the President of the United States demanding remedial action. The indignant will receive a carefully drafted form letter – written by one of many staff members hired for just such occasions – thanking him or her for the expressed concern, and assurances that the government is studying, monitoring, and doing all it can to resolve the problem. Months or years later, the problem may have gotten worse, but if the concerned citizen writes again, he or she will get an updated, albeit similar, postemotional response. Nowadays, one can send one's concerns to the US government via electronic mail, but the response, though almost immediate, is just as postemotional.

Or consider the tight supervision of and near extinction of the art of flirtation in the USA. Even European feminists think that the Americans have gone too far in this regard. In the USA, a male who flirts in any way with female co-workers is opening himself up for a possible lawsuit. Male co-workers are told explicitly in seminars that they must not touch a female in any way, must not look at her, must not compliment her on her appearance, and, in general, must not engage in any sort of behavior that could be construed as offensive. Of course, just about any behavior can and will be construed as offensive by someone. On American university campuses, male professors almost always leave the doors of their offices open when a female student comes to visit during office hours, as protection. Those who pass by the open door might be called on later to testify whether or not anything inappropriate occurred. All this is still in sharp contrast to the collective effervescence of flirtation that still occurs in Europe, at least as of this writing. (But it will not last for long as Americanization sets in.) This American attitude toward flirtation is part of the postemotional mechanization of genuine emotions: Social encounters between males and females must be made smooth, foolproof, problem-proof, highly efficient. There can be no social space for the idiosyncratic emotional interplay that used to occur in mixed gender groups. Now suppose that one decides to adopt this European attitude in America in such a group situation and deliberately engages in flirtation? To be sure, one is defying postemotionalism. But the cost is liable to be great, and in the end postemotionalism will win. A ready-made system exists to deal with such troublemakers, and it will coldly, efficiently, and mechanically punish or eliminate the bad weed.

Finally, one should note that rebelling against the McDonaldization of society may be unsavory, even anti-social and criminal. Thus, the Unabomber's manifesto is essentially an attack on the McDonaldized aspects of modern society, but he has murdered people as part of his attempt to start a revolution. Nationalism is another form of resisting McDonaldization, but it can and has led to genocidal excesses. (And nationalism itself has been automatized and feigned, as in the case of Serbian nationalism in the 1990s: Serbs' history lessons dating back to 1389 and the Ustasha regime clearly follow the format of a well-rehearsed formula.) Resistance to the McDonaldization of society is a complex matter, and resistance to the McDonaldization of emotions is more complex still.

Nevertheless, despite these reservations, I will attempt to follow today's conventional style and analyze the possible positive aspects of postemotion-alism and to search for ways that it might be resisted in the event that it is perceived negatively.

Orwell on the Cult of the Machine

George Ritzer in *The McDonaldization of Society* and George Orwell in chapter 12 of *The Road to Wigan Pier* both address the extension of the machine model from industry to the social realm. Whereas Ritzer believes that one can try to resist McDonaldization despite his claim that the escape routes from rationality have been rationalized, Orwell concludes that the machine is invincible. My own conclusion is closer to Orwell's, with the caveat that postemotionalism might one day be overcome by genuine emotions if the collective consciousness, collective effervescence, and the category of the sacred can be jump-started back into life. Let me repeat that neither Ritzer nor Orwell makes the conceptual leap that is the subject of discussion here, the mechanization of emotions. Yet their analyses serve as precursors to the postemotional concept. And Orwell's analysis of the cult of the machine serves as a precursor to Ritzer's concept of McDonaldization.

Orwell's intent in *The Road to Wigan Pier* is to resuscitate socialism because the masses resist it as 'bound up, more or less inextricably, with the idea of machine-production.'[8] Socialism as a world-system implies machine-production because it demands constant intercommunication, centralized control, equality, uniformity of education, and so on. I am less concerned with Orwell's defense of socialism than with his intriguing sociological link-age between socialism and the machine. I intend to extend this linkage to emotional life and the machine.

Orwell expresses beautifully the typical modernist faith in the progress that will come with the machine:

All the work that is now done by hand will then be done by machinery; wood or stone will be made of rubber, glass or steel; there will be no disorder, no loose ends, no wildernesses, no wild animals, no weeds, no disease, no poverty, no pain – and so on and so forth. The Socialist world is to be above all things an ordered world, an efficient world.[9]

Many of these predictions have come true since Orwell made them in 1937. The credo he summarizes can be found refracted in slightly different forms in the treatises on modernity by Keith Tester and Zygmunt Bauman, which have been discussed earlier. Orwell, Tester, and Bauman, among others, clearly envision the modernist as the perfect 'gardener' who will clear away the weeds and create the perfect garden. But it is not just socialism (for Orwell) or Communism (for Tester) or Nazism (for Bauman) that expresses this modernist cult of the machine. Emotional life in Western, democratic, industrialized countries has finally come under the spell of the machine.

Thus, postemotionalism is a system designed to avoid emotional disorder; to prevent loose ends in emotional exchanges; to civilize 'wild' arenas of emotional life; and, in general, to order the emotions so that the social world hums as smoothly as a well-maintained machine. What Marcuse called the happy consciousness must be maintained at all costs. Psychiatric patients are therefore given 'medications' that suppress their irksome and very emotional symptoms. Political correctness ensures that nothing unpredictable happens emotionally in a social interaction. I recall how David Riesman urged me to go into sociology because, he said, it was still like the 'Wild West,' as opposed to the tightly controlled disciplines such as psychology and economics. In sociology, he said, one could still make discoveries, and one could still obtain emotional satisfaction from pursuing one's chosen guiding star. Alas, twenty years after he made that statement, it seems that sociology is becoming more mechanical too. Social control has now invaded almost every realm of emotional life: Parents must worry what their children tell their teachers about their family lives (for even if parents are not abusive and do not use drugs, children still have vivid imaginations). Everyone must wear seat belts in their cars, but everyone must put on 'emotional belts' in their offices as well. Work, family, play, leisure, church: these and other social domains increasingly come to resemble the functioning of a machine based on pre-determined rules for engaging in emotional exchanges. For example, until recently short commuter flights in the USA did not follow the same rules that govern longer jet flights between cities. The stewards and stewardesses on commuter flights seemed more approachable, friendly, and idiosyncratic than their counterparts on regular flights. But in recent years, the airline personnel on commuter flights are forced to present the same 'safety information' in exactly the same way that they do on longer jet airplane flights. The last bastion of spontaneous collective effervescence that centered on the anxiety of flying, and that often led to dark humor on commuter flights, has been commodified and pre-packaged, with the result that passengers exhibit the same bored chagrin to the official safety presentations that they do on longer flights. Airline stewards and stewardesses exhibit the 'managed heart':[10] They have rehearsed in advance the possible problems that might arise on a flight and the appropriate emotional reactions to each.

Orwell notes that mechanical progress tries to create a world in which 'nothing goes wrong.'[11] The machine must be foolproof. Machine culture must guarantee the same predictable bus trip every time, the same hamburger, the same quality of television reception, and so on. Now all this has its positive aspects when contrasted with the unpredictability of travel in traditional times, or the anxiety of eating in unknown restaurants, or the irritation one still experiences in developing countries when television programs do not follow the published schedule, or, worse, when they go off because of frequent, unpredictable blackouts. Still, Orwell thinks that in pre-mechanical days the traveller was really living while travelling whereas modern, mechanical travel is 'a kind of temporary death.'[12] Suppose that one wants to experience the genuine emotions of pre-mechanical days. Orwell writes:

> Here am I, forty miles from London. When I want to go up to London why do I not pack my luggage on to a mule and set out on foot, making a two days' march of it? Because, with the Green Line buses whizzing past me every ten minutes, such a journey would be intolerably irksome. In order that one may enjoy primitive methods of travel, it is necessary that no other method should be available. No human being ever wants to do anything in a more cumbrous way than is necessary. . . . In a world where everything could be done by machinery, everything would be done by machinery.[13]

Let us extend Orwell's insight to the realm of emotional life. Engaging in flirtation or engaging one's university students emotionally by going out with them for a beer after class are the emotional analogues to packing one's luggage on a mule instead of taking the bus. Life is so much easier and efficient so long as one does *not* flirt or try to be friendly with students. This is because, as with the many problems that could go wrong with the mule, so many unexpected things could happen with the emotional interplay with one's students. Some could get emotionally attached to the instructor, demanding his or her time in the future, or advice in personal matters, or embarrassment in the eyes of one's colleagues if they misconstrue his or her emotions, and so on. Genuine emotional life is a cumbersome, time-consuming, and unpredictable state of affairs. Better to just get on the bus. Better to just follow the postemotional code of behavior and be 'nice' but uncommitted to students.

Those who would defend the mechanized cult of political correctness might point out that they prefer this state of affairs to traditional times in which authority figures seduced innocent females or spouted anti-Semitic remarks in class or otherwise made hurtful statements. Fair enough. But such an attitude is not fundamentally different from a modernist person's preference for a standardized hamburger versus an unpredictable meal, or a bus trip versus a trip on a mule. At least in traditional times one could identify the anti-Semite or sexual pervert or other deviant and society had norms to deal with such phenomena. In contemporary times, by contrast, these and other obnoxious character traits and attitudes are submerged for the most part, at least while the machinery of social interaction is running smoothly. Yet with this mechanical metaphor, as with any machine, there is always the possibility of mechanical breakdown. When one's word processor breaks down, for example, one is liable to lose all of one's creative work in one moment. When the social machinery breaks down, as it did at the reading of the verdict following the Rodney King trial in Los Angeles, long-repressed emotions can erupt suddenly into riots and other forms of social upheaval. Even in the arena of international politics, one could extend this metaphor to conclude that the machinery of various security arrangements such as NATO and the CSCE are on the verge of breakdown, and that widespread social upheaval is on the international horizon.

Orwell notes another impediment to breaking free of the cult of the machine. The mechanization of the world forces people to develop habits of the mind (Orwell is so similar to Veblen in this regard) that are as difficult to break as any other habits. Orwell writes:

> As a single instance, take taste in its narrowest sense – the taste for decent food. In the highly mechanized countries, thanks to tinned food, cold storage, synthetic flavoring matters, etc., the palate is almost a dead organ. . . . And what applies to food applies also to furniture, houses, clothes, books, amusements and everything else that makes up our environment. There are now millions of people, and they are increasing every year, to whom the blaring of a radio is not only a more acceptable but a more normal background to their thoughts than the lowing of cattle or the song of birds. The mechanization of the world could never proceed very far while taste, even the taste-buds of the tongue, remained uncorrupted, because in that case most of the products of the machine would be simply unwanted. . . . But meanwhile the machine is here, and its corrupting effects are almost irresistible. One inveighs against it, but one goes on using it.[14]

Again, I agree with Orwell, and think it would be interesting to extend his insights to the realm of emotions. What are the emotional equivalents to the corruption of taste represented by canned food, chewing gum, machine guns, telephones, and fast cars? I think a possible reply includes: pre-packaged news, recourse to humanitarian organizations versus individual compassion, standardized birthday parties, dating services, the greeting card industry that standardizes the 'right emotion' for the 'right occasion,' and the code of political correctness. With the passage of time, one gets habituated to having one's emotions manipulated and will object to being forced to engage in collective effervescence to experience real emotions in the same way that the modernist is irritated by a bird's song but enjoys listening to the radio as background noise. Thus, imagine the work that would be involved in seeking out the full extent of the news through contacting experts on one's own rather than just accepting what one reads in the newspaper. Even reading the newspaper is time-consuming and cumbersome. Ritzer is right that television news – which is the primary source of news for most efficiency-minded Americans – gives one 'News McNuggets,' not news.[15] And junk-food journalism has permeated even the newspapers. Imagine the inefficiency of travelling to Bosnia to deliver toys on one's own instead of writing a check to a relief organization. Or all the work that used to go into cooking for and arranging a family birthday party versus writing a check to McDonald's. The contemporary person who prefers letter-writing to telephone conversations or communication on the Internet would be regarded as odd. And so on. In all these cases, one would be forced not only to expend great effort and consume much of one's precious time in maintaining genuine emotions, but one would also have to engage many other people in collective effervescence and the excitement of discovering the truth or cheering up a Bosnian child or participating fully in the birthday of one's own child. Extending Orwell, I believe that many if not most people today would prefer the postemotional route in these and other circumstances if for no other reason than the reason of habit.

Thus, to turn back the tide of postemotionalism would be the equivalent of smashing every machine invented after a certain date and smashing the habits of the mind that surround them. In the emotional realm, one would have to smash every postemotional formula for social interaction invented after a certain date and also smash the habits that go along with such interaction. Such a task seems simply impossible. Every smashed machine and smashed postemotional formula would be replaced almost immediately by a new one. To be fair, such progress has made life easier and more efficient, as promised, even in the emotional realm. Marcuse was right about happy consciousness producing a society without opposition. But progress has also ruined the emotional palate and made social life bland and nearly dead. No matter how one feels about such progress, its course apparently cannot be reversed.

Orwell shared the resistance of the masses to mechanized socialism although he did not succumb to fascism. He sought to uncover what he thought were the emotional ideals of socialism, justice and liberty. More than fifty years after Orwell wrote this essay, it seems that the masses are still resisting socialism, albeit the most recent versions of socialism such as the welfare state and big government. This sentiment was undoubtedly behind the rise of the Republican Party in the USA during Bill Clinton's failed experiment in communitarianism. But as of this writing, the American masses are wanting to have their cake and eat it too. Opinion polls began to swing back in support of President Clinton as the Republicans began to put their revolution into effect by slashing the welfare state. Ironically, it seems that the masses have become habituated to the mechanized state even as they think they want to return to the good old days.

But the more important point is that in contemporary times the distinction between the political Left and Right is fading. Extremists on both sides of the political spectrum call each other fascists. Justice and liberty are hailed as goals by both sides of the political spectrum, only these terms mean widely different things to them. Both sides of the political spectrum assume a mechanized model of centralized government control that extends to thought and feelings. And both sides know that to achieve these goals they must present a 'nice' image to the masses. Thus, in recent American politics, the conservative Newt Gingrich has been described as being 'Clintonesque' while President Clinton comes across as being too conservative for many liberals.

Actually, a third force is slowly, almost imperceptibly, but steadily filling the vacuum created by widespread public cynicism concerning the political Left as well as the Right. That force is nationalism. In the USA, the emergence of

African-American nationalism has surprised many analysts who had assumed that, following Martin Luther King Jr, race relations were on the mend. In the United Kingdom, an unforeseen consequence of European unification has been the resurgence of Scottish nationalism as many Scots have realized that their collective emotional needs are met better in the European Union than in the United Kingdom. A few years ago, Canadians did not take nationalism in Quebec very seriously, but the near secession of Quebec recently has made them aware that even modern Canada holds the potential for Balkanization. Serbian nationalism has already been treated at some length and requires no further comment. I hold that the unexpected eruption of nationalism throughout the Western world is the real resistance front to postemotionalism. Of course, it is an open question whether it will succeed in resisting postemotionalism or whether it, too, will become mechanized, McDonaldized nationalism.

Resistance and Acquiescence to Postemotionalism

I travelled to Holland in October 1995 to give several talks on postemotionalism. It seemed to be a busy time for travel to and from the United States: Over 170 heads of state travelled to the USA to commemorate the fiftieth anniversary of the United Nations. It was a postemotional spectacle: The UN's colossal failures were dressed up as far-reaching achievements. Richard Holbrooke and his staff were engaging in so-called 'shuttle diplomacy' between the USA and the Balkans. But in addition to this *literal* travel, there seems to be a *metaphorical* travel of American ideas occurring as well. McDonald's restaurants are cropping up all over Holland, have already nearly obliterated Parisian cafés, and are slowly taking over the rest of the world. As I have already noted, McDonald's is more than a restaurant: It is an American idea, a veritable symbol of the McDonaldization of society. David Riesman wrote long ago on the 'Nylon War' in reference to the widespread cultural influence of American nylon stockings on the rest of the world following World War II.[16] Following the Cold War, we have the McDonald's War, and McDonald's is winning.

The idea behind McDonald's is to replace traditional ways of thinking as well as eating with standardized, rational, coldly efficient ways of doing things. McDonald's represents America not only as an artefact but as the ethos of tearing down trees, destroying old churches that are hard to maintain, and, in general, of eliminating the old to make way for the new and calculatedly 'pleasant.' To be fair, both McDonald's as the restaurant chain and McDonaldization as a process are often preferable to old-fashioned restaurants or ways of doing things. Anyone who has had the experience of trying to order a meal in the woefully inefficient Communist countries will no doubt appreciate McDonald's. Nevertheless, McDonaldization as a process is destructive: trees are cut down to erect buildings, flower stalls are eliminated, the homeless are forbidden to display their desperation on downtown streets, and so on.

Every war has its resistance movement, but where is the cultural resistance to postemotionalism? My Dutch friend and sociologist Jacques Janssen and most of the Dutch professors and students in my audiences all became agitated when I spoke of the Americanization of the world. They cited the need to maintain Dutch culture in face of the new cultural onslaught. Driving from Amsterdam to Nijmigen, Jacques lamented the appearance of every McDonald's by the highway, as if these restaurants represented a new colonization. In Nijmigen, he took me to see the statue of Charlemagne and I remarked, 'I can't see it because of all the trees.' He answered, 'The Dutch like trees,' and we laughed together. Another Dutch friend, Theo, described vividly for me the recent floods in Nijmigen, and the controversy over rebuilding the dikes. The controversy was not over whether to build them, but *how* to build them without destroying trees and the natural beauty. As Jacques's son explained to me over dinner, he didn't want some ugly efficient dikes, but charming efficient ones. Finally, I remember walking with Jacques and Theo in Amsterdam and seeing flower stalls.

The Dutch point out that Holland has always been Balkanized into three separate societies but that until recently they were held together by a mutually respected ethic of tolerance.[17] For example, it was possible for Dutch Catholics to carry on an almost exclusively Catholic existence in their separate schools, clubs, and entertainment yet still think of themselves as Dutch. However, Dutch sociologists claim that the ethic of tolerance, a key component of what might be called Dutch Civil Religion, is now breaking down. Therefore, although the Dutch whom I met all felt that Americanization and McDonaldization should and can be resisted by Dutch culture, it is difficult to see how, if the meaning of this culture has been problematized.

It's impossible not to like the Dutch, for even when one complements them for being tolerant and charming, they are self-effacing and still *more* charming: They reply that they had to become tolerant given their crowded living conditions and geographical location; they point to their Nazi collaboration as evidence of non-toleration; they even point to their genocide in Indonesia as an evil for which they feel collective guilt. My American, British, and French audiences have never returned a compliment by self-scrutiny of the evils their nations have committed.

While I was in Holland, a scandal emerged regarding the role of Dutch UN peacekeeping troops in handing over the 'safe area' of Srebrenica to Serb General Ratko Mladić, who was later indicted for ordering crimes against humanity in that Bosnian town. The general Dutch reaction seemed to be one of shame and anger at the behavior of the Dutch soldiers, but still more anger at UN bureaucracy that would not send in air strikes to defend the Dutch in trying to protect the Bosnians. For the purposes of the present discussion, it is important to ask: How could the Dutch soldiers have resisted the cold logic of the UN in concluding that the fall of Srebrenica was not all that important, even though the UN's prestige was allegedly on the line because it established Srebrenica as a safe area? The UN, like any other modern institution, has many public relations specialists on its staff who are skilled at smoothing over and McDonaldizing any such 'embarrassments.' The Dutch soldiers could have martyred themselves in Srebrenica in order to uphold the UN mandate. That would have been heroic, but, having cited martyrdom over a noble cause as an option, one cannot easily imagine such an event occurring in postemotional society. Martyrdom is an old-fashioned virtue predicated on passionate *commitment* to a belief or value regardless of cost. But passionate commitment is problematic in postemotional society. Additionally, such defiance of the UN in the cause of enforcing an existing UN mandate would have confused the masses emotionally. The UN enjoys generally high ratings in Western opinion polls despite its many failures throughout the world. Defying the UN, even for principled reasons that transcend the UN, would be futile. The most likely scenario might have been: The UN is a nice, good institution, so the Dutch were wrong to oppose it.

On the other side of the Atlantic, yet another postemotional spectacle was underway, namely, the Balkan peace talks that were held in Dayton, Ohio. When President Tudjman allegedly drew a map in London for Liberal Democrat leader Paddy Ashdown in early 1995, in which he divided Bosnia-Herzegovina between Croatia and Serbia, he was assailed as Milošević's equivalent in the American media. A few months later, the American President, Bill Clinton, proposed a similar ethnic partition of Bosnia. But the American media did not assail the American President; instead, he was hailed as a peacemaker. The postemotional culture industry can use the same set of facts (in this case, ethnic partition) to vilify or glorify a person or cause or nation. The ethnic partition of Bosnia was being served up by the Americans as a political McDonald's 'happy meal,' allegedly the 'only' solution to the 'tribal' warfare among Serbs, Croats, and Muslims in Bosnia. Yet this 'happy' solution destroys the sovereignty of Bosnia-Herzegovina; rewards Serbian aggression; contradicts the West's ostentatious 'commitment' to multicultur-alism; and seeks to obliterate a tradition of ethnic tolerance in Bosnia[18] that rivals the Dutch tradition of tolerance. Inner-directed types of previous gen-erations who were committed to multiculturalism would probably have concluded that it would be an unconscionable proposal, no matter how it was dressed up for public consumption. (So that we do not view the past nostal-gically, one should note that racist inner-directed types would have fought just as passionately for partition.) The more important point is that in the post-other-directed era, which is supposed to be guided by the ethic of tolerance, there is no basis for a firm commitment to any position: Most opinion-makers quickly got on the bandwagon of 'peace.' Who could possibly oppose peace (even if it might be construed as an unjust peace)?

Nor is President Clinton's postemotional packaging of his peace arrange-ment in Bosnia substantially different from other foreign policy packaging, such as Haiti. US troops went to Haiti in 1994 ostensibly to restore democ-racy, despite CIA reports that the then exiled President of Haiti, Jean-Bartride Aristide, had dictatorial tendencies. More than a year after the US military occupation of Haiti, reports resurfaced that these tendencies were evident once more. In both Haiti and Bosnia, President Clinton tried to package as 'peace' and 'democracy' US military support of regimes that were anything but peaceful or democratic.[19] Despite initial grumbling, both Congress and the US public supported him because the happy consciousness associated with the concept of peace immediately vanquishes passionate opposition.

During President Clinton's televised speech to the American people on 27 November 1995, in which he explained the Bosnian peace plan, he referred to it repeatedly as 'the right thing to do.'[20] Interestingly, this is a phrase used in recent television advertisements used to promote the consumption of oatmeal. President Clinton used the rhetoric that Robert N. Bellah discovered in his research on American Civil Religion, including: 'our [American] values,' 'America has always been more than just a place,' 'peace,' and the 'power of our ideas.' The Croats, Bosnian Muslims, and Serbs were referred to as 'warring ethnic groups' and 'three warring parties.' President Clinton pledged that the USA would help Bosnia 'build a peaceful, democratic future.'[21] In Riesman's terms, it was a 'nice' speech. But in this postemotional instance, American Civil Religion was being used to solidify Serbian gains achieved through international aggression, and at least one of the 'warring parties,' the Bosnian Muslims, consistently stood for a multicultural and pluralistic Bosnia.

Contrast President Clinton's speech with the President of Bosnia-Herzegovina, Alija Izetbegović's plaintive, lengthy, denunciation of the ethnic partition of his country, made at the UN festivities mentioned above and repeated in Dayton. Izetbegović comes across as charming, even if his cause is as pathetic and doomed to failure as Greenpeace protesting French nuclear testing in the South Pacific or environmentalists who chain themselves to trees to prevent their destruction. In contrast to President Clinton, President Izetbegović emerged as inner-directed through his insistence on justice and multiculturalism. Izetbegović resisted, but his resistance did not have a chance to succeed in postemotional society.

In summary, it seems very difficult to find illustrations of cultural resistance to postemotionalism because the happy consciousness is a society without opposition. Effective opposition cannot be mobilized against anything that is 'nicely' packaged. Yet the pre-packaged post-emotions clearly come across as hollow. Thus, regarding the consummation of the Balkan Peace Plan discussed above, note the lack of joy at this prospect of 'peace' on the part of all those involved except the Serbs. The end of World War II was celebrated with gusto. Most people have seen the famous photograph of a US soldier kissing a woman in Times Square in New York City to celebrate peace after Hitler was defeated. But after the Dayton agreement: Americans are not happy about the 'peace' in the Balkans because they worry about American soldiers getting killed; Croatians are not happy about it because the plan gives Serbs territory adjoining Croatia and thereby threatening Croats for generations to come; the Bosnian Muslims are not happy because their country has been partitioned. Only Radovan Karadžić expressed glee, stating that the Serbs got what they wanted. The postemotional cultural industry has not yet mastered the ability of manufacturing joy.

Postemotional Commitment

From Riesman and Marcuse I have extended the idea that other-directed niceness and the happy consciousness make autonomy and resistance to postemotionalism problematic because one cannot succeed in getting indignant at the nice and happy in a society based on simulation. Postemotional society is a society without opposition. There is yet another reason why cultural resistance to postemotionalism is difficult if not impossible: Passionate commitment to a cause or value or belief has evaporated for individuals as well as groups and organizations.

The contemporary impossibility of making commitments to anything or anyone can be found in many social arenas. Consider the contemporary marriage vow as an illustration of postemotionalism. Many couples formalize pre-nuptial agreements as to how property will be divided after divorce. Even couples who do not take this legalistic step often marry with the idea that if the marriage does not 'work out,' they will divorce. In class discussions of marriage as a social institution, my university students express openly this reliance on divorce as an escape hatch from commitment. In the USA, half of all marriages end in divorce. When the survivors of these broken marriages take a vow to love someone until death do them part, the vow surely must seem somewhat hollow. In general, contemporary weddings give the impression that the bride and bridegroom are mouthing words that neither really believes – except in a Disneyesque, postemotional sense. The contemporary wedding is often a postemotional exercise in trying to imitate traditional commitment.

Even dating has been transformed in postemotional societies. Increasingly, young people no longer 'make dates' and no longer 'go out' together. These are vestiges from the inner-directed era: The 'date' from previous generations required a minimal amount of commitment that is anathema nowadays. Postemotional adolescents plan events where they can 'be together' and 'see' each other without using the d-word (date). The old question 'are they dating?' has become 'are they seeing each other?' They may or may not see each other following the event. It is understood that either party can stop 'seeing' the other at any time. This state of affairs is different from some ultra-liberated Scandinavian countries where couples live together hardly ever thinking of getting married. The new postemotional type is still willing to 'live together,' so long as it is understood that either party may still wish to 'see' (date) other people.

Corporations also illustrate this sense of not really meaning what they promise. For example, many products are sold with a money-back guarantee in the event that the consumer is dissatisfied with the product in any way. But corporations do not lose money on this institutionalized hollow promise because most consumers in other-directed societies would be too embarrassed to return a product for the sole reason that they no longer like it. (Of course, there are those curdled indignants who make a habit of complaining about most of the service and products they consume, but they seem to be relatively few in number, and are dismissed as cranks.) Those consumers who do return a product typically find that the implicit 'fine print' in the 'unconditional' guarantee does have costly or time-consuming conditions so that it is cheaper to buy a new product without complaining.

Contracts in contemporary societies are just as problematic. What seems on the surface to be a binding commitment between two parties often turns out not to be binding because of the 'fine print' and because armies of lawyers are trained to find loopholes in contracts.

It is common practice in the USA for large corporations to lay off workers who are about to be entitled to pensions, and all workers know that the commitment of the corporations for which they work is to make a profit providing for the worker's well-being. The business world has nothing similar to the tenure system in Western universities, itself subject in recent years to strident calls for its abolition.

International agreements and international security arrangements are just as susceptible to this postemotional tendency toward the broken promise. For example, the Poles in the 1990s regard as hollow NATO's promise to defend them against a resurgent Russian imperialism following NATO's debacle in Bosnia. The UN Charter stipulates that the right to self-defense is inherent, but this crystal-clear fact did not enable Bosnia-Herzegovina to get the illegal arms embargo imposed on it to be lifted. Diplomats the world over know that the real motor driving both NATO and the UN is the USA, and the historical record of American commitments is one of broken promises, from the treaties signed with Native Americans to international treaties.

The underlying reasons for the reality of the broken promise in contemporary times stem from the many social forces that have been uncovered in the course of the present discussion: The other-directed type is seduced by so many choices and options that the idea of commitment to one of these is out of character. Postmodernism conceived as a social movement has enshrined ambivalence and ambiguity as social virtues. Durkheim wrote that the idea of the contract was sacrosanct in traditional societies, but the general disappearance of the sacred in contemporary societies renders the contract profane.

In general, commitment presupposes traditional or inner-directed conviction, passion, and rigidity. In stark contrast to these virtues (or vices) held by previous generations, contemporary societies foster openness to many points of view and many possibilities, processed feelings, and flexibility. Thus, commitment becomes yet another phenomenon for the postemotional type to imitate.

Concluding Thoughts on the Americanization of the World

Throughout this discussion, I have followed the trajectory from Tocqueville through Riesman and Arnold Toynbee to Baudrillard that the USA serves as the cultural center of the world. Some authors find this assumption problematic and prefer to speak of the Japanization of the world. But Japan's technological influence internationally is still an aspect of its self-conscious imitation of America. Japan is not a center of cultural transformation in the world. In Communist countries especially, the USA was the promised land above all else because it symbolized the freedom, progress, and tolerance that the Communist version of mechanical culture lacked. About this America persons in Communist nations had to whisper quietly in a small circle of trusted friends and among family members. America also dawned on Communist as well as non-Communist peoples through Disney cartoons, drinking Coca-Cola, wearing blue jeans, and, most recently, consuming McDonald's hamburgers. The music which many persons grew up on in Communist nations was also North American or English: Bob Dylan and the Beatles early on, and, more recently, Leonard Cohen, Bruce Springsteen and Nirvana. Thomas Cushman has published an excellent ethnography of the Soviet underground rock music counterculture which basically idolized American music as a symbol of authenticity.[22] This is understandable given the social climate of fear and mistrust that ruled the Soviet Union. Children growing up in Communist countries learned the names of the stars of the US National Basketball Association. Those who were privileged enough to play tennis and could afford tennis shoes used Wilson and Reebok. Ironically, the youth in formerly Communist nations grew up Americanized despite the Iron Curtain. The Iron Curtain could keep people in, but it could not keep American culture out.

This might be construed as a genuinely positive aspect of postemotionalism. For if Disney cartoons, Coca-Cola, Nirvana, and other icons of American culture are part of the mechanized model of emotional packaging in the West that has been discussed throughout this book, they simultaneously served as 'sacred' totems of freedom in the formerly Communist world. Who doesn't recall the excitement of Soviets lining up for hours to experience McDonald's in Moscow as a way of experiencing America? It is ironic that the kitsch products of American postemotional culture were perceived as symbols of authenticity and freedom in totalitarian societies.

In Communist schools, things were completely different. There existed two Americas, one to be used (even if not respected) and the other to be constantly criticized in order to uphold the virtues of Communism. Everyone liked American Westerns, for example, because comrade Tito adored them as did the entire Communist nomenklatura. One was allowed to like Coca-Cola, tennis rackets, jeans, and Reeboks so long as one did not go overboard. But one was not allowed to admire the American style of democracy, federalism, freedom of the press, and human rights. Capitalism was depicted in Communist schools as a form of evil, something like the ninth level of

Dante's hell. The images of America that Communist governments beamed to their own people were America's exploitation of the poor, its constant class struggle, bourgeois decadence, and constant moral crises.

One must keep in mind that although Communism was a Western cultural product brought to the Soviet Union by the Bolsheviks in a sealed train, as Keith Tester eloquently observes in his book *The Two Sovereigns*, it did not function as the smooth-running machine that it was intended to be. Only the institutions of terror were efficient. Nearly everything else was so hopelessly backward that it was a wonder that anything in the Soviet Union functioned. George Ritzer expresses this insight eloquently:

> One can argue that communism constituted a barrier to rationalization; as a result such societies failed to McDonaldize. Thus, Communist societies tended to be characterized by inefficiency, incalculability, unpredictability, and to be relatively backward (except in the military) in introducing advanced technologies. As a result, at least in part, of the failure to rationalize, Communist societies suffered the wide range of economic (and social) problems that forced them to abandon their economic system and move toward a more market-like economy, a system that at least resembles a capitalist system. In other words, Russia and Eastern Europe are now rushing head-long in the direction of greater rationalization.[23]

Soviet Communism was a modernist system grafted clumsily onto a traditional and inner-directed culture that often operated in pre-modern ways. Thus, the America that people in Communist countries admired was conjured up from their emotional, pre-modern fantasies. They could not imagine that the real America had achieved the mechanistic goals that Communism could not.

After the fall of the Berlin Wall, perestroika, and glasnost, the Americanization of cultural life in formerly Communist nations entered a new phase of intensity. Satellite TV was available to those who could afford it; CNN now entered homes in formerly Communist nations; personal computers and the modem became available. The USA sent teams of free-market consultants to the formerly Communist nations. Political consultants gave lectures and advice on human rights, democratically run elections, First Amendment rights, and other tenets of American Civil Religion. But the masses in formerly Communist nations soon realized the hardness and harshness of postemotional Americanization. For in the interest of the smoothly running machine, it did not matter to the consultants whether pure capitalism produced homeless people, made day care unaffordable in nations where everyone felt that day care was a natural right, eliminated free and universal health care, and, in general, produced sudden and great social hardships. Suddenly, people in former Communist nations were divided into Americaphiles and Americaphobes. The Americaphiles were former Communists who still had the old social networks as well as old money that enabled them to make a profit using American values. The Americaphobes were the rest of the population who found that they could not survive under this new 'freedom' and began to express nostalgia for the good old days of Communism.

And this is where matters stand at the present time. The formerly Communist world has discovered the real, metallic feel of America. The poor and disadvantaged in the USA have known it for a long time. It is an open question whether Americanization will triumph after all or whether the discontented in formerly Communist nations will retreat into nationalism and new forms of authoritarianism.

Parting Thoughts

Anyone who has read through this book is bound to feel frustrated and perhaps even indignant at this point. The argument presented here is unsettling, to the author as well as the reader. For I have argued that things have gotten worse than George Orwell imagined. From the control of thoughts and the mechanization of social life that he observed, society has moved to the manipulation of emotions and the rational control of emotional life. If any of this is true – and the reader will have to determine this for him- or herself – surely it calls for a reaction that goes beyond the acceptance of a new form of victimization. Has postemotional humanity been sentenced to a life of powerless inside-dopesterism in which it is manipulated by 'nice' agents of authority? What can be done?

It may seem that my conclusions about the possibility of autonomy are completely pessimistic, even nihilistic. But that is not really the case. The careful reader will have noted the many occasions in the course of this book where I pointed to possible avenues of escape into authenticity: collective effervescence, qualitative field work, dialogue, *caritas*, and so on. Clearly, I have stated if not implied that the O.J. Simpson trial should have been about Simpson's guilt or innocence; that the focus in Bosnia should have been on stopping genocide; that Russia might have become more 'like us' if 'we' had tried to understand the Russians first; and so on for the many other illustrations that were used in this book. Yet the purpose of this book has been confined mostly to outlining the parameters of postemotional society, to suggest that it exists and that postmodernism and other existing conceptualizations of society are becoming increasingly irrelevant. My thesis may, in fact, be proved incorrect by others. But if it is correct to any degree, the first step toward eventual emancipation from postemotionalism must include realization that the problem exists. And this realization must involve heart as well as mind.

Notes

1. See George Orwell, *Homage to Catalonia* (New York: Harcourt Brace, 1980).

2. Stjepan G. Meštrović, *Genocide After Emotion: The Postemotional Balkan War* (London: Routledge, 1996).

3. George Ritzer, *The McDonaldization of Society* (London: Sage, 1992).

4. Ibid., p. 19.

5. Ibid., p. 23.

6. Chris Rojek, *Ways of Escape: Modern Transformations in Leisure and Travel* (Lanham, MD: Rowman and Littlefield, 1994).

7. Ritzer, *The McDonaldization of Society*, pp. 183–5.

8. George Orwell, *The Road to Wigan Pier* (New York: Harcourt Brace, [1937] 1958), p. 188.

9. Ibid., p. 189.

10. Arlie Hochschild, *The Managed Heart: Commercialization of Human Feeling* (Berkeley: University of California Press, 1983).

11. Orwell, *The Road to Wigan Pier*, p. 193.

12. Ibid., p. 200.

13. Ibid.

14. Ibid., p. 204.

15. Ritzer, *The McDonaldization of Society*, p. 57.

16. In David Riesman, *Individualism Reconsidered and Other Essays* (Glencoe, IL: Free Press, 1954).

17. See especially Arend Lypharat, *The Politics of Accommodation: Pluralism and Democracy in the Netherlands* (Berkeley: University of California Press, 1968).

18. As argued by Noel Malcolm, *Bosnia: A Short History* (New York: New York University Press, 1994).

19. Larry Roghter, 'Tensions in Haiti Increase Sharply, Imperiling Peace,' *New York Times*, 30 November 1995, p. A1: 'Even as the United States prepares to send troops to Bosnia, the Clinton Administration suddenly finds itself struggling to prevent the unraveling of a fragile peace that began here barely a year ago.' Clarence Page, 'Haiti Illustrates Democracy Takes Time,' *Houston Chronicle*, 30 November 1995, p. 42A: 'President Clinton's attempt to turn the nation's eyes to Bosnia only makes recent unrest in Haiti more significant, since failure of American policy in Haiti can only make Congress even more reluctant to get involved in the far-away Balkans.'

20. 'Clinton's Words on Mission to Bosnia: "The Right Thing to Do,"' *New York Times* 28 November 1995, p. A6.

21. Ibid.

22. Thomas Cushman, *Notes From Underground: Rock Music Counterculture in Russia* (Albany, NY: State University of New York Press, 1995).

23. Ritzer, *The McDonaldization of Society*, p. 148.

Subject Index

Name Index